The Unmanageable Consumer

The Unmanageable Consumer

Second Edition

Yiannis Gabriel and Tim Lang

SAGE Publications

London ● Thousand Oaks ● New Delhi

First published 1995
Reprinted 2002, 2003
Second edition first published 2006

 SAGE Publications Ltd
1 Oliver's Yard
55 City Road
London EC1Y 1SP

SAGE Publications Inc.
2455 Teller Road
Thousand Oaks, California 91320

SAGE Publications India Pvt Ltd
B-42, Panchsheel Enclave
Post Box 4109
New Delhi 110 017

British Library Cataloguing in Publication data

A catalogue record for this book is available from the
British Library

ISBN-10 1-4129-1892-8   ISBN-13 978-1-4129-1892-3
ISBN-10 1-4129-1893-6   ISBN-13 978-1-4129-1893-0 (pbk)

Library of Congress Control Number: 2005932913

Typeset by C&M Digitals (P) Ltd., Chennai, India
Printed in Great Britain by Athenaeum Press, Gateshead
Printed on paper from sustainable resources

Contents

Acknowledgements

In writing this book, we have been helped by many people who have encouraged us to collect our thoughts; or discussed all or parts of our thesis; or fed us ideas, papers and facts; or suggested avenues of reading and research; or all of those! Our thanks to them all, and in particular to: Richard Adams, David Albury, David Barling, Walden Bello, Helen Bold, Eric Brunner, Martin Caraher, Liz Castledine, Charlie Clutterbuck, John Cousins, Ross Cranston, Guy Dehn, Martine Drake, Ignacio Peon Escalante, Jane Gabriel, Steve Fineman, David Gee, David Grant, Edward Goldsmith, Andrew Graves, Robin Grove-White, Rob Harrison, Corinna Hawkes, Nick Hildyard, Colin Hines, Aubrey Greenwood, Candido Gryzbowski, Uri Huta, Mika Iba, Michael Jacobson, Martin Khor, Richard Lamming, Simon Lang, Jerry Mander and all at the International Forum on Globalization, David McNeill, Angela McRobbie, Pradeep Mehta, Melanie Miller, Erik Millstone, Sally Moore, Geoff Mulgan, Helena Norberg-Hodge, Michael O'Connor, Hugh Raven, Geof Rayner, John Richard, Jeremy Rifkin, David Robins, Freida Stack, Frank Trentmann, Margaret Ubabuko, Andrew Ward, Lori Wallach, Tony Webb, Diana Whitworth and everyone in the world consumer movement we have talked and debated with over the years, too numerous to mention! Our thanks, too, to our editor, Delia Martinez Alfonso, and all the people at Sage.

Preface to the Second Edition

The Unmanageable Consumer was published in the mid-1990s, a period dominated by claims of the triumph of the consumerist West. In the midst of excitement about what was seen as an uncontestable hegemony of consumer capitalism, the book warned that 'any triumphalism about Western style consumption is misplaced. The future of global consumption must remain the object of questioning on economic, cultural, environmental and moral grounds' (p. 5). Unlike some, we felt that the 1990s was a 'troubled time in the world'. Over a decade later, few would dispute that times are indeed troubled or that Western-style consumerism is facing and creating serious threats. These range from ecological crises such as climate change and resource shortage to financial and political uncertainties, including an escalating and still dangerous dependency on oil.

The last 10 years have seen extraordinary social and economic changes that have reframed the nature of consumption worldwide. The emergence of China, India and other developing countries as huge consumer markets and producer hotspots has extended the reach of contemporary consumerism. Political realignments worldwide have spawned new outposts of consumption and new black holes of deprivation, while generalized uncertainty has tempered some consumers' appetites. Major technological innovations, notably the Internet, have turned many homes into retail outposts, while digital photography and MP3 players have revolutionized patterns of consuming images and music. Education and health provisions have become yet more commodified, with students and patients viewing themselves as consumers. At the same time, anti-globalization movements with an anti-consumption message have, at times, assumed centre-stage in politics, offering at least a glimpse of opposition to mainstream consumer capitalism. Overall, the last 10 years have seen a substantial expansion of consumerism into new areas, countries and homes, and an escalation of potential checks from environmental and political uncertainties.

In the same period, academic writing on consumption and the accompanying fetishization of the consumer has sky-rocketed in new consumer-oriented journals and books. Cultural studies has dissected shopping malls as cathedrals of consumption and students of organization have focused on the limits of the ethos of customer service. Identity construction has come to be viewed increasingly through the prism of lifestyles. Choice, modelled on the affluent consumer experience, has become the central tenet of many political and ethical discourses. At the same time, there is an increasing awareness among academics of the ecological limits to the consumerist orgy, which are already alarming observers of climate change, raw materials and natural resources such as soil, water and air. In addition, there is the continuing sore of billions of people subsisting at a level of bare survival.

When we originally wrote *The Unmanageable Consumer*, we put forward an unfashionable thesis. We argued that the notion of the consumer was an intellectually unstable entity, which summed up a central dilemma for late 20th-century capitalism – whether to treat people as controllable or free. We proposed, not least in the title of the book, that, in spite of the best attempts to seduce them, coax them or chide them, consumers consistently proved themselves unpredictable, contradictory and unmanageable – that they displayed many different faces and images. We also argued that far from disappearing from sight, work remained a fundamental part of people's everyday experience and that production and consumption were intrinsically interlinked through the deal pioneered by Henry Ford – alienating work in exchange for ever-escalating material standards. We observed that this Fordist Deal was fragile and could be dislocated by sudden events. We signalled some of the shortcomings of choice as a universal value, obscuring all others. We argued that citizenship is far from dead as a force in political arenas and that international relations could not be reduced to political deals aimed at improving consumer choice, by removing trade barriers. We anticipated the continuation of a viable critique of rampant consumerism, building on the legacy of decades of struggles against the impact of industrialization and widening social divisions and inequalities.

Events in the last 10 years have strengthened our commitment to these arguments. An increasing number of academic voices are now challenging the political and ideological primacy of 'the consumer'. The unmanaged and unmanageable dimensions of consumption signalled by our book are gradually gaining wider recognition, not least due to the urgency of environmental constraints. That said, in certain ways our analysis of future trends could be accused of having been premature. In particular, in our concluding chapter, we were perhaps too eager to discern signs of a twilight of consumerism which has yet to materialize. Indeed, it is accelerating in both developed and developing worlds.

It is now time for some re-evaluation. Is consumer capitalism in the process of reinventing itself, in ways that transcend the crudity of mass production and mass waste? Are environmental and ethical costs finally being internalized into the prices of goods and services paid by consumers? Is the moral outrage against sweatshops finally curbing some of the worst excesses of consumer capitalism? Is quality of life assuming a greater prominence over sheer weight of amounts consumed? Our inclination is to answer all these questions with a qualified 'no'. This new edition brings the book up to date, while leaving the essential thesis, scope and arguments unchanged. If anything, we believe that accelerated consumption poses bigger risks in the 21st-century than it did at the end of the 20th-century. The unmanageable consumer continues to pose many threats for the survival of the planet, social justice and human happiness. We hope that the account that we give here deepens engagement with the urgent policy debates on the containment of the negative aspects of consumerism, while enlarging and democratizing its positive aspects.

Introduction: The Faces of the Consumer

The consumer is now a god-like figure, before whom markets and politicians alike bow. Everywhere it seems, the consumer is triumphant. Consumers are said to dictate production; to fuel innovation; to be creating new service sectors in advanced economies; to be driving modern politics; to have it in their power to save the environment and protect the future of the planet. Consumers embody a simple modern logic – the right to choose. Choice, the consumer's friend, the inefficient producer's foe, can be applied to things as diverse as soap-powder, holidays, healthcare or politicians. And yet the consumer is also seen as a weak and malleable creature, easily manipulated, dependent, passive and foolish. Immersed in illusions, addicted to joyless pursuits of ever-increasing living standards, the consumer, far from being a god, is a pawn, in games played in invisible boardrooms.

The concept of the consumer sits at the centre of numerous current debates. Policy-makers, marketers, politicians, environmentalists, lobbyists and journalists rarely lose the consumer from their sights. The supermarket has become a metaphor for our age, choice, its consumerist mantra. A new way of thinking and talking about people has emerged, which engulfs all of us. By the beginning of the 21st-century, we had learnt to talk and think of each other and of ourselves less as workers, citizens, parents or teachers, and more as consumers. Our rights and our powers derive from our standing as consumers; our political choices are votes for those promising us the best deal as consumers; our enjoyment of life is almost synonymous with the quantities (and to a lesser extent qualities) of what we consume. Our success is measured in terms of how well we are doing as consumers. Consumption is not just a means of fulfilling needs but permeates our social relations, identities, perceptions and images.

The consumer has also assumed centre-stage in academic debates. If the 19th-century tradition of social theory and political economy approached people primarily as workers and creators of wealth, consumption is the focus of much 21st-century theorizing. Psychologists have redirected their sights towards an understanding of what drives modern consumers. Cultural theorists have increasingly recognized the spirit of our age (whether described as late modernity, post-modernity, or advanced capitalism) not in modes of production, government, class structure or art but in modes of consumption, lifestyles and identities. Following the collapse of communism in the Eastern bloc, consumerism was commonly described as the unchallenged ideology of our times. Its scope constantly stretched to incorporate new geographical areas, such as Far Eastern countries, new spheres of social relations, like health and education, and new social spaces, like homes and the countryside.

Discussions about consumption and consumerism are rarely value-neutral. Some commentators celebrate the rise of the consumer; having lost faith in religious or political recipes of salvation, the consumer is seen as the mature individual who seeks to enjoy life by making choices and exercising freedom. Others lament consumerism as the final stage of commodification, where all relations between people are finally reduced to usage and exploitation, in which the consumer is easily co-opted. The consumer is not merely an object of theorizing, but almost invariably a central character from a story; now a hero or a heroine, now a victim, now a villain, now a fool, but always central. In some stories, consumers feature as sovereign, deciding the fate of products and corporations at a whim, in others they feature as duped victims, manipulated by producers, advertisers and image-makers. In some, they feature as callous villains, indifferent to the plight of the planet or those less fortunate than themselves, in others as addicts, pursuing a chimera that only reinforces their despair.

This book was written because we believe that the word 'consumer' is now so overused that it is in danger of collapsing into meaningless cliché. At one level, to state that someone is a consumer is almost as meaningful as acknowledging that she or he is a living being. We all consume the same way that we all breathe, since life without consumption is as impossible as life without respiration. Plants and other animals consume too. Why then has 'the consumer' in our culture become so loaded with meanings, assumptions and values? From where does this idea draw its power?

In this book, we argue that different traditions or discourses have invented different representations of the consumer, each with its own specificity and coherence, but wilfully oblivious to those of others. Some conservative economists, for example, have invented the consumer as a decision-maker and an arbiter of products while some consumer activists look at the consumer as a vulnerable and confused being, in need of help. Many cultural theorists look at the consumer as a communicator of meanings sustaining the social fabric, while most ecologists reproach consumers for their reckless and selfish behaviour. In this way, the concept of the consumer appears to have lost its specificity. It can enter different social and cultural agendas, including those of cultural theorists, Marxists, journalists, publishers, advertisers and politicians across the spectrum with apparent equanimity, in seemingly perfect accord. The consumer can mean all things to all people.

The theoretical softness of the concept of the consumer (its readiness to act as an obedient and polite guest in almost any discourse) is accompanied by a moral hardness which it can readily assume. In reviewing what other thinkers have written and after considering the common usage of the term, we became and still are impatient with one-dimensional views, whether they demonize or romanticize the consumer as if in consuming, people transcend every other level of social existence. Paradoxically, love and fear of consumption cross conventional political and economic boundaries. Religious authorities can side with ecologists in denouncing excessive consumption, while co-operative socialists and free market conservatives can join hands to celebrate consumer power.

We believe that it is time different traditions of defining the consumer started to take notice of each other. Our first object therefore is to identify, disentangle and juxtapose approaches to contemporary consumption that are rarely found within a single book. Our discussion will address diverse features of consumption ranging from gifts and bargain-hunting to cashless systems of exchange, from fashion and fads in the First World to the effects of Western consumerism for the Third World, from the class dimensions of consumption to children as consumers, from the semiotics of modern advertising to the scope and limitations of the law as an instrument of consumer protection, from the concept of choice to debates about free trade and protectionism.

A crucial feature of this book is that we examine not only different academic and everyday discourses on consumption, but also the views and ideas of organizations and activists who represent or claim to represent consumers. The consumer movement is sometimes referred to as consumerism, but also the word 'consumerism' can be used to refer to a life excessively preoccupied with consumption. This book is not a sociological study of the consumer movement, but it does address that movement's contribution to defining and shaping contemporary consumption by championing consumer rights. We will sketch an ideological map of the consumer movement since its early beginning in the 19th-century, describing four successive worldviews in consumer advocacy, all alive today: co-operation, value-for-money, anti-corporatism and 'new wave', alternative or ethical consumption. Each of these traditions, and the organizations that still carry them forward, has proffered distinct analyses and interpretations of the position of the consumer in society. These vary hugely from reformist to radical, from pragmatic to visionary, from global to local and from class-, gender- and race-bound to highly individualist.

The book's structure is an attempt to organize a truly prodigious, though sometimes chaotic, array of arguments according to the underlying image of the consumer which inspires and drives them. Thus, after Chapter 1, which investigates the emergence of contemporary Western consumption, each subsequent chapter until the final one presents a distinct portrait of today's consumer, as it emerges from the writings of academics, journalists, advertisers, consumer advocates, policy-makers and others. We portray in succession the consumer as chooser, as communicator, as identity-seeker, as victim, and so forth. It will quickly become evident that each of these portraits highlights a different feature of the consumer's physiognomy, while at the same time obscuring others. We discuss the tensions and contradictions inherent in each portrait and examine the tendencies of each to mutate into or confront different ones. We observe how critical discontinuities and anomalies in a particular tradition of consumer studies are overcome by simply switching from one consumer representation to another. We look, for example, at how the consumer as explorer turns identity-seeker or how the consumer-chooser turns into victim. We argue that each one of these portraits has strengths as well as weaknesses and we try to evaluate each.

Our own purpose, however, is not merely to recreate these images, compelling though they be, nor to criticize each one of them from the vantage point of another. In spite of their considerable complexity, we shall argue that all of these portraits are too tame, predictable and one-sided, failing to come to terms with the fragmentation, volatility and confusion of contemporary Western consumption.

By stirring various traditions together, we are seeking to reclaim some theoretical recalcitrance for the concepts of consumption and the consumer. We would thus like to re-inject some critical edge and prickliness into the notion of the consumer that it has lost by being all things to all people. We introduce the concept of the 'unmanageable consumer' to express this recalcitrance, a refusal on our part to allow the idea of the consumer to become domesticated and comfortable within parcelled discourses.

But there is another quality that we seek to capture through the concept of unmanageability, one that pertains not to the concept of the consumer as it features in academic, political and cultural discourses, but rather to the vital unpredictability that characterizes some of our actions and experiences as consumers, both singly and collectively. As consumers, we can be irrational, incoherent and inconsistent just as we can be rational, planned and organized. We can be individualist or may be driven by social norms and expectations. We can seek risk and excitement or may aim for comfort and security. We can be deeply moral about the way we spend our money or quite unfettered by moral considerations. Our feelings towards consumption can range from loathing shopping to loving it, from taking pride in what we wear to being quite unconcerned about it, from enjoying window-shopping to finding it utterly boring, from being highly self-conscious about the car we drive to being quite indifferent to it. Such fragmentations and contradictions should be recognized as core features of contemporary consumption itself, hence the pertinence of the idea of the unmanageable consumer.

To portray consumers as unmanageable does not seek to overlook the difficulties many people have in making ends meet, the lack of choice that we experience due to the oppressive burden of social expectations or the indignity of rank poverty. Nor does it skim over the immense resources and effort deployed to observe, monitor, survey, forecast and control our behaviour as consumers, in short, to manage us. Like today's worker, today's consumer is over-managed, prodded, seduced and controlled. Never before has one's every purchase been so closely observed, each credit card transaction so closely dissected, each movement monitored on close-circuit TV. In the pages of this book, we will encounter countless modes of consumer management coming from diverse quarters. Consumers, however, do not always act as predictably as would-be managers desire. The very fragmentations and contradictions that characterize our actions as consumers enable us from time to time, in devious, creative and unpredictable ways to dodge management devices and evade apparatuses of monitoring and control.

Ultimately, our actions and experiences as consumers cannot be detached from our actions and experiences as social, political and moral agents. The fragmentation and contradictions of contemporary consumption are part and parcel of the fragmentation and contradictions of contemporary living. Being a consumer dissolves neither class membership nor citizenship; it is not the case that at one moment we act as consumers and the next as workers or as citizens, as women or men or as members of ethnic groups. We are creative composites of several social categories at the same time, with histories, presents and futures.

But the most important reason for writing this book has been our desire to explore the qualities of fragmentation and unmanageability of contemporary Western consumption as part of a long-term historical process. Today's Western consumer is often treated as the terminus of a historical process, which will be duplicated in other parts of the world. Alternatively, Western consumption is viewed as culpable for the escalating plunder of vast sections of the Third World and the continuing deprivation of its inhabitants. We want to emphasize that today's Western consumption is itself but a stage towards something different. The fact that no-one can be sure about what lies ahead does not imply that we should treat today's Western consumer as the consummation of a historical development. This is a mistake made by some political ideologues in their romanticization of consumer choice and inability to imagine a future different from the present. We wish therefore to re-assert the importance of the debate about the global and historical implications of Western modes of consumption and the legacy that it is likely to leave for future generations.

The meaning of consumerism is framed by its wider political and social context. The demise of the Soviet Union and the end of the Cold War at the end of the 1980s signalled to many observers the triumph of Western consumer capitalism. Equally, the spectacular rise of the economies of the Asia Pacific region was seen as confirmation that the only meaningful choice left to nations (now that the choice of capitalism versus socialism was foreclosed) was that between consumer capitalism and poverty-ridden, corruption-rife under-development. Instead, we argue that any triumphalism about Western-style consumption is misplaced. The future of global consumption must remain the object of questioning on economic, cultural, environmental and moral grounds. The rapid globalization of production and markets heralds a decline in some of the conditions that fuelled the rise of modern consumerism: steady jobs, full employment, high wages, rising standards of living, and so on. The efforts of advertisers, publishers and trend-setters to entice consumers to resume the riotous pace of spending are not consistently successful. Major economies like those of Japan, France and Germany have faltered, while the USA itself stuttered in the aftermath of the bombings on September 11th, 2001. In the wake of insecurity about jobs and countless cautionary tales of debt and bankruptcy, some perceptive commentators talk about consumers suffering from spending fatigue. Some politicians are quick to despair about consumers doing their bit for the economy. Some consumers have become notably reluctant to consume. As earlier generations of workers had been accused of being work-shy by their bosses, so consumers can be castigated for being spend-shy and failing in their duty to keep the economy going.

The core assumptions of consumerism have also come under scrutiny. The foolishness of pretending that the natural environment contains inexhaustible resources and has unlimited tolerance to abuse has become patently clear. The notion that everyone in the world could 'enjoy' Western standards of living without leading to an environmental and ecological catastrophe seems increasingly blinkered. Even the axiomatic equation of quality of life with wealth has started to be questioned, as some vanguard consumer groups continue to say, 'Consume less'. While we cannot see the end of Western consumerism yet, its future and pattern can no longer be taken for granted. For the time being, consumerism, far from resting on its laurels, seems to be going through a period of well-earned malaise.

This book argues that the fragmentation and unmanageability of the consumer are features of this malaise. As long as the consumer could confidently look forward to a future of greater prosperity and affluence, the issue of defining the consumer seemed pedantic. Today, however, defining the consumer has become like a Rorschach Test, the psychologist's tool, where individuals are invited to say what they 'see' in the shape of an inkblot; the idea is that what they each 'see' betrays their state of mind. Similarly, to ask what the consumer is invites us to explore ourselves, our notions of society and our outlook on life. One's tendency is always to search for meaning, cohesion and transparency where there may be doubt, ambiguity and uncertainty. By accepting fragmentation and unmanageability, this book invites the reader to unravel some of the paradoxes that make up contemporary consumption and to assess their implications for the future. Are we going to witness the consumer's resurgence, metamorphosis or demise?

CHAPTER 1

The Emergence of Contemporary Consumerism

There is little sign that most of the populace wish for anything other than a continual increase in the availability of such products and the benefits felt to be received by their possession.

Daniel Miller, 1987: 185

C O R E ARGUMENTS

Five meanings of the term consumerism are introduced, tracing some continuities in consumption patterns, but also identifying some new qualities of its contemporary forms. The 20th-century was characterized by a 'Fordist Deal' under which enhanced standards of living compensated for alienated work. This deal has unravelled with the new global division of labour. The major challenge for consumerism in the future looks likely to arise from its environmental impact, partly as a result of the spread of Western consumerism worldwide.

Since the 14th-century, the word 'to consume' in English has had negative connotations, meaning 'to destroy, to use up, to waste, to exhaust'. By contrast, the word 'customer' was a more positive term, implying 'a regular and continuing relationship to a supplier'. The unfavourable connotations of the word 'consumer' continued to the late 19th-century. Gradually, the meaning of 'to consume' shifted from the object that is dissipated to the human need that is fulfilled in the process (Williams, 1976: 69). It is mainly since the 'Roaring Twenties' (1920s) in the USA that the meaning of consumption has broadened still further to resonate pleasure, enjoyment and freedom (Lasch, 1991). Consumption moved from a means towards an end – living – to being an end in its own right. Living life to the full became increasingly synonymous with consumption.

By the beginning of the 21st-century, this had changed. The consumer has become a totem pole around which a multitude of actions and ideologies are dancing. Whether en masse or as an individual, the consumer is no longer a person who merely desires, buys and uses up a commodity. Instead, as we shall see in subsequent chapters, we encounter the consumer in turn as one who chooses, buys or refuses to buy; as one who displays or is unwilling to display; as one who offers or keeps; as one who feels guilt or has moral qualms; as one who explores or interprets, reads or decodes, reflects or daydreams; as one who pays or shop-lifts; as one who needs or cherishes; as one who loves or is indifferent; as one who defaces or destroys.

Like the words consumption and consumer, the word consumerism is part of different intellectual traditions that for a long time have knowingly or unknowingly disregarded each other. As a result, the word consumerism has come to mean different things to different people in different contexts. Even within academic research, the word consumerism has acquired a number of distinct uses. It is common when talking about consumerism to slip from one usage to another, hardly being aware of doing so. It is instructive, however, to try to disentangle some of the different meanings that the term has acquired. We discern at least five variants, some of which overlap.

1   **Consumerism as a moral doctrine in developed countries**. In developed countries, consumption has come to embody a moral doctrine; with the demise of the Puritan ethic of self-denial, consumption has emerged virtually unchallenged as the essence of the good life. According to this view, consumerism is the vehicle for freedom, power and happiness. All of these things lie in the consumer's ability to choose, acquire, use and enjoy material objects and experiences. Within this discourse, style, taste, fantasy and sexuality have come to the forefront; gender makes an intermittent appearance; class has unjustly tended to be obscured.

2   **Consumerism as the ideology of conspicuous consumption**. In addition to defining the meaning of good life (as above), consumption has come to supplant religion, work and politics as the mechanism by which social and status distinctions may be established. Display of material commodities fix the social position and prestige of their owners.

3   **Consumerism as an economic ideology for global development**. With the collapse of the Communist bloc and its productionist rhetoric ('forever more tons of steel per head'), consumerism, the pursuit of ever-higher standards of

living in ever-less regulated markets, is seen as supplying the ideological force underpinning capitalist accumulation in the global system dominated by transnational corporations. It has become a key feature of international relations from trade and aid to foreign policy. The nurturing of consumers is seen as the key to economic development in countries as diverse as those of the old Soviet bloc, Latin America, Asia and Africa.

4   **Consumerism as a political ideology.** Formerly the hallmark of the political Right, this form of consumerism is increasingly embraced across the political spectrum, in high-, medium- and low-income countries alike. The modern state has emerged both as a guarantor of consumer rights and minimum standards and also as a major provider of goods and services. Accordingly, consumerism has entered the realm of party politics. Many right-wing political parties in the West adeptly shifted their rhetoric from paternalism to present themselves as parties of choice, freedom and the consumer. Old socialist parties belatedly started to shake off their image as champions of the so-called nanny state and its association with patronizing attitudes towards what people need and sanctimonious admonishments against pleasure. According to this view of consumerism, the marketplace supplies increasingly glamorous, stylish goods, while the state is seen as providing shabby, run-down services, from which proper consumers seek to buy out, if they can afford it. It is, therefore, the new role of the state to create markets and market disciplines out of what were previously seen as public goods or services.

5   **Consumerism as a social movement seeking to promote and protect the rights of consumers.** Consumer advocacy, dating back to the co-operative movement in the 19th-century, has developed with changing patterns and scope of consumption. Some consumer advocates today are moving from concerns over quality and 'value-for-money' to a critique of unbridled consumption in a world of finite resources and a fragile natural environment. Currently consumer advocacy seeking a better deal for the consumer co-exist uneasily alongside a new wave consumerism with its radical and ethically driven agenda.

Each of the chapters of this book introduces a different face of the consumer and a distinct variant of consumerism. We will therefore not narrow our discussion by offering a strict definition of consumerism. We embrace the variety and nuances in the term in order to draw the connections between the five meanings above. In this way, we will develop a more complex account of consumerism, as a phenomenon that both describes social reality and also shapes our perceptions of social reality. In all its meanings, consumerism is neither ethically nor politically neutral, and is therefore a terrain to be contested and argued over. Our object is not merely to clarify current and past debates on consumerism and consumption, but to explore the contradictions harboured by contemporary consumption patterns, the limits to consumerism and the forces that are likely to oppose it in the future.

The rest of this chapter sketches the emergence of Western consumerism. We examine the circumstances that fostered it and argue that the 21st-century looks like being a period a considerable malaise for consumerism. In the next 50 years, it is almost certain that consumerism, as we currently know it, will have peaked and that affluent societies will be forced to enter the currently uncharted waters of 'post-consumerism' (Lansley, 1994: 234–8). Environmental, population and political factors are likely to conspire to deliver this. It is also possible that the centre of gravity of rampant consumerism will migrate from the de-industrializing West to the rapidly industrializing East. The paths are unclear.

The Fordist Deal and Contemporary Consumerism

How did it all start? Contemporary consumerism in all its current diversity is unthinkable without the unwritten deal pioneered by Henry Ford for his employees: *ever-increasing standards of living in exchange for a quiescent labour force*. Ford offered his workforce the carrot of material enjoyment outside the workplace as compensation for the de-skilling, control and alienation that he imposed in the workplace. He also recognized the potential of his workers as customers, once they rose above mere subsistence. 'If you cut wages, you just cut the number of your customers' (Barnet and Cavanagh, 1994: 261). Since that deal was struck, consumerism has come to signify a general preoccupation with consumption standards and choice as well as a willingness to read meanings in material commodities and to equate happiness and success with material possessions (Lebergott, 1993).

The Fordist Deal linking consumption to the labour process highlights three dimensions of 20th-century consumer capitalism that are rarely addressed together. They will be at the forefront of our discussion throughout this chapter. The first is its *historical* character. Consumerism did not appear already shaped and formed in advanced industrial societies. It was prefigured in earlier societies (McCracken, 1988; McKendrick et al., 1982; Mukerji, 1983; Williams, 1982). Contemporary consumerism is the product of long-term historical changes. Fordism (as a phenomenon embracing both production and consumption) signalled the transformation of consumerism from an elite to a mass phenomenon in the 20th-century in advanced capitalist societies (Williams, 1976). A very different picture emerges if, instead of approaching contemporary consumerism as the terminus of economic and cultural trends, it is looked at as transitional, that is, having to reinvent itself or being overtaken by other social forces.

The second dimension of contemporary consumerism is its *global* nature. While consumerism touches the minutiae of everyday life, it is a global phenomenon in many different ways. It underlines the interconnectedness of national economies, it affects rich and poor alike, it shapes international trade and (as the wars in the Middle East have demonstrated) politics and peace (George, 1992; Gray, 2003) The major players in the consumerist game, the transnational corporations, are global players, the stakes are global stakes and the implications of the game itself are global (Barnet and Cavanagh, 1994; Castells, 1996, 1997, 1998; Held, 1999; Held and McGrew, 2000; Sklair, 1995). By the end of the 20th-century, just 200 corporations accounted for a fourth of global economic activity. Using World Bank and Fortune 500 figures, the Institute of Policy Studies compared the relative power of the top national economies and corporations and produced a composite Top 200. This found that:

> Of the 100 largest economies in the world, 51 are corporations; only 49 are countries (based on a comparison of corporate sales and country GDPs). [...]

> The Top 200 corporations' combined sales are bigger than the combined economies of all countries minus the biggest 10.

The Top 200s' [companies and countries] combined sales are 18 times the size of the combined annual income of the 1.2 billion people (24 percent of the total world population) living in 'severe' poverty.

While the sales of the Top 200 are the equivalent of 27.5 percent of world economic activity, they employ only 0.78 percent of the world's workforce. (Anderson and Cavanagh, 2000: 3)

Consumers themselves are aware of globalization, increasingly encountering goods that are both similar and familiar all over the world.

This connects with the third dimension, sharply highlighted by the Fordist Deal, the vital links between contemporary consumerism and *production*. To be sure, a central feature of consumerism is the separation of the at times squalid circumstances of the production of commodities from their glamorized circulation and sale (Bauman, 1988; Du Gay, 1996b; Frenkel et al., 1999; Korczynski, 2001, 2003; Korczynski et al., 2000; Lasch, 1991; Sturdy et al., 2001). Yet, patterns of consumption are crucially linked with developments in the nature of production. The consumer is ultimately the same person as the worker or manager now threatened by continuous mechanization of production and distribution or by the flight of capital to lower wage economies. Equally, international capital has a lot at stake in seducing the displaced peasant and exploited workers of the Third World and converting them into consumers aspiring after Western standards (Bello, 2002; Durning, 1992; George, 1988; Norberg-Hodge, 1991; Seabrook, 2004; Sklair, 1991).

The History of Consumption

Much consumer research looks at consumers a-historically; it also approaches consumption as a set of patterns detached from other cultural practices. This is the approach adopted both by market researchers and by the compilers of official government statistics who monitor spending power, spending patterns and changes in buyer behaviour. On such data, many great corporate and state decisions are based – whether to launch a new product; whether to expand into a new market; whether to tax this product or that service; whether the economy is 'overheating' or 'under-consuming'; whether shifts in spending will last; whether this kind of expenditure should be encouraged or discouraged, and if so how.

Expenditure data can be extraordinarily dry and seemingly lifeless, until placed in an historical context. Some social historians have devoted considerable effort to identifying changing patterns of spending across the centuries. John Burnett, for example, identifies several distinct phases of the cost of living in England. For about 100 years following 1280, his starting point, prices fluctuated by 50 percent to 100 percent around a constant level. From 1380 to 1500, prices stabilized, and were mainly affected by years of harvest failure. From 1500 to the 1650, prices went up six fold, but remained constant from 1650 to the latter half of the 18th-century, then shooting up by the 1820s. The next major period of inflation followed the First World War, when they rose, only to crash dramatically in the 1930s and then rise again following the Second World War. Through these changes, according to Burnett, the cost of living for people in Southern England rose 40 fold between the mid-13th and mid-20th centuries (Burnett, 1969: 328).

What the cost of living panorama fails to show is the changing nature and meaning of consumption through the ages. As Burnett himself has argued, 'we cannot compare the cost of a mediaeval peasant's cottage with a modern council house, or of the Wife of Bath's habit with a miniskirt, in any meaningful way: all are typical enough of their times, but the times have changed' (Burnett, 1969: 10–11). Recognizing the limitations of focusing mainly on living standards, a number of authors since the 1980s have explored the social meaning of consumption in different historical periods. These authors have studied moments in history when consumption achieved extraordinary opulence and importance, at least for select social strata. In a pioneering study, McKendrick probed into the demand side of the early industrial revolution, notably the commercialization of fashion, which turned the British bourgeoisie into avid spenders (McKendrick et al., 1982). Rosalind Williams looked at the rampant consumerism of the Parisian bourgeoisie and the arrival of mass consumption through the institution of department stores in the late 19th-century (Williams, 1982). Mukerji went further back and examined conspicuous consumption among Elizabethan nobility, fuelled by the discovery of 'fashion' and the arrival of nouveaux riches (Mukerji, 1983).

What sets modern consumption apart from earlier patterns is not merely the growth of spending power across social classes and strata, but, more importantly, the experience of *choice* as a generalized social phenomenon. No earlier period afforded social masses the choice of what to spend surplus cash on after the means of subsistence had been met. This is well illustrated by the decline in the proportion of household expenditure on food. In Britain, at the start of the 20th-century, working-class consumers were spending around a half to two-thirds of their income on food (Burnett, 1969). By the middle of that century, food on average claimed only a third of household expenditure. By the beginning of the 21st-century it was nearer one tenth (National Statistics (Great Britain) and Great Britain Dept. for Environment Food & Rural Affairs, 2004). True, for the least well off, the proportion of expenditure spent on food might be twice or three times that of the rich, but even for them, the cash available for other forms of consumption are of an order that most 19th-century consumers and many 20th-century consumers in developing countries would find inconceivable. Similar, if less pronounced, decreases have been noted in most industrial countries (Lebergott, 1993: 77–83).

By the 1960s, Burnett could note an astonishing shift in consumption patterns compared to the past:

> Far more than ever before goes on services and entertainment, taxation and the various forms of saving, less on the traditional luxuries, drink and tobacco, but much more on 'conspicuous consumption' – dress, personal possessions and adornment of the home. With the exceptions of domestic help and private educational expenses … it would be a fair generalization to say that contemporary spending habits have moved towards what was formerly regarded as the typically middle-class pattern and away from the traditional working-class pattern. (Burnett, 1969: 319–20)

The Emergence of Contemporary Consumption

Most commentators on consumption agree that, following the Second World War, there was an explosion of consumption in the industrialized nations. Many industries, such as automobiles, chemicals, domestic appliances, electrical and electronic goods, took off, fuelling as well as feeding off a culture of consumerism. The basic bargain on which consumerism flourished was a more docile workforce in exchange for ever-increasing standards of living, referred to earlier as the Fordist Deal.

Because Fordism makes the reproduction of labour power and mass consumption a decisive basis for the process of accumulation and valorization, it must aim for a tendentially unlimited expansion of consumption, it systematically institutionalizes 'wish production' and it constantly extends needs. These can only be satisfied in commodity form, which produces ever-new needs. The 'endlessness of needs' introduced with Fordist society, the limitless nature of consumer demands inherent in the Fordist model of consumption, contains an inbuilt tendency to a material 'demand inflation'. ... [This] binds the structure of the Fordist individual with consumerism, which may certainly be politically stabilising, but also has an economically precarious effect' (Hirsch, 1991: 168).

Governments became vital parties to the Fordist Deal, leading some commentators like Hirsch (1991) and Jessop (2001) to speak of the 'Fordist State'. Governments became guarantors of full employment: 'Work and you will be able to consume; consume and you will be in work' (Bunting, 2004). Following the post-Second World War reconstruction, politics in the affluent world came to be dominated by governments' credibility, whatever the hue, to deliver on promises to improve living standards (Hobsbawm, 1994: 579ff.). Political economy became a constant 'compare and contrast' exercise between the different types of contract with consumers (Hampden-Turner and Trompenaars, 1993). This was signalled in the UK by the defeat of the Labour government in 1950–51 whose seemingly endless policy of frugality since 1945 was swept aside by the Conservatives' promise of a better deal for the consumer (Hennessy, 1992) and in the USA by the post-war continuation of the 'American Way of Life' that began before it (Mander, 1991: 21–4).

In economic geographical terms, the world's economy is now dominated by regional trading blocs, in North America around the USA, in Europe around a golden 'triangle' of London–Bonn–Milan, and in the Far East, initially around Japan and increasingly around China and India. All such blocs are deeply in love with the consumer. Much is made of the differences between them, particularly in regard to their emphasis on the role of government, the price of their labour and their consumers' spending power. It is less often remarked that all these blocs, in spite of their political and other differences, offer their populations not dissimilar versions of the consumer dream: pleasure through spending.

Throughout the period referred to by Hobsbawm (1994), as the Golden Age of the West (1947–72), this policy was highly successful, with ever-increasing opportunities for consumers to spend on goods such as records, clothes, homes, cars. By the 1960s, standards of living as measured by traditional indicators of consumption had improved spectacularly, with the USA, as so often, leading the way (Lebergott, 1993). In 1920, 16 percent of US households had a phonograph; by 1960 31 percent had one (Lebergott, 1993: 137). In 1900, only 20 percent of US households had a horse. In 1920, 26 percent had a car and by 1989, nearly 90 percent had one. In 1925, 10 percent of US households had a radio; by 1990, 99 percent had one and 98 percent had a television.

Internationally, the USA led a common emerging pattern among rich countries. By 1960, 93 percent of US households had hot running water, in the UK 77 percent had, in the Netherlands 67 percent, France 41 percent, West Germany 34 percent. Fifty-five percent of US households had a washing machine, 45 percent in the UK, 69 percent in the Netherlands, 32 percent in France and 36 percent in West Germany. Seventy-seven percent of US households had a car, 35 percent in the UK, 26 percent in the Netherlands, 40 percent in France and 26 percent in West Germany (Lebergott, 1993: 111). It is this explosion of consumer spending power that is now promoted in the fast developing Asian countries.

Time studies offer another way of looking at changes in people's behaviour as consumers, signalling the rise of Western consumerism. The major trends here have included for substantial savings of time spent on domestic labour accompanied by considerably increased amounts of time spent on transport, shopping and working (Bunting, 2004). There are national differences here, with Anglo-Saxon economies promoting long working hours, while European polities seek to defend a social model of progress that includes shorter working weeks, longer holidays and more time spent with families.

Gershuny has also drawn attention to wide variations by social class; for example, British working-class housewives saw a decline in their domestic work time from the 1950s until the mid 1970s, whereas middle-class housewives saw a twofold increase (Gershuny, 1992: 16). He insists on a general increase of time spent on consumption activities:

> Productivity growth (at work) leads to a need for more time to consume the social product. Consumption takes time: the more we produce, the more time we need for consumption. Working time reduction, in short, is a phenomenon of a deeply materialist society. (Gershuny, 1992: 21)

Time studies, like those pioneered by Gershuny, provide interesting information. Like expenditure figures, however, they stop short of unravelling the motives and sentiments of the consumer. Both traditions of studying consumer behaviour indicate how consumers 'vote' in the marketplace, not why they do. The picture that emerges is that in advanced capitalist societies, people spend more money on more goods and spend more time spending money. But what of the meanings of these goods? Are the luxuries of yesteryear still regarded as luxuries, or have they become necessities? And is time spent shopping to be regarded as leisure time or as domestic labour time? Is time spent driving an expensive car (or a cheap one) to the supermarket (or to work) to be seen as enjoyable consumption or as routine drudge? Such questions cannot be answered by economic studies alone. The role of consumption within ideology should also be addressed.

Consumption and the New Conservatism

The emergence of modern consumerism can hardly be reduced to spending patterns. Equally, it should not be studied outside the ideological context of the Cold War. Throughout this period, glamorized consumption of the West as depicted in advertisements and celebrated in television series, was at least as potent an ideological weapon in the super-power confrontation as space exploits or gold medal hauls in the Olympic Games. The patent effectiveness of Western free enterprise in supplying a plethora of constantly mutating and highly desirable consumer products was held as final evidence of the superiority of capitalist market forces, entrepreneurship, free trade and political systems. Chronic shortages of consumer goods, perennial queues and the absurd inefficiencies of the Soviet bogeyman became as important a part of Western propaganda as civil rights abuses and political oppression. Since then, of course, the Chinese economic success has indicated that its brand of Communism was not intrinsically hostile to expanding consumer markets; certainly, it seized the opportunity to recast itself as the efficient low-cost labour, reliable source of cheap luxuries to the rest while also fuelling its own consumerist boom.

But the eulogies of Western consumerism set against the alleged bleakness of the communist system did not merely originate with the propagandists of the Cold War. Scorning a long sceptical and critical tradition from the 19th-century to the present, which included Alexis de Tocqueville, Max Weber, Georg Simmel, Thorstein Veblen, R.H. Tawney and culminated in André Gorz and Herbert Marcuse, many Western economists found much to celebrate in consumerism. To them, the planned economies of the Soviet bloc provided a tangible model against which positive comparisons could be made. Milton Friedman and Friedrich Hayek, for instance, argued that consumers under Soviet-style command economies can only walk down the 'road to serfdom'. Command economies offer next to nothing, Friedman argued, compared to Western economies, which gain under 'co-operation through voluntary exchange', that is, voluntary associations through the free market's price mechanism (Friedman and Friedman, 1980: 3–14). Raymond Aron, no uncritical celebrant of Western consumerism, noted that under the old Soviet system:

> consumer choice has been almost completely eliminated. The distribution of national resources between investment and consumption is dictated by the planners, and even the distribution of resources between various sectors of industry, or between industry and agriculture, is not determined by the consumers. (Aron, 1967: 109)

In Soviet economies, it was a political choice not to give consumers choice. The state controlled the price of goods, taxing the difference between what it bought and sold products for. Thus planners had the power to decide 'whether or not to satisfy the desires of this or that category of consumers' (Aron, 1967: 110). Socialist economists joined in the critique of Soviet-style planned economies. Alec Nove, long before the demise of the USSR, pilloried the idiocy of giving the planner primacy over the end-user. Power over economic activity in the USSR, argued Nove, would ultimately have to be given to the consumer. 'To influence the pattern of production by their behaviour as buyers is surely the most genuinely democratic way to give power to consumers. There is no direct "political" alternative' (Nove, 1983: 225).

Nove lived long enough to see his prognosis come true. The Soviet system could not last without the market mechanism, continuously failing to meet the aspirations of its consumers. He would have been critical, however, of those like Stanley Lebergott who, since the collapse of Soviet economies at the end of the 1980s, have been singing the praises of the market. Lebergott, a US free market economist, argued that the consumer-led market economy is simply the best *social* system. Others have been devised, but only when the consumer is in the driving seat is the 'pursuit of happiness' successful and egalitarian. His missionary fervour in favour of consumerist culture led him into some well-known mine-fields. For example, he exalted the wide availability of affordable cars to the US consumer, which extended the privilege of travel from the rich to all social strata. If 'tons of steel per head of population' was the sign of economic prowess and social progress for the old-style Soviet planners, for Lebergott 'cars per head of population' was the measure of happiness, freedom and social justice (Lebergott, 1993). Along with ideologues of the conservatives then known as 'the New Right', Lebergott idolized motor-cars, choosing to ignore their social and environmental dysfunctions, the injuries and death that they cause, the frustration of traffic jams or lengthy journeys to work, to school or to the shop. For him, as for Margaret Thatcher, the motor-car epitomized the freedom of private consumers to go where they please, without relying on government, business or anyone else to run the buses, coaches or railways on time.

Throughout the Reagan–Thatcher years of the 1980s, a backlash against Keynesian economics in the West ushered in a phase of almost unchallenged supremacy for the free market. Consumerism shifted from an ideological weapon in the Cold War to an ideological weapon for the New Right. It became fashion-able for apostles of the free market on both sides of the Atlantic to view con-sumers as the storm-troopers of freedom. Their foes were no longer Soviet-style planners, but social-democratic politicians who supposedly wished to tax citizens, in order to provide whatever provisions – housing, health, education, railways, parks, roads – they believed were needed. The 1970s and 1980s saw the spectacu-lar resurrection of Adam Smith, a selective reading of whose ideas provided the gospel of the New Right. Markets work, leave everything to the market, became the cry. Adam Smith was right:

> It is not from the benevolence of the butcher, the brewer, or the baker that we expect our dinner, but from their regard to their own interest. We address ourselves, not to their humanity but to their self-love, and never talk to them of our own necessities but of their advantages. (Smith, 1970[1776]: 119)

Adam Smith's prototypical consumers did not have to contend with advertisers enticing them to have a second and a third dinner, let alone to 'graze' on snacks all day long; nor were they faced with different brands of meat, beer and bread, each proclaiming its own personality. But Smith's present-day enthusiasts believe that neither the increasing concentration of economic activity nor the effects of mass media and advertising undermine the fundamental value of markets in ensuring efficient economic activity.

Consumerism and the Mass Media

The role of the mass media and advertising in fuelling and sustaining contem-porary consumerism has been widely debated and contested. What is beyond doubt is that consumerism, in its many guises, found in the mass media the ideal vehicle both for its self-definition and for its dissemination. Modern consumerism really takes off with the growth of effective advertising campaigns, where the systematic moulding of consciousness can take place. Modern media of mass communication enabled advertisers to capture the attention and imagination of millions, to stop chance dictating how a product is seen and to shape thoughts and actions in particular ways. Raymond Williams suggested that the development of modern commercial advertising is highly significant in the creation of consumerism. Under late 19th-century capitalism, mass manufacture was related to the satisfaction of relatively fixed needs. Early forms of advertising were primarily meant to notify potential customers about available supply (Williams, 1976: 69). Modern advertising, on the other hand, is forged on the assumption that consumers have different means of satisfying needs; indeed, that consumers can derive pleasures and satisfactions that have little to do with needs. Modern advertising makes no secret of its aim to stimulate desire rather than to propose the means for satisfying needs (Lury, 1994, 1996, 2004).

Much has been written about the genius and creativity of marketing as well as about the effectiveness of the techniques used. These techniques have become increasingly indirect and sophisticated, relying on product placements, texting, the creation of rumours and systematic manufacture of fashion in goods. Advertisers regularly counter criticisms that they manipulate the public and generate artificial needs for spurious products by pointing at the numerous failed campaigns and at advertisements that backfired. They also like to argue that today's 'sophisticated consumers' are not easily taken in by crass salesmanship, that advertisements today are a subtle art form, stimulating thinking and providing humour and entertainment. Some of these arguments will be examined in detail in the chapters that follow. While it is wrong to attribute to advertisers demonic powers of deception and persuasion, it is equally wrong to overlook the cumulative effect of advertising on culture. Irrespective of whether a campaign is successful, whether an advertisement is witty or mundane, whether it is addressed to a mass or a niche market, the cumulative effect of advertising is to associate commodities (and especially brands) with meanings, that is, to turn commodities into what Baudrillard called sign values (Baudrillard, 1988b[1970]). Whether one is looking for happiness, identity, beauty, love, masculinity, youth, marital bliss or anything else, there is a commodity somewhere that guarantees to provide it. Through advertising, meanings are spuriously attached onto commodities, which are then presented as the bridges to fulfilment and happiness (McCracken, 1988).

The effects of advertisements on the 'unsophisticated' consumer are even more far-reaching. Mendelson and his co-researchers (Mendelson, 1992) voice a common concern that children are especially vulnerable (Mendelson, 1992). Advertisers, they argue, use two approaches to sell products to children: normal advertisements and programme-length commercials that promote action figures and products related to the show.

> Young children are unable to distinguish between programs and commercials and do not understand that commercials are designed to sell products. This observation suggests that any advertising directed are young children is inherently unfair. (Mendelson, 1992: 343)

Thus the culture of consumption is reproduced within each generation. This culture is exported to the Third World with equal facility. In her study of Ladakh culture in Nepal, Helena Norberg-Hodge (1991) charted the impact that television had on a society previously locked into its extraordinary frugal ecological way of life for centuries. Within a few short years from the introduction of television, children, aged 6 or less, started to see their own food as primitive and backward, refusing to eat what had been eaten for centuries and had been regarded with pride. In many other areas of consumption, Western goods came to be regarded as modern, civilized and desirable while their traditional counterparts were dismissed as backward and uncivilized. In a couple of decades, that culture was broken up irreversibly (Norberg-Hodge, 1991). While Norberg-Hodge acknowledged the role of other agents in such a cultural invasion, her research highlighted the power of the media and Western advertising and acts as a particularly striking reminder of the likely effects on local cultures of further globalization of the mass media through satellite and cable systems (Barnet and Cavanagh, 1994: 137–60).

Consumerism at the Fin-de-siècle

The 1980s is retrospectively recognized as the moment of triumph for consumerism. The old moral restraints on consumption (such as remnants of frugality and thrift associated with the Protestant work ethic, guilt, or vestiges of snobbery vis-à-vis conspicuous consumption) were swept aside by an extraordinary, credit-led consumerist boom (Lee, 1993). Successful businessmen, and a few businesswomen, emerged as cultural super-heroes, temporarily joining film and sports stars. Greed lost some of its pejorative, puritanical connotations. The other side of the coin in the 1980s in the West was a crumbling social infrastructure, a squeeze on social services and a sizeable proportion of the population that was kept out of the consumer party (Mack and Lansley, 1985, 1992; Townsend, 1979, 1993; Toynbee, 2003). At the end of the 20th-century, according to Zygmunt Bauman (Bauman, 1992) the 'new poor' were defined not by absolute standards of deprivation but by the lack of choice and their dependence on state provisions. In a strange way, the new poor not only did not spoil the party for the rest, but on the contrary tended to make it sweeter. According to Bauman, the poor were seen as failed consumers who stumbled in their exercise of choice and were then forced to accept the state's choices on their behalf:

> The radical unfreedom of welfare recipients is but an extreme demonstration of a more general regulatory principle which underlies the vitality of the consumer-led social system. (Bauman, 1988: 69)

In the 1990s, the atmosphere changed, nowhere better indicated than in the tougher tone of many advertisements. Martin Davidson, a former advertising executive, commented on how the advertising industry responded to this new brashness with hard threatening images, which underlined the risks and dangers of modern life, inviting consumers to join the select ranks of 'survivors' who can join the party. In the following passage, he observed this change in a well-known series of British vodka advertisements:

> There was a new hardness in the air, particularly manifest in the images we confronted in the ads. Lifestyle had become a commodity in its own right. Take Smirnoff, the vodka that for years sent itself up with a campaign style that was the epitome of camp (all those 'I thought X was Y until I discovered Smirnoff'). 'Just good friends' [the replacement advertisement

series] has, however, thrown this all over. This was 80s consumerism in its new guise. For a start it looks different; its production values are affected anti glam, and the strapline throwaway cryptic. [...] This is life underground, on the edge, on the up, utter self-confidence even when narcissistically threatened. (Davidson, 1992: 67–8)

The consumerist party ended abruptly with the end of the 1980s boom. It was ironic that just as the collapse of the Soviet empire came as final confirmation of the superiority of the Western economic and social system (at least for Francis Fukuyama (1992) and those like him), the West was entering a period of recession, accompanied by profound self-doubt and unease. The recession had several distinct features compared to earlier ones. For one, it affected strata of society – managerial, professional, home-owning, thoroughly middle-class – which had rarely experienced the reality or even the threat of unemployment in recent times. Hardship, privation and feelings of profound economic insecurity were more widespread and more pervasive. On both sides of the Atlantic, the spirit of the times appeared to be captured in the poetic justice seen when some of the abrasive 'yuppies' of the 1980s fell on hard times. Even those spared the direct effects of the recession seemed to be afflicted by an ethic of parsimony. Surprisingly, even as signs of recovery were heralded, Western consumers found it hard to re-discover their appetite for spending. The term 'spending fatigue' made an appearance (see Lansley, 1994).

The 1990s witnessed the appearance in Europe of US-style cheap mass retail outlets, substantially undercutting the prices of both high-street shops and out-of-town supermarkets. They also witnessed consumer spending on basics, such as food, being concentrated into fewer supermarket chains competing, or at least giving the impression of competing, for the first time in ages on price (Competition Commission (UK), and Dept. of Trade and Industry (UK), 2000; Raven, et al., 1995). Words like 'savings', 'value', 'free', 'unrepeatable offer', and so on, reappeared in advertisements. These trends made us ponder in the first edition of this book whether that phase marked a blip, a crisis or the twilight of consumerism. In retrospect, our diagnosis of generalized uncertainty owed more to our focus on North American, British and Japanese consumerism than on the rest of the globe.

In the 2000s, the picture is more mixed. American consumerism resurged on the back of a vast array of new products, such as mobile phones, computers and electronic goods, new forms of distribution, mainly through the Internet, and new forms of consumer credit. A low value of the dollar, huge military spending and colossal trade and budget deficits have further heated consumer spending. Starting from different levels, the UK along with some of the economies of former Soviet-bloc countries have also seen unprecedented consumer booms. China and India, at least their elites, joined the big spending consumer societies, helped by tariff reductions and globalized supply chains. By contrast, other countries saw major reversals. France, Germany and several countries of 'old Europe' saw their consumer spending squeezed and their economies static. Argentina and many South American countries have regressed to under-development, while much of Africa remains consigned to near or just above subsistence consumption. Japan continues to stagnate (UNDP, 2001).

There is no agreement on whether the current mixed picture for consumerism will continue or whether we are at the point of a more fundamental structural change in the nature of consumption. American neo-Cons, like their partners elsewhere in the world, are determined to keep their faith in the market to right itself and are unwilling to be dragged by fainthearts back into Keynesian state investment to create demand. Europe is caught in the midst of another heated debate between a social vision for capitalism with an enduring role for the state or whether it should move towards an Anglo-Saxon model of unbridled markets. Many Europeans appear unwilling to relinquish their rights and responsibilities as citizens in favour of accepting as consumers the beneficence of markets.

China and the rapidly industrializing nations of the Far East offer new market opportunities for Western businesses and producers. The prospect of more than 1 billion consumers in China owning washing-machines and driving cars is one that fills them with excitement, even as it concerns ecologists, already worried by the damage caused by the world's first 1 billion members of the excessively consuming class. China, India and other Asian nations doubtless represent the new terrains of consumerism, displaying a voracious appetite for prestigious Western goods and rapidly replacing local markets with Western-style shopping complexes and hyper-markets. Whether these nations will come to the rescue of consumerism in the West is rather more doubtful. Their economic success, based on their ability to supplant the West as centres of manufacturing industry, strikes at the heart of the Fordist Deal on which contemporary consumerism has been based. Workers and managers in the core businesses of the Fordist Deal (cars, household and electrical goods, chemicals, textiles, ship-building, and so on) have suffered as their industries have contracted ('downsizing'), rationalized production techniques to use fewer production centres or seen their centres shifted to the new manufacturing boom areas of the Far East, the newly industrializing countries (NICs) (Broad and Cavanagh, 1993; Lang and Hines, 1993). As capital was attracted away from the old manufacturing centres to areas where wages are low and where standards of welfare and protection for the workers and the environment are laxer, new areas of economic activity appeared to take some of the slack, sustaining high levels of consumption among new groups of aggressively spending nouveaux riches.

Production and Consumption

When writing the first edition of this book, we envisaged two major structural obstacles to the continuing hegemony of the Fordist Deal and Western consumerism at the end of the 20th-century. These were, first, the new global division of labour, following the loosening of trade barriers at regional and global levels, and second, environmental limits, exhaustion and degradation associated with rampant consumption. In the 21st-century, looking back, we can say that we over-emphasized the importance of the first factor and under-emphasized, if anything, the second. In spite of the continuing drain of jobs from the industrial to the developing countries, new areas of economic activity have provided substantial compensation and opportunities for earning. Many Western consumers may no longer enjoy 'jobs for life' enabling them to make long-term spending plans. However, in Anglo-Saxon countries, work opportunities in the new knowledge and information industries, the media, education, health, tourism, sport and entertainment have enabled many of them to sustain spending sprees of conspicuous and luxurious consumption.

The precept 'the producer is also the consumer, the consumer is also producer', held somewhat different meanings to Henry Ford and Karl Marx. Yet they were both clear that work and consumption are closely interlinked activities. Unlike some sociologists who have viewed consumption as supplanting work as a source of meaning and identity in people's lives, work and consumption form a unity that becomes reconfigured in different historical periods. If the Fordist Deal offered stable, well-paid, deskilled, alienated jobs in exchange for uniform and methodical mass consumption, post-Fordism augurs a new deal whereby unpredictable employment in highly visible front-line jobs fuels a wide variety of lifestyle consumption patterns. Identities, instead of emerging out of steady jobs, steady class positions and predictable consumption aspirations are being forged from a variety of transient lifestyle options that include work, sexuality, leisure pursuits, choice of brands and so forth. While in countries like Germany and Japan, increasing casualization of work has tempered the appetites of many consumers, in Anglo-Saxon countries it appears to have had the opposite effect, unlocking new forms of hedonistic consumption. 'While the going is good, enjoy what you have' appears to be the dominant motto.

In *The Corrosion of Character: The Personal Consequences of Work in the New Capitalism*, Richard Sennett (1998) argues that new flexible work arrangements promote a short-term, opportunistic outlook among employees, one that undermines trust and loyalty. Insecurity and fear are endemic. Careers become spasmodic and fragmented, their different steps failing to generate cohesive or integrated life-stories. Exposed to intrusive monitoring of performance, employees feel constantly on trial, yet they are never sure of the goals at which they are aiming. There are no objective measures of what it means to do a good job, and those celebrated for their achievements one day easily find themselves on the receiving end of redundancy packages the next. Showing eagerness, being willing to play any game by any rules, looking attractive and involved, while at the same time maintaining a psychological distance and looking for better prospects elsewhere, these are the chameleon-like qualities of the new economy. Above all, the opportunism of the new economy means being constantly on the look-out for new opportunities and never being satisfied with what one has. The missed opportunity represents the ultimate failure in this state of affairs. Constant job moves, preoccupation with image and the look of CVs/resumés, absence of commitments and sacrifices, these stand in opposition to traditional family values of duty, commitment, constancy and caring.

Sennett illustrates his arguments with a few well-chosen case studies. Wherever he focuses, Sennett observes different elements of the same picture – flexibility, dictated by global markets and ever-changing technologies, promoting opportunism, short-termism and insecurity while destroying values, trust, community and caring. A deep anxiety and insecurity permeates workplaces. This, by itself, is not new. Earlier generations of employees worried; they worried because of the vagaries of the labour markets, social injustice and lack of control over their fate. Today's employees, however, perceive themselves as having *choices*, which can make the difference between success and failure. 'I make my own choices; I take full responsibility for moving around so much' (Sennett, 1998) says one of Sennett's interviewees, who seems to abhor dependency above all else.

Sennett displays no interest in linking these aspirations and experiences of people as workers with their aspirations and experiences as consumers, but the links are clear. *Choice* is once again the key word and experience – choices of lifestyles, of brands, of partners and so forth. Opportunism rules along with an acceptance of highs and lows. Instead of a coherent linear life story, today's consumers, just like their alter-egos, today's producers, accept uncertainty and insecurity, creating multiple and overlapping storylines with themselves as central characters. Thus the volatility of consumer demand and the flexibility of organizations and consequent casualization of work feed off each other, creating a new configuration for the unity of production and consumption that, far from undermining consumerism, sustains it.

Environmental Limits to Consumerism

If casualization of work has not brought about the slow-down of consumption that at one moment it appeared poised to do in the mid-1990s, the severity of looming ecological crisis is likely to prove a more serious obstacle. It has now become almost universally uncontested that the single collective brake on future unbridled consumption is its environmental impact. To consume is to use resources. There is no aspect of consumption that does not have an environmental implication. Making, moving and marketing goods has a footprint, using space, energy and human labour. When this book was first written, the evidence was already strong that there might be finite limits to population, oil/energy availability, other raw materials and the earth's capacity to absorb pollution and waste. By the start of the new century, that evidence had got much stronger (Global Environment Facility, UNEP: GEO Section, and UNEP: Division of GEF Coordination, 2002; Millennium Ecosystem Assessment (Program), 2005). And the evidence for 'new' pressures, notably climate change, had persuaded even short-termist politicians and commentators to see the connections between consumption and environmental degradation. The environmental impact of consumption is forcing us to reformulate what is meant by human and social progress.

The challenge of creating modes of consumption that are at least environmentally benign, and at best environmentally beneficial, is now the great challenge of the age. The drivers for this challenge are increasingly clear. For instance, the world currently has 6 billion people to feed, many of whom it fails to do (while overfeeding others). This is anticipated to grow to 9 or 10 billion by the middle of the 21st-century (UNFPA, 2004). Industrial countries, far from being sheltered from such demographic pressures, will experience a drop in productive population and a simultaneous growth of elderly and dependent people.

Since the 1970s, an emerging environmental movement coupled with a now forgotten hippie reaction to materialism had decried the ecological impact of unfettered consumption (Fritsch, 1974; Meadows and Club of Rome, 1972). As one of the earliest and most trenchant critiques put it, 'the combination of human numbers and per capita consumption has a considerable impact on the environment, in terms of both the resources we take from it and the pollutants we impose on it' (Goldsmith et al., 1972: 2).

Thirty years on, the questions regarding the capacity of the earth to maintain its population have grown. The debate is no longer just about absolute levels of population or just about the exhaustion of particular types of raw materials, but about the continuing impact on the ecosystem of reckless consumption in the developed world and desperate attempts to escape poverty and hunger in the developing world. Even if the planet can sustain twice or three times its present population, it is patently unequipped to sustain it at the present level of the wasteful and polluting lifestyles of the affluent nations (Johnson, 1992). Early pessimists argued starkly that 'if we attempt to preserve the consumer economy indefinitely, ecological forces will dismantle it savagely' (Durning, 1992: 107). Optimists, on the other hand, continue to place their faith on technical fixes (cleaner cars, recycling, energy-conservation etc.), on the resourcefulness of markets in finding rational solutions (Cairncross, 1991: 153ff.; von Weizacher et al., 1996) and, less conspicuously, the determination of governments to see that the poor, the disenfranchised and the starving, at home and abroad, are kept at bay.

Since the (re)birth of a modern environmental movement (Pearce, 1991), the environmental critique of consumerism has moved from being a minor irritant to a business associated with hippies to being a major challenge. The Western model of consumerism is, like a junkie, dependent on oil not just to make, but to move and market goods. Despite denials from political leaders in the USA and UK, there seems little doubt that the invasion of Iraq and overthrow of Saddam Hussein was partly, if not wholly, driven by the need to retain Iraqi oil for Western use (Gray, 2003). Water wars loom, as climate change and soil depletion threaten the capacity of agriculture to supply enough food for everyone (Lang and Heasman, 2004). These adversities will become considerably exacerbated by climate changes that will render much land uninhabitable, enhance desertification and accelerate water use and add to pressures on migration. Some commentators anticipated widespread social and political unrest, possible wars and serious economic dislocation that are unlikely to leave consumerism in its current patterns.

Although there is wide agreement about the environmental 'tipping points' that are likely to change policy and the direction of current consumerism, there is surprisingly less political expression of the environmental critique of consumerism. Those arguing a fundamentalist 'back to nature' position and 'a plague on all consumption' position are so far less represented in governments than those promoting either a continued right to consume ad nauseam or a 'light' green, ameliorative approach. Some, in the corridors of power, know that the environment will sooner or later halt current consumption, but they prefer to back a compromise position: the promotion of more energy efficiency and tougher recycling, resource reuse, and so on. The challenge, according to this technocratic response, is not whether to use the environment, but how to use it well, efficiently and effectively.

If their formal political impact has so far been modest, bit by bit, environmentalists have re-opened a fundamental ideological critique of Western consumption: that it damages even as it gives pleasure to the consumer; that it carries a likely seed of its own undoing; that the nature and scale of production now threatens the maintenance of present styles of consumption. In an appeal to business to change the direction of consumption, Hawken was early to argue that contemporary capitalism is ecologically unsophisticated, reducing everything to crude annual indicators of profit and loss that are unable to account for the longevity of by-products of consumption such as toxins in the environment.

> Our current system [of managing toxins] is based on the fascinating reverse of responsibility and accountability. If my dog gets loose and bites someone, I have to pay, but if a corporation's chemicals get loose and poison groundwater, rivers, fish, and ultimately humans, it is we, the citizens, who pay. (Hawken, 1993: 70)

Ironically, the unparalleled period of post-war consumption meant that, by the early 21st-century, the word 'consumer' has regained its older, destructive connotations, as a result of the environmental critique. Concern for the environment draws together people from across the conventional political spectrum. Whether a green movement can redefine politics, consumption and the nature of the good life or whether it will be compromised and incorporated is still unclear. In many democratic countries there are Green political parties, but they generally remain small, despite prophecies that the Green movement is the greatest ideological adversary to global capitalism, following the collapse of communism (Sklair, 1991: 71ff.). The Greens are fashioning a vocabulary deeply critical of consumerism and a global consciousness ('we are all fellow travellers on spaceship Earth'). They may be able to tap into the old tradition that sees progress as having limits and views overweening desire as calling for retribution (Lasch, 1991). Today's reckless consumption certainly has to be paid for sooner or later. The goods we consume, not just their wrapping paper, ends up in the refuse tip and landfill sites are now themselves ecological sores, reminders that today's pleasure can be tomorrow's pollution.

Capitalism has responded to the growing and strong evidence about consumption's environmental impact in a variety of ways. If there are fewer captains of industry or politicians today than in the 1990s who deny the importance of the environment, there are still lamentably fewer prepared to question the right to consume on environmental grounds. Indeed, Western capitalist cheerleaders are, at the time of writing, redoubling efforts to encourage consumers to consume more to maintain economic activity and continue to pursue narrowly defined progress, while at the same time beginning to focus on the urgent need to tackle climate change as though this has nothing to do with consumerism.

Looking Ahead

At the start of the 21st-century, Western consumerism is definitely facing structural uncertainty. It is threatened by technological, economic, but especially environmental and demographic forces. To argue that the future shape of consumption is forged by the free actions of sovereign consumers in the world's marketplaces is no longer a plausible policy. Consumers are daily involved in numerous choices, often unaware of their environmental impact, let alone being willing to pay or otherwise take full responsibility for it.

As we shall see in the next chapter, there are serious limits to both range and types of choice available to consumers. Consumerism is the outcome of a complex interplay of forces – political ideology, production, class relations, international trade, economic theory, cultural and moral values. The rest of this book explores these themes by looking at various faces of the contemporary consumer. Each chapter is a variation on a theme, probing deeper into what is meant by the consumer and consumerism. In the last chapter we shall return to address the questions raised in the first two.

CHAPTER 2

The Consumer as Chooser

The ancient Greeks were right. The ideal of the chosen life does not
square with how we live. We are not authors of our lives; we are not
even part-authors of the events that mark us most deeply. Nearly
everything that is most important in our lives is unchosen. The
time and place we are born, our parents, the first language we
speak – these are chance, not choice. It is the casual drift of things
that shapes our most fateful relationships. The life of each of us
is a chapter of accidents.

Gray, 2002: 109

CORE ARGUMENTS

Choice is the concept that has come virtually to define contemporary
consumption, assuming different psychological, cultural and economic
dimensions. However, there are now serious questions about whether
choice constitutes a supreme and uncontested value for individuals or
societies. While constituting the basis of today's freedom and driving
economic development and progress, choice is shown to have a darker
side as well as different negative consequences for individuals and
economies.

Choice lies at the centre of the idea of consumerism, both as its emblem and as its core value. The principle advantages of choice can be summed up in a few brief notions:

- All choice is good; the more choice there is for consumers, the better for consumers.
- Choice is good for the economy; it is the driving force for efficiency, growth and diversity.
- A social system based on choice is better than one without; choice is the supreme value.
- Consumer capitalism means more choice for everyone.

In this chapter, we explore from where the idea of choice draws its power, and ask why it seduces consumers, politicians and intellectuals alike. We question whether all choice is the supreme value that it is meant to be, by examining three distinct intellectual traditions that address it: psychological, cultural and economic. We do not deny the reality of choice for many consumers, but we argue that the limitations of choice are as important:

1   Choice without information is not real choice. Almost everyone agrees with that. The contention starts over what sort of information is appropriate, how much, in what format and given by whom.
2   Choice between similar options is only choice in a marginal sense, like choosing between Tweedledum and Tweedledee. It can be psychologically significant to the chooser, but of minor social or historical significance.
3   Choice limited only to those with resources undermines the advantages of choice for all. It helps to be rich, but to be rich is not a pre-condition for happiness through choice.
4   The overabundance of choices leads to diminishing returns. It leads to fears of failing, worries about choosing the right option. This applies not just to major decisions (for example, marriage, career, house, holiday), but to trivial ones (for example, which dish to order from a menu).
5   Choice can be used as a smoke screen for shedding responsibility or for deception. If one is seen as actively choosing a particular option, one is expected not to complain when it goes wrong; for example, if a cosmetic operation leads of complications or if a used car turns out turns out wrong.

It is hard to stand back from the notion of choice. Choice is inextricably linked with morality, notions of right and wrong, good and evil. Even those who set out to take morality out of the study of choice, back into it themselves. Others who deride choice as a mere bourgeois illusion would be up in arms if their choice of newspapers or TV channel or books was restricted. Choice is something one gets used to, which why it is a sensitive issue. As individuals, everyone likes to believe that they have choices, even if they do not exercise them. The last thing they will surrender when everything else is lost is their right to choice. Pandora's Box was Zeus' gift to Pandora, a valuable receptacle containing all the blessings of the gods; when opened, everything escaped, with the exception of hope. Like Pandora, today's consumer may be at risk of losing all the blessings for the sake of retaining choice.

Exploring Choice

Every shift in culture invents or reinvents an image of the consumer and applies it to the act of choosing. Trains of academic thought can be traced from theoretical origins through to marketing application. Games theory, a perspective that analyses interactions as a sequence of moves, was taken up and developed in defence studies and ended up being applied in marketing, the consumer being seen as a game player, someone who seeks to win in the consumption game. The consumer has also been modelled now as a probability estimator, now a risk-taker and now an uncertainty reducer, as though these were mutually compatible. Even the choice of something as mundane as breakfast cereals has been submitted to such modelling (Mitchell and Boustani, 1992). The researchers inform us that perceived risks are financial, physical, social, psychological and time. Consumers therefore adopt risk-reducing strategies, drawing upon formal and informal information about products, brand loyalty, the image of the store from which it was bought, price, promotions and advice from sales assistants.

Another model of choice has consumers as problem-solvers; how they choose depends on how they frame the problem and the consequences of buying this rather than that product (Burton and Babin, 1989). Apparently, they are also information-seekers and processors (Coupey, 1994; Coupey and Narayanan, 1996). Bettman argues that conceiving of the consumer as 'having goals, taking in information, actively processing and interpreting that information, and selecting alternatives' is superior to other psychological models in that it depicts the consumer as chooser as engaged in an active process, which cannot be said of classical behaviourist analyses where the consumer is seen as stimulus-bound (Bettman, 1979: 346).

When choosing a holiday from a tourist operator, for instance, the information that would-be customers seek is, from the operator's point of view, infuriatingly complex. One study found that choice depended on gender, age, previous visits to the destination, type of accommodation used, frequency of vacation trips per year and the likelihood of revisiting the location. We learn, too, that consumers are told they *ought* to be information-seekers. By shopping around for a car, for instance, and by pretending to be a sophisticated would-be purchaser, they can get a better deal (Jung, 1988).

We learn, too, that consumer choices can be a vehicle for social contact. One study of 'lonely people' found that they went out shopping looking for social intercourse (Forman and Sriram, 1991). With retailing being increasingly automated and with pressure on staff to be more efficient, the total needs of customers are ignored at the retailers' peril, warned this study. The arrival of the Internet has transformed shopping as an opportunity for social contact. The Internet has become a vehicle for social contact (for example, chat-rooms, blogging, e-mails) and has further alienated the customer–shop interface. It has also given an extraordinary new power to customers, enabling them to comment and criticize products and services in ways that can be shared with other consumers.

Others argue that choosing betrays consumers as pragmatic, consciously judging goods as meeting or failing to meet desired purposes. When they choose, they are influenced by how the product meets what they want, its social value, the ability of the product to arouse curiosity and meaning among others, its emotional value and its suitability for the task envisaged (Sheth et al., 1991). Market researchers have been keen to explore the changes in consumer motives and context, and they are reported almost before they have become discernible trends. Thus at the height of the 1980s consumer boom, we learned that consumers choose ethically (Moyle, 1990); environmentally (Rock, 1989); but at the same time, that their choices are swayed by a variety of factors from check-out technology in retailing (Powderley and MacNulty, 1990) to music in stores (Yalch and Spangenberg, 1993; Yalch and Spangenberg, 2000).

With all this inquiry into the everyday act of choosing, it is perhaps surprising that consumer choice has been described as schizophrenic (Gelb, 1992; Kardon, 1992). This image is as much a reflection of the marketers' frustration about consumer behaviour towards brands, as of the complexities of people's behaviour as consumers. But underlying many of these different appeals and metaphors for consumer choice is an assumption that choice is undertaken on rational grounds; the entire marketing enterprise depends on and perpetuates this notion (O'Shaughnessy, 1987: 79–97). Modern texts on consumer choice are full of flow charts, diagrams and decision-trees, and little sign of randomness or whim. The intellectual task for marketers is to find order and reason in what might appear emotional or unreasonable.

The Rise of Product Choice: Fact and Fantasy

Just as the notion of choice goes almost unquestioned within consumer studies, in spite of the frustration it causes, so, too, it is taken for granted that choice has increased with the growth of product ranges. 'These days, there is so much more choice' is such a common assertion. Older generations say it to the younger. Some postmodernist theorists, as we shall see shortly, unite with market researchers and with the neo-Cons and the New Right ideologues to celebrate choice. Consumer theorists join in the celebrations, recognizing that most consumer organizations would be redundant without choice in the marketplace. Consumer advocates are more measured in their acclaim. Choice, yes; endless choice, no. John Winward, then Director of Research at the UK Consumers' Association (now 'Which?') argued in the early 1990s that consumer organizations like his own can only be effective in providing information on goods and services for consumers to choose between if there is large-scale production. This ensures a number of broadly comparable options for every type of purchase. Post-Fordism, with its proliferation of niche products, makes product comparison more difficult and encourages endless fine-tuning of products to fit market gaps. Thus, it poses a major threat to the existence of consumer organizations that evaluate and compare products for their members (Winward, 1994). Indeed, in most countries, membership of consumer organizations has declined, even as their profile as pundits and media commentators on products has grown. For the postmodernists, on the other hand, the demise of mass markets opens up unique opportunities for exercising consumer choice. Each commodity becomes a unique 'sign', capable of carrying virtually any meaning dreamed of by advertisers or arbitrarily imposed by the consumers themselves.

But is it true that product variety is growing? Much depends on the timeframe of the analysis or the income level of the consumer. Compared to the Middle

Ages, there is an increase in the choice of cars and transport, of course. Growth of choice and variety depends on how you look at products. Are the 10 different variants of a car model or the 10 detergents on a shelf different products?

In a rare and fascinating attempt to assess whether consumer choice has increased in one country, Finland, Mika Pantzar of the Finnish Consumer Research Centre concluded – accurately but unsensationally – that the picture was mixed. For some products the range had increased, but for others it had declined. In 1980, there were 10,000 grocery shops in Finland. At the end of the decade there were only 7000 (Pantzar, 1992). But the number of daily goods in Finnish shops had increased, from around 2,600 in 1960 to an estimated 10,000 articles by the year 2000. 'Every day one new product appears in the shops, and every 3rd day one product disappears' (Pantzar, 1992: 349).

The modern European hypermarket now offers around 30,000 different items as well being a source of other products and services. However, within product categories, the top brands dominate, leading analysts to argue that this apparently prolific choice under one roof disguises concentration of control (Lang and Heasman, 2004). Certainly, even though there may be thousands of products competing for the attention of consumers, it is a tiny handful of retailers who mediate the relationship between producers and consumers. One business study of the European food market found that in Europe (then 15 member states), there were 3.2 million farmers, around 240,000 processors, 600 retailer chains, but just 110 combined 'buying desks' (consortia of retailers' contracts and specifications officers) that interface with 250 million consumers through 170,000 shop outlets (Lang, 2005). This study concluded that the role of retailers and their buying desks was the new power in the consumer–producer interface.

There is an extraordinary fixation within consumerism on ever-increasing ranges of manufactured products, when natural products are disappearing at an alarming rate. Conservationists are deeply concerned about the decline of species and varieties of both animals and plants, wild and cultivated or domestic. In the UK, according to the charity Common Ground, there are 2000 varieties of apple in the national collection that have been grown commercially or for domestic use, yet just nine varieties dominate commercial orchards today (Paxton, 1994: 10). The rhetoric of diversity is belied by a tendency to monoculture, with many processed food products being based on, or including, a very restricted number of key ingredients. A distinction therefore can be made between the appearance of choice and its substratum.

Even accepting consumer product choice at face value, John Benson in his review of consumption in Britain 1880–1980, like Pantzar in his of Finland, points to the contradictory trends in consumer choice (Benson, 1994). Compared to the 1860s, British shoppers in the 1960s spent less of their income on shopping because they had more fixed costs (housing, and so on); yet new product ranges had also emerged. Women, for instance, saw a broadening of choice in cosmetic and sanitary protection products in the post-Second World War period, where there had been little before, but a decline in food shops coupled with a rise in the range of foods on sale in the remaining shops (Benson, 1994: 75). Range of choice frequently diminishes for consumers, when the rhetoric suggests it only increases. In most affluent societies, the number of shops selling basic goods such as food, furniture, textiles, has declined, and consumers have to travel further to get to the shop. There is increasing ecological concern about the necessity of consumers having to use a car to be able to shop, the costs of transport are externalized, with the retailer benefiting from apparent 'bargains' because the consumer has no choice but to pay for a car and, as taxpayer, pay for the road infrastructure, burdens not internalized in the cost of goods (Pretty et al., 2005; Raven et al., 1995).

Choice Inequality

If choice is unevenly distributed across product ranges, as we have suggested, it is infinitely more unequally distributed across sections of the population, indeed across the globe. Nowhere is this more starkly evident that in the global distribution of food. While Western consumers may deliberate over 16 brands of breakfast cereal, other consumers face a different predicament. According to UNICEF, one in five people in the developing world suffer from chronic hunger – this represents some 800 million people in Africa, Asia and Latin America. Over 2 billion people worldwide subsist on diets deficient in vitamins and minerals essential for normal growth and development, and for preventing premature death (Commission on the Nutrition Challenges of the 21st Century, 2000: 19).

There is more than enough food to go around, yet many are starving. UNICEF has long argued that this is the 'paradox of plenty' (UNICEF, 1992: 29). Even in rich countries, as throughout the world, the poorer people are, the worse the diet they eat, yet the more proportionately they pay for it, the more of their household income goes on food, and the worse time they have shopping for it. So there is a choice, but not equality of choice (Dowler et al., 2001). The key barrier to consumer choice is money. The message? If you want choice, and who doesn't, you have to get out there and get going. Money gives choice. Choice gives freedom. Whatever the area of consumption, from crime-protection to clothes, from health to education, from cultural industries to cars, money is the final arbiter.

The politicians, however, artlessly disregard this reality and elevate choice to the standing of an unqualified value. Since the earliest attempts to bring the state into consumer affairs (see Chapter 7, 'The Consumer as Victim'), choice has been a cornerstone of political rhetoric. President John F. Kennedy's oft-quoted consumer message to Congress in March 1962 is a classic statement in this vein. He proposed four rights (Tiemstra, 1992: 11):

- the right to accurate and complete information about products at the point of sale;
- the right to products that are reasonably safe in their ordinary and foreseeable uses;
- the right to choose among products of different specifications; and
- the right of consumers to be heard by government regulatory bodies.

Similar emphasis on choice was accorded on the other side of the Atlantic in the National Consumer Council's principles, which are as follows (National Consumer Council, 1994: 14):

- **Access**: can people actually get the goods or services they need or want?
- **Choice**: is there any? And can consumers affect the way goods or services are provided through their own decisions?

- **Safety**: are the goods or services a danger to health or welfare?
- **Information**: is it available, and in the right way to help consumers make the best choices for themselves?
- **Equity**: are some or all consumers subject to arbitrary or unfair discrimination?
- **Redress**: if something goes wrong, is there an effective system for putting it right?
- **Representation**: if consumers cannot affect the supply of goods or services through their own decisions, are there ways for their views to be represented?.

The Psychology of Choice: Agent or Object?

And what has been the intellectuals' position on choice? They have tended to argue that choice is determined, as we will see now by exploring three different traditions. The first is the study of the cognitive and social psychological processes by which consumers make decisions or judgements. The second centres on the cultural context of consumer choice. And the third is the debate on whether choice matters in economic or political-economic theory.

From promising roots at the start of the 20th-century, the psychology of choice has diminished into mundane laboratory studies of decision-making: why this product was chosen rather than that. More recently, focus groups have become the guinea pigs on which new market ideas are tried and where new product ideas are sought. The trajectory of psychology from a discipline interested in Big Ideas to a discipline concerned about 'marginal differences' in behaviour is illuminating. Psychology started the 20th-century with such promise – the unlocking of human motivation, no less – and ended a servant to mass consumer enterprises. And yet, the rise and fall of psychology's interest in consumer choice has an important tale to tell: that in the 20th-century, which saw the meteoric rise of the rhetoric of choice, applied psychologists spent much of their time studying what factors determine choice. Motivation, whether applied to the individual as producer or consumer, became the key to constraining, guiding and controlling choice. Psychologists became merchandisers of meaning (Sievers, 1986). For much of late 20th-century psychology, the study of behaviour had become a study of control, along the path laid by F.W. 'Speedy' Taylor, the father of time and motion studies. For Taylor, the purpose of what became known as industrial or occupational psychology was to remove the unpredictability of the human factor in production. The uses of modern psychology emerged as remarkably prosaic. When applied to consumers, this psychology was to help producers understand how consumers discriminate between products. Such was the point of studies like that of R.L. Brown in the 1950s on whether the wrapper on a loaf of bread can influence consumer perception of freshness (Brown, 1958). The answer was that it can; consumers judged wrapped bread, whether one day or two day old, as equally 'fresh' as freshly baked bread! The uses of this type of psychology for advertising and marketing was even then exciting those who saw it as an aid to moulding consumer consciousness.

In contrast to the noble tradition in psychology, pioneered by William James for whom 'the mind selects' (James, 1891: 285), and '… no two men are known to choose alike' (James, 1891: 289) kept alive by existential and humanistic psychology (Armistead, 1974), a large section of modern psychology sought to manage choice and thereby diminish it. For behaviourist psychology, choice was merely learned behaviour, an act of discrimination between stimuli (Hull, 1974). From this perspective, choice was an almost outmoded notion. It was what students did when sitting multiple-choice tests, such as to see whom in a group they are attracted to or repelled from! (Secord and Backman, 1964: 239). Choice operates within limits set by superior forces, in this case the psychologist.

The other major tradition in psychology, depth psychology, found the promise of marketing applications even more alluring than did the behaviourists. Since the 1950s, a section of depth psychology has applied itself to promoting specific products by connecting them to unconscious desires or by presenting them as substitute gratification for repressed or unexpressed wishes. The sexualization of everyday objects (fast cars, big cigars, lipsticks, and so on) was one of the outcomes. Thus, within psychology, there was a strange truce on the subject of choice between the two dominant schools, psychoanalysis and behaviourism, with both stressing the management of and, on occasions, the constraints on choice. Even as these two schools of thought were availing themselves to the management and control of choice, humanistic psychology could naively argue that, other things being equal, humans always choose love rather than hate, affection and meaning rather than fear (Maslow, 1970[1954]: 275ff.). Maslow argued that some choices were healthier for the human than others. Give people the choice and they mostly make the right one, allowing each person to grow psychologically, to become more adjusted, content, at ease, less selfish – a far cry from the brash world of marketing psychology.

The Mass Psychology of Brands

By the 1950s, consumer psychology had already taken shape, focusing, as one textbook put it, 'on the *consumer* of the products and services produced by the enterprise. ... The psychologist applies scientific methods in the effort to understand factors affecting the behavior of individuals in their roles as consumers' (Fleishman, 1967: 735). Drawing on the experimental tradition of behaviourist and animal psychology, this industry-oriented approach was dedicated to finding out who the consumers are (their psychological profile, income, class, and so on); how they decide between goods (studying issues like what sources of information do consumers trust, when is information about products worthy of confidence); but above all on how consumers may be influenced by personality, family, group and peer group dynamics, leaders, as well as by mental processes, such as cognitive dissonance (Britt, 1966, 1970).

Much of this research was, and is, ad hoc and borrowed from other academic disciplines (Foxall, 1977: 1 and 19). Its model of influences on consumer choice was no great advance on commonsense. Foxall, for instance, talks of a combination of social structure and individual influences affecting the buying process, which he sees as going through four stages: perception of want, pre-purchase planning, the purchase itself, and post-purchase behaviour such as repeat purchases (Foxall, 1977: 22). Along with many others, his model of choice hardly goes beyond the tautology of 'to choose is to buy and to buy is to choose'.

The purpose of explorations into consumer preferences and the use of techniques like product testing, design and evaluation was to aid marketing and the central mission of the enterprise. This approach was pioneered for social psychologists in the American Soldier study conducted during the Second World War, when they undertook the largest empirical study until then ever conducted, to find out what made soldiers more efficient (Madge, 1963: 287ff.). Famously, they found that high on the priority list of soldiers on a beach-head during an invasion was the desire for a Coke (Social Science Research Council (US) and United States Army Service Forces: Information and Education Division, 1949). Half a century after that milestone study, in 1993, the Consumer Psychology Division of the American Psychological Association was happy to be described as 'the prime force' behind the then 10-year-old annual Advertising and Consumer Psychology Conference (Aaker and Biel, 1993).

The marriage of consumer psychology and business was complete and one of its first offspring was the obsession with brands and the power of advertising to place them. Brand research was 'needed' to understand 'consumer pull', how consumers can be drawn to purchase particular brands through advertising. The methods to test for niches in the market and the effectiveness of marketing, such as consumer panels and 'blind' tests, were falling into place. These could be applied to products as diverse as shaving creams, foods, colas, cigarettes and beers (Fleishman, 1951). Even as consumer choice was being extolled, an entire market research industry was emerging, monitoring every consumer move. By the 1990s, the Landor ImagePower Survey, for instance, was tracking over 10,800 brands in 14 developed economies (Aaker and Biel, 1993).

Choice henceforth was defined in brand terms. Choice meant switching between brands, an advertising effect and thus theoretically subject to influence (Deighton et al., 1994). Brands took on a human aspect and choice of brands, like choice of friends, was seen as a personality-dictated affair. Brands were even, as we noted earlier, the object of consumer schizophrenia (Kardon, 1992). Brands take on independent lives of their own, being ascribed financial value in themselves. The power of brand anthropomorphism was such that when confectionery giant Nestlé bid for Rowntree in 1988, at twice Rowntree's pre-bid stock value, Nestlé argued that the Rowntree brands such as Kit-Kat were worth it. By the mid 1990s, the issue of brand value continues to be a sensitive issue. In the globalization process, the notion that choice might not be brand-dominated was explosive. IBM, hitherto one of the highest value brands, saw its brand value go negative in 1994, having been estimated as the third most valuable globally only the year before. The cola market previously dominated by a mesmerizing tussle for market share between the two global giants, Pepsi-Cola and Coca-Cola, began to be undercut by retailer 'own brands' mostly made by the Canadian company, Cott.

The Future of Brands

It is now being argued by some commentators that 100 years of brands may be drawing to a close. The phenomenal success of Naomi Klein's book *No Logo: Taking Aim at the Brand Bullies* (2000) has highlighted a change in public sentiment. No longer is it unfashionable to argue, as we did in the first edition of this book, that brands are oppressive and gloss over more complex and fraught supply-chain relations. Klein's book became a focal text for an anti-consumerist ethos that sought to challenge the hegemony of brands and the violence of fashion and styles. It also captured a mood that was first expressed in a politically significant way in demonstrations against the GATT (General Agreement on Tariffs and Trade) trade talks held in Seattle in December 1999. While not making much of a dent on the sale of brands, Klein's book was instrumental in capturing an anti-corporate sentiment and helped voice a dissatisfaction with the power of brands. This was not what the brand psychologists had either anticipated or wanted in the decades of brand build-up and ascribing monetary value to brands.

The 'No Logo' ethos, despite its success in capturing imaginations has not made much of a dent in the continuing rise of brands (Gilmore, 1999, 2003). 'Own label' products, however, have grown on the back of the retailers' increasing power at the expense of manufacturers (Randall, 1994; Randall and Chartered Institute of Marketing, 1990; Seth and Randall, 2001). Changes in retailing have encouraged consumers to purchase 'own label' products, thus undermining the value of some bigger brands. For all this, a fierce campaign is being staged to capture consumer spending and link it with particular brands. The decline of brands seems unlikely. Belief in consumer choice and the power of brands remains an article of faith not only for market researchers and their psychological gurus, but also for corporations most consumers.

Sir Michael Perry, the Chairman of Unilever, one of the world's biggest brand owners, summed up this article of faith well in his presidential address to the 1994 UK Advertising Association, stating that 'brands – in their small way – answer people's needs ...' (Perry, 1994). His argument deserves full quotation as a classic statement of the creed vis-à-vis the consumer:

> In the modern world, brands are a key part of how individuals define themselves and their relationships with one another. The old, rigid barriers are disappearing – class and rank; blue collar and white collar; council tenant and home owner; employee and housewife. More and more we are simply consumers – with tastes, lifestyles and aspirations that are very different.

> It's a marketing given by now that the consumer defines the brand. But the brand also defines the consumer. We are what we wear, what we eat, what we drive. Each of us in this room is a walking compendium of brands. You chose each of those brands among many options – because they felt 'more like you'.

> The collection of brands we choose to assemble around us have become amongst the most direct expressions of our individuality – or more precisely, our deep psychological need to identify ourselves with others. (Perry, 1994: 4)

He added:

> Our whole skill as branded goods' producers is *in anticipation of consumer* trends. In earlier appreciation of emerging needs or wants. And in developing a quality of advertising which can interpret aspirations, focus them on products and lead consumers forward. (Perry, 1994: 18, our emphasis)

Our judgement is that while brands come and go, while they are resisted by sections of the populations on ideological or price grounds, they continue to be major influences on consumer choice. Even the retailers' own brands have themselves become brands and spawned sub-brands.

Advertising: the Systematic Moulding of Consciousness?

As we stated at the opening of this chapter, information is a pre-condition for real choice. One can make choices but if one lacks information about alternatives, their pros and cons, their uses, side-effects and dysfunctions, the results of these choices can range from inadequate to catastrophic. Moreover, information can create false choices or guided choices concealing rather than elucidating the full range of options. The relationship between information and choice is captured in the Chinese story recounted by Gregory Bateson (Bateson, 1972: 208). A guru shows a stick to his pupil and says 'if you say this is a stick, I will beat you with it; if you say this is not a stick, I will beat you with it'. The lesson the guru was trying to teach was not to fall for false choices. A sensible pupil should say anything he wished other than the two 'choices' proffered by his master. Is the advertisers' project anything other than the drawing of false choices?

Is the message from psychology that consumer choice is moulded, limited and manipulated? The tendency of the academics is to answer yes. Choice has become a code for something else. The practitioners from advertising and marketing, however, are more guarded. On the one hand, they argue that their professional skills can work (or they would be out of a job). On the other hand when accused of manipulation they assure that their powers are limited to choice between brands. These battle lines are old and heat up periodically, notably in both Australia and the UK over advertising targeting children with less than wholesome food (Dibb, 1993; Packard, 1981[1957]).

An unalloyed notion of choice is untenable. For consumers to be sovereign, they would have to have a wide range of options, an unlimited amount of information and an unlimited amount of money. They would also have to be immune to temptation. In the words of E.J. Mishan, an economist, nothing could be further away from reality.

> ... [U]nless the wants of consumers exist *independently* of the products created by industrial concerns it is not correct to speak of the market as acting to adapt the given resources of the economy to meet the material requirements of society. In fact, not only do producers determine the range of market goods from which consumer must take their choice, they also seek continuously to persuade consumer to choose what is being produced today and to 'unchoose' that which was being produced yesterday. Therefore to continue to regard the market ... as primarily a 'want-satisfying' mechanism is to close one's eyes to the more important fact, that it has become a want-*creating* mechanism. (Mishan, 1967: 147ff.)

Look at the complexity of the information required on something as 'simple' and 'everyday' as choosing what to wash clothes with. Journals and consumer magazines are full of reports on tests on machines and detergents. One, for instance, compared 11 non-phosphate detergents with 12 phosphate-containing ones and found that in soft water there was no difference. In general, phosphate-containing detergents gave somewhat better results in warm water, but detergents using bleach didn't make clothes any whiter than non-bleach containing powders (Brown et al., 1993). A follow-up study by the same researchers, compared 11 'unbuilt' liquids and six 'built' liquids. In soft water, there was no difference between the liquids, whether warm or cold washed, except for a elaleuca oil-based detergent, which was significantly better in hot water. Unbuilt liquid detergents worked a bit better in warm and hot water, but not to a statistically significant degree (Cameron et al., 1993). Who, pray, knows the difference between 'built' and 'unbuilt' liquids? And what is elaleuca oil? What difference does this knowledge make? What are the effects of not knowing this kind of data? Should the consumer, like the pupil of Bateson's Chinese guru, 'choose' to ignore manufacturer's advice, for instance on temperature control? The answer is no (Cunliffe et al., 1988)!

The consumer society, glorifying choice, bombards its consumers with information rationalized as aid to choice; this simultaneously underlines how under-informed they are and creates an information overload that cannot possibly enhance their decision-making. This is partly due to rapidly changing product ranges and specifications and partly due to changing social relations. People in affluent consumer societies rarely live with extended families from whom they might learn what to buy, how to approach the purchasing; that is, they lack the knowledge-base for making informed consumer choices (Galbraith, 1974: 59–60). Instead, they live surrounded by messages that undermine the potential for autonomous judgements and objects that seduce even as they appear to be chosen.

Choice in Cultural Studies

Seduction is the point on which numerous cultural theorists of consumption converge. Many of these writers are either postmodernists or in debate with postmodernist ideas. Postmodernism has been notoriously difficult to pin down. Here is one attempt at a definition:

> an intense concern for pluralism and a desire to cut across the different taste cultures that now fracture society; an obligation to bring back selected traditional values, but in a new key … ; an acknowledgement of difference and otherness, the keynote of the feminist movement,… ; the re-enchantment of nature … ; and the commitment to an ecological and ecumenical world view … . (Jencks, 1992: 7)

Bauman as well as Baudrillard, two key figures in this area, argue that much modern consumption unfolds in the realm of seduction, where goods are not chosen for their uses but act as objects of fantasy. Choice is an illusion, but like all illusions serves as a mechanism of control. Seduction is one major mode of control for Bauman, the one that applies to those people with the means to scrutinize, to fall in love and to purchase goods, that is, those who can easily persuade themselves that they are choosing. By contrast, the 'new poor', disenfranchised from choice, by being dependent on the state for their livelihood, a livelihood devoid of choice, are controlled through repression (Bauman, 1988, 1992). Giddens takes a less stark view. For him, the contemporary individual pursues an unending project of self-creation through a continuous making of choices; many, if not the majority of these choices are consumer choices:

> On the level of the self, a fundamental component of day-to-day activity is simply that of choice. Obviously, no culture eliminates choice altogether in day-to-day affairs, and all traditions are effectively choices among an indefinite range of possible behaviour patterns. Yet, by definition, tradition or established habit orders life within relatively set channels. Modernity confronts the individual with a complex diversity of choices and … at the same time offers little help as to which options should be selected. (Giddens, 1991: 80)

For Giddens, like Sartre, 'we all not only follow lifestyles, but in an important sense are forced to do so – we have no choice but to choose'. Lifestyles are routinized practices around which they define themselves:

> Each of the small decisions a person makes every day – what to wear, what to eat, how to conduct himself at work, whom to meet with later in the evening – contributes to such routines. All such choices (as well as larger and more consequential ones) are decisions not only about how to act but who to be. (Giddens, 1991: 81)

This choice, however, is not open to everyone. 'To speak of a multiplicity of choices is not to suppose that all choices are open to everyone' (Giddens, 1991: 82). Choice is an indicator of the demise of traditional society; plurality of choice is both oppressive and exciting. The world is now characterized by an accentuation of difference and the opportunity for people to create their own niches, rather than be controlled by mass markets. Consumption is an opportunity to display one's identity (see Chapter 5, 'The Consumer as Identity-seeker'). Many postmodern theorists stress the creative opportunities of contemporary consumption. Other cultural theorists stress the culturally determined nature of consumption. Bourdieu, for instance, uses the term 'habitus' to indicate a modest but significant elbow room for choice afforded to each individual by his or her social class or stratum. Tastes in food, films, music, art, photographs, and so on, are social demarcators, generally accounted for by a person's 'cultural capital', that is, his or her educational level or occupation (Bourdieu, 1984). Others are still more determinist (Douglas and Isherwood, 1978). (See Chapter 3, 'The Consumer as Communicator'.)

These different tendencies within cultural theory – culture as choosing versus culture as ordained – offer a central insight into modern choice. The tension is important. Never has there been so much; never so little. As Giddens notes:

> Modern social life impoverishes social action, yet furthers the appropriation of new possibilities; it is alienating, yet at the same time, characteristically, human beings react against social circumstances which they find oppressive. Late modern institutions create a world of mixed opportunity and high-consequence risk. (Giddens, 1991: 175)

According to Rutherford, contemporary culture has changed the rules of consumption. 'It's no longer about keeping up with the Joneses, it's about being different from them' (Rutherford, 1990: 11). Interest in difference as a central feature of consumption long pre-dates postmodernism; it can be traced back to Veblen's and Simmel's pioneering portrayals of consumption styles at the turn of the 19th- and 20th-centuries. For postmodern theorists like Baudrillard, however, difference is the *only* object of consumer choice. In other words, people buy goods solely to be different from others. The futility of this project is self-evident, though the project of difference remains (Baudrillard, 1988b[1970]: 45). The fascination of choice persists, but choice itself is transformed in most postmodern writings into whim and caprice. Postmodernists have been hugely interested in the effects of mass media and the designer industries from art to architecture and fashion (Harvey, 1990). Sophisticated, culture-literate consumers can share the architect's jokes or the designers' references, as they observe (consume) the postmodern building (a shed with a graeco-roman portal) or a clothing outfit with different time references (hippie skirt worn with leggings, working men's boots and a body top). Choosing between goods becomes a cerebral in-joke, an impudent guesture whose ultimate rationale lies in 'why not?'. Choosing becomes a witty tour of the cultural supermarket; if it degenerates into whim and fancy, 'why not?'. 'Anything goes' becomes the postmodern slogan, *par excellence*.

The Costs of Choice and Freedom

Bauman, almost alone among postmodernist thinkers, develops a highly sophisticated but also profoundly ambiguous position as regards consumer choice. He argues that choice, and especially consumer choice, is the foundation of a new concept of freedom: 'In our society, individual freedom is constituted as, first and foremost, freedom of the consumer …' (Bauman, 1988: 7ff.). This freedom, however, is not distributed evenly: 'Those who rule, are free; those who are free, rule' (Bauman, 1988: 23). Modern capitalism, says Bauman, has opened up the possibility of choice to ever-increasing numbers of people, offering 'a wider than ever space …, the rapidly expanding, seemingly limitless, world of consumption' (Bauman, 1988: 57). By the same token, however, the very system that offers 'a lot of choice and makes him a truly "free" individual, also generates on a massive scale the experience of oppression' (Bauman, 1988: 50ff.). Bauman argues that precisely because of the importance of choice; those excluded from making choices automatically become disenfranchised and oppressed (Bauman, 1992).

The key to this type of choice is not political struggle for the acquisition of communal rights (like those in Britain that ensured the Magna Carta or the anti-colonial struggles of the 20th-century in India or the anti-apartheid road in South Africa), but the marketplace. 'The consumer market as a whole may be seen as an institutionalized exit from politics; …' (Bauman, 1988: 82). Yet, this freedom is no less sweet than that that drove the French Revolution:

> What makes the freedom offered by the market more alluring still is that it comes without the blemish which tainted most of its other forms: the same market which offers freedom offers also certainty. It offers the individual the right to a 'thoroughly individual' choice; yet it also supplies social approval for such choice, thereby exorcizing that ghost of insecurity … People are thus pulled to the market by a double bind: they depend on it for their individual freedom; and they depend on it for enjoying their freedom without paying the price of insecurity. (Bauman, 1988: 61)

This double bind of choice lies at the heart of Bauman's ambivalence. Here is the price of consumer freedom:

> Thick walls are an indispensable part of consumer society; so is their inobtrusiveness for insiders. … Consumers rarely catch a glimpse of the other side. The squalor of inner cities they pass in the comely and plushy interior of their cars. If they ever visit the 'Third World', it is for its safaris and massage parlours, not for its sweatshops. (Bauman, 1988: 92)

He is right. Consumer activists, especially the new wave and those in developing countries, constantly remind us of this cultural paradox (see Chapter 9, 'The Consumer as Activist'). Bauman's approach to choice resonates with approval and disapproval. Choice, even when exercised, has its downside. More than many theorists, he acknowledges the contradictions of choice. Choice is imagined, yet real; choice liberates some, but exacerbates the oppression of others.

Choosing as Economic Welfare

In contrast to cultural theorists, neo-classical economists start with the assumption of choice and explore its implications. They take a consistent, if narrow, approach to choice. The fact that resources are scarce and human wants are infinite means that economic agents have to make choices, to allocate the scarce resources between competing uses. 'Every choice involves a range of alternatives' says one economic textbook (Anderton, 1991: 1). To choose one object or course of action means the potential benefit of others is lost. This is the key economic notion of opportunity costs, the benefit forfeited by not choosing the next best alternative. Faced with the choice of buying one out of many newspapers, the opportunity cost of making that choice is the loss of not being able to read the others. To the economists, choice has by definition a downside.

Since the pioneering work of Herbert Simon, economists have also been concerned with establishing the practical psychological and organizational limits to rational decision-making. Simon's concept of 'bounded rationality' sought to highlight that even 'rational' actors will make a choice when they find an alternative deemed good enough instead of endlessly seeking the perfect option (Simon, 1947). Some economists push this notion further, arguing that the economics of consumer behaviour should take greater account of the limits to choice and constraints on choice. Deaton and Muellbauer, for instance, write that '... the part played by preferences in determining behaviour tends to be overestimated' (Deaton and Muellbauer, 1980: 3). The economic factors influencing this limited choice are more important: budgets, information, uncertainty. A consumer has no way of knowing which companies have the 'best' prices for a good (Deaton and Muellbauer, 1980: 410), an information vacuum which the value-for-money consumer advocates try to end through their testing procedures and magazines. But Deaton and Muellbauer are right; unless everyone has the consumer magazine, unless the information is completely up to date, inevitably prices and specifications of the goods will require checking. In theory, the consumer can be helped with information. In practice, choice is doomed to be a stab in the twilight. Subsequent information may always undermine the confidence in the choice. Uncertainty 'is pervasive in almost all decision-making', they say (Deaton and Muellbauer, 1980: 380). The ice cream may melt before it is eaten; its taste may not be what is expected. There is risk in all choice. More recently, Deaton has placed even more stress on consumer risk. Choice, he suggests, is 'volatile'; how much should be consumed now, rather than saved or deferred till later? Consumers look into the future even as they gingerly consume in the present (Deaton and Muellbauer, 1980: 104).

This model of consumer choice stands in opposition to more traditional views, such as Samuelson's confident assertion that modern economics is the study of 'how ... we choose to use scarce productive resources with alternative uses, to meet prescribed ends ...' (Samuelson, 1970: 13). Galbraith, in contrast, has suggested that 'the best economic system is the one that supplies the most of what people most want' (Galbraith, 1974: 1). In spite of this view, Galbraith recognizes that the imagery, if not the reality, of choice is extremely powerful, which is why those with power such as monarchs have so often denied that they have it.

Galbraith presses his attack by pointing out that everything can be explained and explained away by choice. If someone is abused, they asked for it. If there is pollution from consumption, it was the public's choice. The ideology of choice, Galbraith argues, is highly 'convenient' to those with power. Even though at one time when firms were smaller and markets less oligopolistic, consumers might have been sovereign, today that is impossible. Markets are dominated by relatively few producers rather than millions of individuals making choices. In the USA even by 1970, the 333 corporations with assets of more than $500 million owned 70 percent of all assets employed in manufacturing (Galbraith, 1974: 43). By the 1990s, according to the United Nations (UN), the top 500 corporations of the world controlled over half of world trade (Lang and Hines, 1993: 34) but employed only 0.05 percent of the world's population (Hawken, 1993: 92). While many corporations may have downsized and outsourced some of their labour processes, the concentration of market share has continued apace in almost all consumer sectors.

Economists are divided over the extent, the value and the reality of choice. The critics, from liberals such as Galbraith to the modern ecological economists such as Ekins, deny that free choice is possible, because there is no perfect competition (Ekins et al., 1992). The neo-classicists, on the other hand, drawing from the theories of Adam Smith and Ricardo, argue that politicians' duty is to remove barriers to perfect competition in order to allow growth and the market to work their wizardry over scarce resources and infinite wants. They 'assume an ideal of the world and then explain deviations from the ideal' (Abolafia and Biggart, 1992). Unhindered choice is a restatement of the ideal, as Douglas and Isherwood remarked: 'The theory merely assumes the individual to be acting rationally, in that his choices are consistent with each other and stable over the short time that is relevant' (Douglas and Isherwood, 1978: 19).

Choice, the State and the New Right

For some economists, choice is no longer just a means, whether towards economic development or individual happiness. It has become an end in its own right. Nowhere is this clearer than in the writings of the political economists of the New Right who were so influential in shifting political culture from the corporatism of post-war Keynesian economics to the anti-statism of the Reagan–Thatcher years. Economists such as Hayek and Friedman attacked the Keynesian state by celebrating the right of the individual to choose. The purpose of the new political economy, they argued, could only be justified if it increased choice:

> An essential part of economic freedom is freedom to choose how to use our income: how much to spend on ourselves and on what items; how much to save and in what form; how much to give away and to whom. (Friedman and Friedman, 1980: 65)

The main barrier to choice according to these thinkers is the state, which however well intentioned almost inevitably both reduces freedom and fails to deliver what is promised. Far better, therefore, to remove the burden of the state and to structure society to maximise choice and consumer power. Daily experience, said the Friedmans, suggests that consumers can make both sensible and elegantly simple choices.

> When you vote daily in the supermarket, you get precisely what you voted for, and so does everyone else. The ballot box produces conformity without unanimity; the marketplace, unanimity without conformity. (Friedman and Friedman, 1980: 65ff.)

By intervening in the marketplace, the state stops consumers from expressing their values and from using resources accordingly. Critics of state-dominated economies do not necessarily deny the need for social welfare; but they do argue with others over how it should be produced, controlled and delivered (Gray, 1993, 1994). One of the more intriguing and pervasive ideas from the New Right has been the application of consumer choice to welfare. Since the national or local state provide many social welfare services – schools, health, welfare benefits – monopolies tend to build up. This has the advantage of economies of scale, but the disadvantage of diminution of consumer choice. The New Right's solution to this conundrum, besides curtailing state activity altogether and re-building family or community reliance, was to propose vouchers, which the welfare 'consumers' can redeem in whichever way they 'choose'. The argument for vouchers was that they give people room to shop around for services, and to top up with their own savings or income, that is, that they turn recipients of services into proper consumers. In theory, choice is maximized, but in practice, equality declines, and social divisions are accentuated, to say nothing of the extra expense of administering this choice.

The political and ideological obsession since the 1980s with applying choice to all spheres of government has maintained its momentum. Provision of choice is a key rationale – a sales pitch, almost – for the privatization of public utilities, for applying market logic to sectors which perhaps were inappropriate (Hambleton and Hoggett, 1993; Hutton, 1995). Public sector bodies, it is argued, are unresponsive to consumer tastes, have no incentive to raise quality, to lower costs or to innovate (Carruthers and Holland, 1991). The free market is the optimum mechanism for allocating resources, as could be witnessed by the idiocies of the planned economies, which not only failed to get goods to their consumers, but gave their consumers no control over what or how goods are produced.

Even the public sector has not escaped the ideology of marketization and consumer choice with the introduction of internal markets and the New Public Management movement (Ferlie et al., 1996). The previously homogeneous UK welfare system has been separated into 'purchasers' and 'providers' of welfare services. Purchasers have the state-funded budgets with which to buy services from competing providers. Providers may either be state or independent or private bodies. The key purpose of this purchaser–provider split is to engender a contractual relation within welfare services. The purchasers' task is to find the best value-for-money on offer from providers and to ensure the delivery of 'packages of care' to the customer as laid down in the Care in the Community Act 1990 (Barker, 1991).

This application of the notion of choice to public administration ranks as one of the great political experiments by the state machine. This could only happen through a strong central state. It is also a wholly political phenomenon. As a result, perhaps, the love affair with choice in welfare began to raise questions about whether choice is transferable from goods to services. Potter, for instance, questioned whether the principles of consumerism – access, choice, information, redress, representation – are at all applicable to public sector management. He further questioned whether they would yield a shift of power from the service provider to the citizen, let alone mould the service to the consumers' needs (Potter, 1988). Martin points out that the transfer of a consumer choice ideology to the service sector – exemplified by the explosion of interest among marketers of financial and welfare services – has underestimated the considerable differences between services and goods, from the perspective of the consumer (Martin, 1992). Services tend to be intangible (cannot be seen or touched), perishable (expire the moment they are created), inseparable (are produced and consumed simultaneously) and heterogeneous (they vary from service to service). Consumers or would-be consumers of services are forced into a number of conflicting roles, between which they have to learn to discriminate, if they are to exercise consumer choice. However, opposition to the elevation of choice as the determining force for improving public services has also grown (Levett et al., 2003). Some privatization experiences, notably the British rail service and school-meals, have consistently produced lower standards, high costs and public dissatisfaction.

So our review of the political economy of choice returns to where it began; that choice, where it is felt to exist, occurs within limits, that the rhetoric about choice is misplaced, that there is a downside to consumer choice, that choice is a political affair. In practice, there is a tendency for producers to coalesce, for markets to be oligopolistic and dominated by large producers, and for information to be dominated by interests of the seller. We agree with Galbraith that in a true market system, the firm should have few resources to expend on persuading consumers to do other than they want (Galbraith, 1974: 45). Yet we have seen that in the second half of the 20th-century, wholly new opportunities for highly suspect, though systematic, moulding of consumer choices have been opened up.

Which? Or Whether?

From our review of the field of consumer choice, we cannot escape a sense that one type of choice has monopolized the attention of writers, whether psychologists, economists or cultural critics. This has obscured a different type of choice altogether, a more difficult type of choosing, one that involves dilemmas and morality rather than tastes and whim or a desire for difference. In our view, the notion of choice should be reserved for important matters in life, like choosing whether to take a job, whom to marry, whether to have children, whether to move abroad, whether to live in rented accommodation or to buy a house, whether to take on private healthcare insurance or send your children to private school.

So much that is referred to as consumer choice in mature markets and developed economies boils down to relative trivialities, compared to matters of life and death, political and civil rights, or the future of the planet. To us as individuals, it does, of course, matter if we put Mozart or McCartney on the CD player, or buy this linen suit rather than the cotton one, or buy this soap powder over that one, or eat this food rather than that. The deep opposition to lack of consumer choice in communist societies meant that the apologists for Western-style consumer choice have received far less critical attention than they were due. The glorification of consumer choice in the post-Second World War period is symptomatic of a blind spot in Western cultural values, that choice is not only a matter of which product or service to select, but also to whether and how to consume.

We would prefer to think of choice in connection with significant issues in our lives, involving genuine life changes, as when someone chooses to become a vegetarian, having been brought up a meat-eater, or when, as happened to a friend of ours, he decided to buy a pair of shorts to wear in the summer and for the first time to bare his polio-afflicted leg to the eyes of strangers. That is choosing to consume in a more meaningful sense. More everyday concerns regarding preferences among brands or substitute products could be referred to as selection, that is, where one expresses a preference for one among fixed options.

Even manufacturers recognize that the range of options they offer to consumers is often restricted. Ton Otker, Marketing Research Executive for Philips International, is unusual in publicly stating then that the

> harsh reality is that differences between the majority of brands within a given type of product (durable or non-durable consumer products) are actually minimal. … [C]onsumers are basically lazy and prefer to extend existing experience, rather than continually branching out and trying something new … (Otker, 1990: 32)

This type of everyday consumer decision is not sufficiently momentous to make it the basis for a consumer culture. When it mutates onto the political plane, this type of decision turns politics into a spectator sport and politicians into competing brands, a phenomenon already widely observed among commentators as diverse as Hobsbawm (1994), Postman (1986) and Baudrillard (1983). Economists, of course, will continue to build elaborate models on just this restricted type of choice. In our view, the right of individuals to make infinitesimal selections between close alternatives, important though it may be, should not override other vital human interests, priorities and rights. The fetishization of choice is symptomatic of a large hole at the heart of consumerism.

CHAPTER 3

The Consumer as Communicator

Goods assembled together in ownership make physical, visible
statements about the hierarchy of values to which their chooser
subscribes. Goods can be cherished or judged inappropriate,
discarded, and replaced. Unless we appreciate how they are used
to constitute an intelligible universe, we will never know how to
resolve the contradictions of our economic life.

Douglas and Isherwood, 1978: 5

C
O
ARGUMENTS
E

The objects we consume can be seen as a live information system,
through which cultural meanings are conveyed and contested. Fashion
creates distinctions of social status, supplanting older distinctions
based on family lineage or wealth. Goods, such as clothes and cars, as
well as services, such as holiday destinations and meals in restaurants,
tell stories about those who consume them; goods also communicate
emotion and social prestige when exchanged as gifts. The meanings
and messages emitted by particular objects and services, individually or
in combination with others, are widely but imprecisely affected by
advertising that seeks to create stories and narratives within which to
cast them.

How fixed are the meanings and messages communicated by
different objects? There is a continuing argument in the social sciences
over this question. Many ethnographers emphasize the stable and
predictable attributes of material culture, while cultural theorists, especially postmodernist ones, emphasize the transient and volatile nature
of meanings that characterize today's consumer culture.

F̲ew images have dominated discussions of consumption to the same extent as that of the consumer as communicator of meanings. This may be seen as the by-product of the current dominance of language in every cultural debate. It is not merely fashionable to talk of food, clothes, cars, buildings, organizations, politics or even our bodies as 'texts', carrying messages. The idea, according to many cultural theorists, is now that all culture *is* text, using different codes, but subject to very similar rules of syntax and grammar. Language no longer serves as a metaphor for understanding culture (let alone as a mere tool); it has become the central paradigm furnishing core concepts and ideas that then migrate into numerous other cultural debates, redefining the terms of these debates. This chapter explores the strengths and shortcomings of looking at consumption and the world of objects as a system through which we communicate to others as well as to ourselves.

Images of consumers as communicators, using material objects to express social differences as well as personal meanings and feelings, considerably pre-date the present privileged position of language within the human sciences. Simmel's (1971[1904]) theory of fashions as well as Veblen's (1925[1899]) critique of conspicuous consumption both approach material goods not as useful objects aimed at satisfying different human needs, but as signs defining social status, establishing differences and similarities. More recently, anthropologists and sociologists have examined how social differences and status become encoded in systems of dress and clothing, food, transport and other areas of consumption (McCracken, 1988; Sahlins, 1972). An emerging tradition in historiography is currently re-evaluating consumption in the 15th- and 16th-centuries, revealing not only ostentatious displays of wealth, but also a keen awareness of fashions and a rampant consumerism (McKendrick et al., 1982; Mukerji, 1983). Even the supposedly ascetic Protestants in the 17th- and 18th-centuries are gradually being discovered to have cultivated tastes for 'great country houses on their newly acquired estates and filling them with lovely artefacts (portraits, chairs, murals, and chinaware) that testified to their high social position' (Mukerji, 1983: 3). All of these trends have had the effect of dislodging material objects from their automatic linkage with physical and social needs and placing them within a communicative package as carriers of meaning.

In the last quarter of a century, a vast body of literature has focused on the idea of material culture; in other words, the meanings carried by material artifacts, visual representations, images, and so on. Since Barthes' (1973, 1977[1966]) pioneering work on narratives, we have come to appreciate the ability of such artifacts to tell stories that become embedded in the life-stories and identities of the people who use them, display them or appropriate them. Consumer culture, in other words, the sum total of meanings carried by objects, images and signs, is now seen by many as a defining feature of late modernity and the societies many of us inhabit (for example, Appadurai, 1990; Bauman, 2001; Du Gay, 1996a; Featherstone, 1991; Lury, 1996; Miller, 1987; Slater, 1997). In order for objects and images to assume their dominant position as cultural signifiers, their association with human needs had to be dislodged – an item of clothing could not be seen as telling a story about its wearer as long as its primary function was seen as keeping him or her warm, nor could an automobile establish the rank of its owner, as long as it was seen as a machine carrying people from A to B.

The Idea of Needs Goes out of Fashion

Material objects are and have always been central to human communication. We communicate through words, but we also communicate through body language and manners, through gifts, through clothes, through food and through the innumerable items that we use, display and discard every day. Large sections of Homer's *Iliad* and *Odyssey* are devoted to detailed descriptions of material objects, armour, swords, shields as well as domestic objects, each object telling a story (Homer, 1974, especially Rh. XVIII). At a less poetic level, even a sword may serve its aim without actually being used, by communicating deterrence. This appears so self-evident that it is surprising that entire areas of the human sciences have ever been able to study the material world that surrounds us without looking into communication. Yet, large areas of psychology, sociology and economics have in different ways done precisely that. Whether a coat is seen as an item to keep one warm, as the product of a deskilled mechanical process or as an item on an inventory – in all of these instances, its communicative qualities are either ignored or denied. Consider, for example, the opening of Marx's *Capital*:

> The wealth of those societies in which the capitalist mode of production prevails, presents itself as 'an immense accumulation of commodities,' its unit being a single commodity. Our investigation must therefore begin with the analysis of a commodity.

> A commodity is, in the first place, an object outside us, a thing that by its properties satisfies human wants of some sort or another. The nature of such wants, whether for instance, they spring from the stomach or from fancy, makes no difference. Neither are we here concerned to know how the object satisfies these wants, whether directly as means of subsistence, or indirectly as means of production (Marx, 1967[1867]: 35).

Marx and many of those who followed him approached material objects, in the first place, in terms of their usefulness, hence the term 'use-value', and subsequently as things that can be exchanged or traded, hence the term 'exchange-value'. Marx held no naive naturalistic views of the ways objects fulfil human needs, being fully aware both of the social nature of these wants and of the polymorphous usefulness of objects. Nevertheless, he did not inquire into the factors that make objects useful or the manner in which they may satisfy human wants. A weapon, a machine, a coat, a clock, a table and a jewel, are all useful objects having use-values; they cannot be compared with each other until they are treated as exchange-values. Political economy takes no interest in what makes them useful or what uses they may have. 'To discover the various uses of things is the work of history' (Marx, 1967[1867]: 35).

Subsequent authors have distinguished between luxuries and necessities, but the essential link between the usefulness of the object and need of the consumer remained (see Lebergott, 1993). Conservatives prefer the term 'utility' to the Marxist 'use-value'. As we saw in Chapter 2, the two have argued endlessly whether the state or the individual is a better judge of these needs, and whether a socialist or a capitalist production system is better able to satisfy them. Nevertheless, they agreed on seeing objects as the means of satisfying material, psychological and social needs, that is, as things whose primary *raison-d'être* lies in their uses.

Baudrillard has vigorously contested this view, arguing that use-value was always a flawed concept which foreclosed any theoretical study of consumption (Baudrillard, 1988a[1968], 1988b[1970]). By short-circuiting the uses of objects with putative human needs, use-value reduces consumption to a series of tautologies: 'I buy this because I need it; I need it because it is useful to me', 'I buy this because I like it; I like it because it is nice', and so on. The shortcomings of the idea of use-value are laid bare by consumption patterns in the industrial West. The word 'useful' is surely being stretched to excess when applied to video games, olive paté, kitchen gadgets, cigarettes, as well as numerous other objects we consume daily. To describe an expensive pair of running shoes as 'useful for running' or a perfume as 'useful for enhancing one's self-image' collapses either to tautology or to absurdity – a theoretical impasse. To argue retrospectively that such objects fulfil human needs merely highlights the impasse. (For more equivocal arguments than Baudrillard's on the demise of use-value, see Kellner, 1989; Lee, 1993b; Lury, 1996.)

An earlier generation of social critics had also expressed reservations about the idea of goods as use-values. Adorno, one of them, argued that under capitalist accumulation the exchange-value of commodities dominates or even obliterates their use-values. Objects are produced if they can be sold at a profit, rather than because of any social or individual uses they may have. Most commodities, argued Adorno, become detached from their use-value; use-values persist as distant memories lost in the noisy symbolic clout of consumer society, whereas commodities acquire new symbolic meanings and associations (Rose, 1978: 25).

The demise of the concept of use-value, precipitated by Western consumers' apparent willingness or even eagerness to purchase commodities with only the most tenuous use-value or no apparent use-value at all, has opened several possibilities. One is to argue along with Packard (1981[1957]), Marcuse (1964) and Lasch (1980, 1984) that consumers are *victims* (see Chapter 7, 'The Consumer as Victim'), duped into buying more or less useless objects by techniques of mass manipulation and marketing. A less pessimistic option is to argue that the attraction of objects in advanced capitalism lies not in their function but in their aesthetic qualities, the consumer being essentially an *artist* whose purchases constitute the brush-strokes of an on-going creative process; for example, one's home becomes one's creative expression (see Chapter 6, 'The Consumer: Hedonist or Artist?'). Yet another option is to approach the consumer as an *explorer* of objects, as one who goes out shopping 'just to look' or who purchases without any clear notion of what lies ahead but in the hope of discovering something exciting and unexpected; for example, buying a record or a book because you like the cover or title (see Chapter 4, 'The Consumer as Explorer').

The Meanings of Goods

None of these less pessimistic images, however, have quite the currency enjoyed by the image of the consumer as *communicator*. At the core of this image lies the idea that material objects embody a system of meanings, through which we express ourselves and communicate with each other. We want and buy things not because of what things can do for us, but because of what things mean to us and what they say about us. According to this view, goods tell stories and communicate meanings in different ways but every bit as effectively as words. In the first place, material objects stand as evidence that certain events took place, removing ambiguity and fixing meanings. A wedding ring, for example, is the material object that establishes marital status, turning two separate people into husband and wife; its 'use' lies primarily in the story it tells about those wearing it. According to this view, whether a car is a useful device to carry you from A to B is largely irrelevant. There are many ways of going from A to B, and in any event the reasons why one wishes to go from A to B may be related to the availability of a car. A car, therefore, is not a carrier of persons so much as a carrier of meanings about itself, its owner, its manufacturer and the broader culture. It is a part of a symbolic nexus made up of material goods (Firat, 1992; Pandya and Venkatesh, 1992).

The study of consumption as communication proceeds from the cultural values of goods and the meanings that they embody. Economic (exchange) values ultimately derive from cultural values, not from biological or social 'needs':

> One cannot sell objects that do not have meaning to other people. A wad of paper or ball of fluff does not have economic value, unless adopted by an artist for an artwork or otherwise used as a raw material. ... But objects do not have to have absolute cultural meanings in order to sell. A Mexican blanket may be bought in Mexico to be used on a bed for warmth while it may sell in the United States as a wall hanging. People need only find ways to make objects meaningful to make them economically valuable (without necessarily depending on the meanings of their creators). (Mukerji, 1983: 13)

The recognition that goods are parts of a communication system opens great possibilities of explaining the seemingly insatiable character of modern consumption without recourse to concepts of greed and envy, of exploring how different goods may combine to generate composite stories, and of explaining why people may make do without necessities in order to afford luxuries. Finally, it opens the possibility of assessing the impact of image-makers and 'merchandisers of meaning' (Sievers, 1986: 347) without resorting to the idea of manipulation or deception, discussed in Chapter 2.

Communication and Consumption – Some Early Views

Two of the earliest theorists to focus on the communicative qualities of commodities were Thorstein Veblen and Georg Simmel, both of whom were fascinated by the emerging metropolitan lifestyles at the turn of the century, especially the ostentatious displays of wealth pursued by the nouveau riches. In *The Theory of the Leisure Class*, first published in 1899, Veblen explored how, at least for the newly rich, everyday objects lose their functional qualities and become objects of display, establishing the social standing of their owners and users. For the members of the leisure class, the functions of objects are not defined by their uses; their function is to signify that their user does not work with his or her hands, or indeed does not work at all. Goods become status markers, indicating a certain level of income and a lifestyle of leisure. Veblen's conception, as McCracken has argued (McCracken, 1988: 36), did not involve any elaborate theory of communication or any genuine symbolic depth. Goods are 'prima facie evidence' of income, rather than symbols. Fashionable clothes are *insignia* of leisure. Any sensible observer can deduce the wealth of a person by the cost of an item of clothing they wear, without any intricate interpretation or clever decoding.

Veblen shrewdly managed to detach consumption, especially ostentatious and 'excessive' consumption, from notions of greed or acquisitiveness and to account for its driven qualities by linking it to social status. At the heart of his conception lies emulative spending, a heightened propensity to consume in order to keep up with the Joneses. People are tyrannically dominated by fashion, because falling behind the fashion implies one's social decline. McKendrick (McKendrick et al., 1982) has pointed out that what Veblen observed and described is what pioneering entrepreneurs like Josiah Wedgwood had been aware of and exploited for well over a century – that selling pottery, not because of its use-value but because of its snob value, pays (Wernick, 1991). Conspicuous consumption may be aggravated by capitalism, but can be seen as a feature of all cultures; it is based on Veblen's central assumption, that social competition for status induces imitation.

Imitation is a central feature in the other early theory of consumerism, developed by Georg Simmel. Like Veblen, Simmel approached consumption essentially as a process whereby social status and rank are established and communicated. Display is no side-effect of consuming, according to these two views, but its very essence. In an article called 'Fashion' (Simmel, 1971b[1904]), Simmel argued that social groups forever seek to emulate the clothing patterns of their social superiors. However, Simmel argued that status competition inspires not only imitation but also differentiation. The higher social strata seek to distance themselves from their close subordinates by endlessly adopting new fashions and new trends. These act as the new status markers, while yesterday's status markers fall into disrepute to them, even as they are adopted by social groups below them. In this way, imitation and differentiation drive fashion. He wrote:

> The peculiarly piquant and suggestive attraction of fashion lies in the contrast between its extensive, all-embracing distribution and its rapid and complete disintegration; and with the latter of these characteristics the apparent claim to permanent acceptance again stands in contrast. (Simmel, 1971b[1904]: 322)

Leading social groups set new trends in an attempt to distinguish themselves from the masses; the new trends are then adopted by those next in the pecking order until eventually they 'trickle-down' to lower social groups. By this time, the trend-setters have moved onto new pastures. Even more than Veblen, Simmel was able to show that acquisitiveness, the seemingly irrational change of fashions, the psychological obsolescence of outmoded, though perfectly functional commodities and the obsessive interest in style, fashion and trends are all fuelled by an underlying competition for social status and prestige.

Veblen's and Simmel's ideas have had considerable influence on subsequent theories of consumer behaviour. Their plausibility, when applied to many of the goods we consume in everyday life, is remarkable. Consider, for example, the plight of parents whose children nonchalantly discard yesterday's expensive toys only to embrace a new fad, smartly displayed by their friends in the school yard. In the early 1990s, parents of all incomes and classes fought pitched battles in toy shops to obtain the precious sets of 'teenage mutant ninja turtles'; a mass marketing exercise had induced turtle mania to children throughout the Western world. The coveted turtle logos featured on every conceivable item of children's clothes, furniture, kitchenware, and so on. It may seem ridiculous, but any child who failed to sport at least some turtle merchandise could be described as culturally deprived. What was even more remarkable was the speed with which turtles became passé. Within a few months, what had been treasured objects turned into objects of derision. Children who turned up at school still wearing clothes with turtle logos or carrying turtle-emblazoned bags or pencil-cases found themselves teased and ridiculed. It was now the turn of the turtles to become symbols of cultural deprivation. There is nothing new about this phenomenon; whole commercial empires have been built on it, most conspicuously that of Disney (Goulart, 1970).

Holiday destinations can also be seen reflecting status competition among different social groups. New tourist resorts are 'discovered' by the trend-setters, who scorn to visit the mass destinations. Yet, these new resorts gradually trickle down to become mass destinations themselves. Snobbery, hardly concealed contempt and disparagement are reserved for those who cannot afford the new fashionable resorts, even worse to those who have not realized that the resorts they visit are no longer fashionable. Like children's toys, holiday destinations are not innocent or risk-free; they are part of a process whereby meanings of social worth are established and elaborate hierarchies of social standing are sustained.

Simmel, like Veblen, did not develop a theory of how particular meanings come to be attached to particular objects, how meanings migrate across different categories of objects or the changes they undergo as they are interpreted and decoded. Nor did he explore the circumstances under which subordinate groups may choose to reject the fashions set up by their social superiors and set up fashions of their own (something central to the work of Bourdieu and Douglas). He did, however, argue very cleverly that rejection of fashion and affected indifference to it very quickly becomes 'imitation, but under an inverse sign' (Simmel, 1971b[1904]: 307), that is, a fashion in its own right. His views on the fickle, arbitrary quality of fashion anticipated current postmodern thinking on 'the arbitrariness of signs' and 'free-floating signifiers', as we shall see. But the paramount value of his work on fashion lies in its convincing portrayal as at once irrational, capricious, tyrannical but also a central force in our lives as consumers:

> Judging from the ugly and repugnant things that are sometimes in vogue, it would seem as though fashion were desirous of exhibiting its power by getting us to adopt the most atrocious things for its sake alone. The absolute indifference of fashion to the material standards of life is well illustrated by the way in which it recommends something appropriate in one instance, something abstruse in another, and something materially and aesthetically quite indifferent in a third. (Simmel, 1971b[1904]: 297–8)

More Recent Views

The pioneering qualities and originality of Simmel's and Veblen's work is gradually being recognized. Their theories suffer from a number of theoretical shortcomings (McCracken, 1988), yet the fact remains that by looking at the goods that we consume, not as material necessities or useful objects, but as markers of social standing, Veblen and Simmel placed consumption at the heart of social theorizing, long before this became a theoretical fashion in its own right. Their views prefigure many current ideas regarding consumption as a system of communication.

An oft-quoted statement of this position is provided by the anthropologist Mary Douglas and the economist Baron Isherwood in *The World of Goods: Towards an Anthropology of Consumption* (1978). Unlike Veblen and Simmel, however, Douglas and Isherwood argued that there had been too much sniping at excessive consumption. For too long, the study of consumption had suffered from 'a tendency to suppose that people buy goods for two or three restricted purposes: material welfare, psychic welfare, and display' (Douglas and Isherwood, 1978: 3). Much of the sniping would be silenced if consumption was seen as a *live information system*, through which cultural meanings are conveyed and contested. The essence of objects lies in the social symbolism that they carry.

> Instead of supposing that goods are primarily needed for subsistence plus competitive display, let us assume that they are needed for making visible and stable the categories of culture. It is standard ethnographic practice to assume that all material possessions carry social meanings and to concentrate a main part of cultural analysis upon their use as communicators. (Douglas and Isherwood, 1978: 59)

Douglas and Isherwood are more concerned than the earlier theorists about the fine nuances of meanings that may be communicated through material objects, as well as about the creative choices which consumption require.

> The housewife with her shopping basket arrives home: some things in it she reserves for her household, some for the father, some for the children; others are destined for the special delectation of guests. Whom she invites into her house, what parts of the house she makes available to outsiders, how often, what she offers them for music, food, drink, and conversation, these choices express and generate culture in its general sense. (Douglas and Isherwood, 1978: 57)

Instead of passive imitation or compulsive differentiation, they argue that 'the most general objective of the consumer can only be to construct an intelligible universe with the goods he chooses' (Douglas and Isherwood, 1978: 65). Goods not only communicate social categories and hierarchies (for example, superior/subordinate, avant-guard/conservative, new-rich/old-rich) but a highly varied, specific and symbolically charged range of meanings. In this sense, they are far richer than signs or insignia and more like stories through which we communicate with each other and express our emotions. As Miller has noted (1987: 99), children are able to articulate a wide variety feelings and desires through objects at a much earlier age than through purely linguistic symbolism, and although language may supplement the usefulness of material objects in communication, it never quite nullifies it.

Consider, for example, the range of meanings communicated through food, an area of consumption to which Douglas has devoted considerable attention over many years. In her classic article 'Deciphering a meal' (Douglas, 1975), she examined in detail what exactly constitutes a meal. She argued that the definition of a meal varies across cultures and has little relation to the nutritional qualities of what is being consumed. Instead, it depends on the types of utensils used, the kinds of ingredients used, the type of cooking, and so on. These not only differentiate meals from other occasions when food and drink is taken (for example, 'drinks', 'snacks', 'quick bites') but also define what kind of meal is being consumed as well as what the relations are among those who participate. To most middle-class

Britons, a sequence of soup and fruit simply does not constitute a meal, just as eating without utensils cannot be described as a meal (at least until the arrival of US-style 'fast food'). A dish with two staple items on a plate, for example, potatoes *and* rice, sounds a discordant note, just as a misspelt word on a printed page or a mispronounced word in a sentence.

Food on a plate, then, constitutes a system of communication, with its own rules and its own ambiguities. It is a coded message.

> If food is treated as a code, the message it encodes will be found in the pattern of social relations being expressed. ... Food categories encode social events. (Douglas, 1975: 249)

Particular types of meal are signalled through the use of special dishes or trimmings. The use of special items, such as turkey with all the trimmings at Christmas, a roast on Sunday, or a first course followed by an entrée for a dinner party, communicates specific messages. For Douglas, unlike Veblen, ostentation does not necessarily imply social competition, but rather a fixing of meanings. Social and moral judgement is withheld. The use of special cutlery or luxury china during a meal may be less a means of impressing an important guest than a way of stating that a meal is a special one in comparison to other ones.

While Douglas has been persistently critical of Veblen (Douglas and Isherwood, 1978: 4 and *passim*), Veblen's argument about competitive imitation can be seen as a special case of Douglas's more general view that goods establish social categories. For it can hardly be denied that one of the range of social categories which *may* be communicated through a meal is social superiority, especially if a highly ostentatious meal is served to a visitor who can hardly reciprocate at the same level. Nevertheless, Douglas's argument considerably enlarges the communicative potential of material goods, well beyond the establishment of social hierarchies to the general maintenance of meanings. Without material goods, argues Douglas, meanings become unstable, ambiguous, they tend to drift or even disappear. Meanings require rituals to sustain them, and rituals depend on material objects:

> More effective rituals use material things, and the more costly the ritual trappings, the stronger we can assume the intention to fix the meanings to be. Goods, in this perspective, are ritual adjuncts; consumption is a ritual process whose primary function is to make sense of the inchoate flux of events. (Douglas and Isherwood, 1978: 65)

Douglas and Isherwood carry the argument well beyond those of Veblen and Simmel, by highlighting the interconnections of material objects as a feature of their communicative potential, instead of treating each object as a separate icon. Objects do not make individual statements, but rather they communicate together with other objects, just like individual items on a menu or on a plate acquire their significance in the light of the other items. Silver cutlery next to crystal wine glasses and expensive porcelain tells a very different story from silver cutlery in the midst of rustic tableware.

The Diderot Effect and Product Constellations

The combined effect of material objects is graphically captured in what McCracken (1988) terms the 'Diderot unity', prompted by an intriguing observation made by the great French thinker Denis Diderot (1713–84). In a little essay entitled 'Regrets on parting with my old dressing gown', Diderot describes how upon receiving a gift of a magnificent scarlet robe, he discarded his old 'ragged, humble, comfortable old wrapper'. He then started getting dissatisfied in turn with every other item in his study for failing to live up to the splendour of the new item. He therefore set about replacing chairs, engravings, bookshelves and everything else. With every new acquisition, however, he found new things to be dissatisfied with, so that eventually he looked back nostalgically at his study the way it used to be, crowded, humble, chaotic but happy. 'Now the harmony is destroyed. Now there is no more consistency, no more unity, and no more beauty,' he reflected (quoted in McCracken, 1988: 119).

McCracken, prompted by Diderot's reflections, observes that objects do not communicate in isolation but in concert with other objects (the 'Diderot unity'). Once a particular component is replaced, the harmony is undermined, precipitating further changes. According to this view, individual purchases are not motivated by envy or social competition or display, but by an urge for consistency and completeness. The quest for completeness, consistency and unity, is, of course, a driving force in every collector; but it is also a more general cultural phenomenon. Buying a new set of speakers for one's stereo system is likely to lead to dissatisfaction with one's amplifier; the replacement of the amplifier is likely, in turn, to cause dissatisfaction with the other musical components. The owner of a new Rolex watch soon begins to be discontent with his or her modest motor-car and starts dreaming of 'upgrading' it. This phenomenon is well known to advertisers who perennially try to entice us with offers of products that complement or 'bring out the best in' what we already have. Product constellations can be seen as objects that somehow reinforce each other's message and reduce the scope for ambiguity or conflict. Even more commonly, we are enticed with 'complete sets', packages or collections which have already been designed to communicate in unison.

Moving from the public statements of goods in Mary Douglas's arguments to the solitary concerns of Diderot, it may be thought that we have lost sight of the consumer as communicator. After all, Diderot's study, like his dressing gown, were private, not meant for public display. Are there some forms of solitary, personal consumption that simply repudiate the idea of consumption as communication? Douglas and McCracken do not think so. Douglas argues that even the solitary consumers submit to the rules and categories of their culture, when, invisible to others, they eat their meals with knives and forks and shirk away from beginning with pudding and ending with soup, or eating mustard with lamb and mint with beef (Douglas and Isherwood, 1978: 67). Somewhat similarly, McCracken describes goods both as 'bulletin boards for internal messages and billboards for external ones' (McCracken, 1988: 136). Through the goods that we consume, we may be communicating with ourselves, reinforcing social categories and classifications. Like old family photographs that are not for public display, we may use those private goods to remind ourselves of who we are, what we have achieved, what we have lost and what we may wish for the future.

It is questionable, however, whether many consumer goods fall into this category of purely personal story-telling, entirely devoid of a social dimension. Consider, for example, some increasingly popular types of consumption in the West, such as body piercing jewellery or tattoos in intimate places. The very fact that such practices are now seen as fashionable indicates that, for all their privacy and intimacy, they comply with the trends described by Simmel and elaborated by Douglas and McCracken. Like whispered secrets, private and hidden jewellery and tattoos can be seen as a unique type of communication, confirming the special standing of both those who don them as well as of those allowed to see them.

Gifts

Even Diderot, in his solitary study, was hardly removed from a process of communication. In the first place, he was interpreting his friend's opulent gift as a message confirming the eminence he had attained, rather than purely as a token of esteem or as a mere luxury in which he might indulge without further ado. Moreover, through the hapless sequence of subsequent replacements, he might have been seeking to communicate to himself an image of himself as someone who, adorned by his magnificent scarlet robe, deserves something more sumptuous for his den than his simple study of old. His friend's gift turned inadvertently into a Trojan Horse.

If virtually all goods carry meanings, gifts are self-conscious of their meaning-carrying capacities. By their essence, gifts are laden with symbolism, punctuating important ritual occasions, such as weddings, anniversaries, birthdays, name-days, bar mitzvahs, christenings, house moves, Christmas, Mother's and Father's Days, Valentine's Days. Gifts must not be regarded as a small class of objects and exchanges at the margins of consumption. From the 'treats' indulged by parents on deserving children, to flower bouquets dispatched by Interflora, to the purchasing of rounds of drinks or the holding of parties, to corporate hospitality, to the generalized consumer delirium as Christmas approaches, gifts are an important feature of Western culture and a cardinal feature of many others. A new and unique merchandising operation called 'The Gift Shop' has confidently taken its place in shopping malls, high streets and airport lounges. Whole areas of the economy from jewellery and perfumes to book and record tokens, are now fuelled by gift-giving. It is not accidental that the study of gifts has attracted considerable research interest and offers important insights into the consumer as communicator.

Since the pioneering work of Marcel Mauss (1974[1925]), it is widely accepted that gifts, unlike donations, are not just free goods, but parts of reciprocal exchange relations. Gifts reflect the nature and importance of the occasion; they communicate meanings and emotions (such as respect, gratitude, love, and even pity, disdain and scorn), as well as defining the social and emotional distance between giver and receiver. The meanings of gifts are often ambiguous and far from easy to interpret and the choice of gifts can become a cause of major headaches. Yet the very ambiguity in the meanings of gifts makes them highly effective. Like myths, gifts can carry meanings that are once at ambiguous and powerful. And like myths, gifts can reconcile the irreconcilable (Barthes, 1973), bridging vast differences of culture and interest, though of course they can equally lead to gigantic misunderstandings and conflict. For this reason, most of us treat gifts with special respect, as if we recognize that they are a risk. A gift is something that both the giver and the receiver will be judged by. It is also something through which both giver and receiver will judge the other's opinion of them, as well as the importance that the other accords to the occasion. It is not surprising, then, that the amount of time we spend in choosing a present is considerably greater than that which we spend in buying similar items for personal consumption (Pandya and Venkatesh, 1992).

Gifts communicate in many ways and are judged by many of their qualities. Consider one of the simpler ones: price. The price of a gift is an important part of its meaning, yet it can be highly ambiguous. An inexpensive gift from a rich relative may be interpreted as a rebuff, as a discourtesy, as a sign of a loss of money or status on the part of the giver or as a sign of increasing social and emotional distance that the giver tries to establish. Yet an inexpensive gift may equally be accepted with relief for not imposing too severe demands for its reciprocation. A costly gift from a rich relative may be gratefully received with an acknowledge-ment of the relative's superior economic and perhaps social standing. It may, however, be interpreted as an attempt to humiliate, since it may not be recipro-cated in kind. Gifts are a highly delicate area of consumption.

Price is not the only feature by which gifts are judged. Appropriateness, origi-nality, presentation and personal time are highly valued qualities in gifts, as is the personal touch. Children may delight their parents with presents that they make themselves, until somehow they get the idea that things that they make them-selves and are not paid for are not 'real presents'. A less well-off relative may be able amply to reciprocate an opulent present with a less expensive but very well-chosen one, a beautifully wrapped one, an exotic one or one which required a lot of his or her time. Skill, judgement and, above all, time can all enrich the mean-ings of a gift, compensating for its low cost. As Bourdieu (1979) has argued, time can be the most precious of gifts, and the time it takes to locate, to choose, to wrap and to present become parts of the story that the gift tells. The wrapping, the ribbons and cards that accompany a gift are no mere ornaments, but of the very essence.

Nor do gifts cease to communicate once the ritual of presentation has taken place. Some remain as reminders of the occasion or of the giver, keeping or even increasing their symbolic power as the years go by. These are treasured objects, whose damage, theft or loss is experienced as a personal injury by their owner. The anthropologist Levy-Bruhl (1966) noted that in some cultures, everyday objects such as ornaments, clothes and tools, become literally incorporated in the self. In a similar way, Belk (1988) has argued that certain objects (especially things like cars or houses) become vital elements of our identity as if they were physical extensions of our bodies. Lacan (1953) even went as far as to suggest that our car's mechanical failures are exactly equivalent to neurotic symptoms, its fits and starts are neurotic twitches. Such objects clearly provide a bridge between the consumer as communicator and the consumer as identity-seeker (see Chapter 5, 'The Con-sumer as Identity-seeker'). Most gifts, however, have more mundane careers, being used and forgotten, or being sold as second-hand goods at knock-down prices, being given as 'half-gifts' to new receivers or simply being thrown away.

In an intriguing article on consumerism in Japan, Clammer describes how shopping habits are conditioned by the gift economy, 'a perpetual and enormous circulation of commodities – a gigantic kula-ring-like cycle of obligations and rec-iprocities' (Clammer, 1992: 207). Gifts, exchanged by the Japanese on a consider-ably larger scale than most Western Europeans or Americans, come mostly to an inglorious end:

> A certain day each month is 'heavy rubbish day' when unwanted large objects can be put on the sidewalk for collection by the municipal rubbish collectors or by private contractors. The most astonishing variety and volume of things are discarded – furniture, TVs, bicycles, golf-clubs, all kinds of electrical appliances and just about everything that a modern household needs, ... often in almost mint condition. (Clammer, 1992: 208–9)

While from an economic point of view, endless rounds of gift-giving may represent waste and may be dented by recession, in Japan, they strengthen networks of social relations and define social hierarchies in an effective way. In these respects, gifts highlight Douglas's and McCracken's arguments concerning the consumer in the capacity of gift-buyer and gift-receiver as someone who essentially creates, communicates and interprets meanings.

Gifts to Oneself?

Is it possible to give gifts to oneself? Mick (1986) and Levy (1982) have argued that self-gifts differ in character from other personal consumption; they are quite common in Western cultures. Self-gifts can mark special occasions, like private anniversaries or special visits. Souvenirs are often purchased in this way, as markers of specific events. Even more commonly, they appear as rewards for achievement or consolations for failure, re-asserting pride and self-respect. Pandya and Venkatesh give this graphic example:

> In the film 'Crimes of the Heart', Diane Keaton, a lonely middle-aged single woman, thinks her family has forgotten her birthday. She gets a cookie for herself, lights a candle on it and sings 'Happy Birthday' to herself. She gives herself a birthday party the others forgot to give her. Her gift to herself accentuates her loneliness but also affirms her selfhood. There are many such examples of self-gift in real life like vacations as a reward after a year of hard work. But when families discuss their vacations with their friends these often become signs of their status, competition and success. (Pandya and Venkatesh, 1992: 152–3)

Such self-gifts can be seen as part of a continuing dialogue one has with oneself. One can almost imagine old Diderot, ruminating in his study on what should replace the threadbare tapestry hanging from the wall, finally deciding to treat himself to a fine new one. The need we have to present special purchases as treats or rewards highlights the symbolic importance of the objects we purchase. In this way, we use objects to construct meaningful stories about our efforts, our successes and failures and this is one of the factors that doubtless drives modern consumerism. A new CD or video may be thought of as an unnecessary luxury that we resist. If, however, we can present it as the just dessert for a successful effort or as the rightful consolation for an unsuccessful one, it becomes irresistible.

One could very well ask, why do success or failure need be marked in this way, through the use of a newly acquired object? Is it impossible to construct meaningful stories about ourselves and others without the assistance of the objects? For example, is it necessary to mark an important anniversary with a costly gift rather than a kiss and a hug? Why are singing, dancing, poetry and speech-making not adequate enough rituals for a wedding, without having in addition an arsenal of gifts? Is it impossible to construct a story of a meaningful holiday without the material reminders of photographs, souvenirs and other costly tourist paraphernalia?

Objects and Sign-Values

Mary Douglas has argued that material objects are indispensable for fixing the meanings and the categories of events. Long after the singing and the dancing at the wedding has finished, the wedding ring will still be the material evidence of the event. Primitive cultures as well as modern cultures rely on material objects to fix meaning. Baudrillard, on the other hand, whose early studies into consumer culture have much in common with Douglas's, takes a different view. Like Douglas, Baudrillard viewed material objects as forming a system of classification, though his assessment of their value is more ambivalent:

> Objects are *categories of objects* which quite tyrannically induce *categories of persons*. They undertake the policing of social meanings, and the significations they engender are controlled. (Baudrillard, 1988a[1968]: 16–17)

Having convincingly challenged the concept of objects as use-values, Baudrillard approached each object as the carrier of a sign-value. This is where his argument departs from Douglas's view of physical objects as material depositories of social meaning. For Baudrillard, the sign-values of objects are mobile and precarious, more so since the beginning of the industrial era, and infinitely more so at the present time. Like neurotic symptoms, where each symptom can easily be replaced by another (for example, a neurotic cough by may be replaced by colitis), the sign-value of objects can quickly migrate from one commodity to another:

> A washing machine *serves* as equipment and *plays* as an element of comfort, or of prestige etc. It is the field of play that is specifically the field of consumption. Here all sorts of objects can be substituted for the washing machine as a signifying element. In the logic of signs, as in the logic of symbols, objects are no longer tied to a function or to a *defined* need. This is precisely because objects respond to something different, either to a social logic, or to a logic of desire, where they serve as a fluid and unconscious field of signification. (Baudrillard, 1988b[1970]: 44)

Baudrillard is arguing here that for the individual consumer, the desire for a wash-ing-machine may inexplicably be transferred onto a desire for a dress, a record or a car, just as the signifying effect of the washing-machine may be achieved through a dishwasher, a carpet or a ring. Unlike Douglas, who stresses the stabilizing influ-ence of objects, Baudrillard views sign-values as fleeting and migratory. For Douglas, a wedding ring is solid, timeless, reassuring; for Baudrillard, a wedding ring is a transmitter of spasmodic, indistinct and ambiguous messages. This is what makes sign-values both fiercely contested as well as ideally plastic material in the hands of advertisers and marketers. This is also why, in the last resort, they are unable to provide the basis for real identity or selfhood. Ultimately, goods lose all signification, standing for nothing whatsoever beyond themselves. From being depositories of social meaning they become black holes into which meaning dis-appears (Baudrillard, 1983).

Brands, Advertising and the Destruction of Meaning

> If I can describe a cake, a cigarette, a fishing rod, or a bottle of whisky in such a way that its basic soul, its basic meaning to modern man, becomes clear, I shall, at the same time, have

achieved direct communication. I shall have established a bridge between my advertisement and the reader and come as close as possible to motivating the reader or listener to acquire this experience via the product which I have promised him. (Dichter (1960: 92), quoted in Lee (1993a: 150))

Selling things by making them tell stories was well-known to Dr Ernest Dichter, Director of the Institute of Motivational Research. He saw advertising as the art of making commodities communicate to us, by making goods speak with human voices (see Chapter 2, 'The Consumer as Chooser'). Brands were humanized and brand names became condensations of stories. Like the 'crown', which stands metonymically for all things royal, majestic and imposing, brand names become embodiments of special qualities, values and images. Meaning travels from the whole to the part and from the part to the whole. A small bar of soap carrying the logo of Harrods, the famous London department store, becomes the embodiment of the Harrods values, tradition, soundness, and quality, the best of Old British values. By purchasing the small bar of soap, one purchases all that Harrods stands for and makes these attributes of Harrods one's own. Exploiting these metonymic qualities of goods has long been the task of advertisers and market analysts; it has been explored by academics, such as Williamson (1986), Lee (1993a, 2000) and McCracken (1988):

> Advertising works as a potential method of meaning transfer by bringing the consumer good and a representation of the culturally constituted world within the frame of a particular advertisement. The creative director of an agency seeks to conjoin these two elements in such a way that the viewer/reader glimpses an essential similarity between them. When this symbolic equivalence is successfully established, the viewer/reader attributes certain properties he or she knows to exist in the culturally constituted world to the consumer good. The known properties of the world thus come to be resident in the unknown properties of the consumer good. The transfer of meaning from the world to good is accomplished. (McCracken, 1988: 77)

McCracken argues strongly that material objects act as a means of encoding and communicating meanings, but do *not* constitute a language. One of the main differences between language and objects is that objects are constrained in the range of meanings they can assume. In language, onomatopoeic words apart, a particular sound may signify virtually anything, there being no necessary connection between signifier and signified, between word and meaning. Objects, on the other hand, 'bear a "motivated" and "non-arbitrary" relationship to the things they signify' (McCracken, 1988: 132). In this view, a Rolex watch cannot signify a poor man, since a poor man could not afford to buy one. Equally, an inexpensive 'unglamourous' pair of shoes may signify parsimony or poverty or inverted snobbery or various other qualities, but it *may not* by its very nature signify certain things such as wealth, power or discriminating taste in shoes.

Not so, argues Baudrillard, who, since his early book *The System of Objects* (1988a[1968]) has seen brands as capable of telling virtually *any* story, however unconnected to any putative need or use. Even a Rolex may be but a cheap fake, bought at a hundredth of the price, though looking similar. And even a 'real' Rolex may appear as nothing but the kind of model that is much imitated and faked. Once Rolex watches, real and fake, are seen worn on the wrist of any taxi-driver, the meaning carried by them becomes plastic. This argument develops Simmel's idea on the whimsical nature of fashion, whereby anything can become fashionable, provided that it stands out from the rest. Baudrillard takes this argument to its logical conclusion, that signification means simply difference and nothing else. The only meaning that signs retain is their difference from other signs; and this is the end of meaning:

> Diverse brands follow one another, are juxtaposed and substituted for one another without an articulation or transition. It is an erratic lexicon where one brand devours the other, each living for its own endless repetition. This is undoubtedly the most impoverished of languages: full of signification and empty of meaning. It is a language of signals. And 'loyalty' to a brand name is nothing more than the conditioned reflex of a controlled affect. (Baudrillard, 1988a[1968]: 17)

The more brands like McDonald's, Marlborough, Harrods and Nike become temporary depositories of 'meaning' the more emaciated and burnt out the meaning becomes. The more obsessively we interpret, analyse and classify others in terms of the messages emitted by their shoes, their clothes and their preferred drinks, the less we know about them. Ultimately, medium becomes message, signifiers float freely and meaning implodes. Nike, the ancient Greek goddess of victory, no longer stands for victory, for the meaning of victory is swallowed up by the shoe. Clio is no longer an ancient Greek muse; nor do her classical qualities survive in the product; she has become momentarily a French motor-car, a pretty girl, a youthful longing, a clever advertisement, before she is drowned by the noise of other brands, lost and forgotten.

In Baudrillard's view, within the media-dominated world of Western societies, boundaries between reality and representation, substance and image, have imploded, just like the difference between the real and the fake Rolex. A photograph no longer captures the essence of a real event, nor does it claim to do so. A photograph becomes pure image, the product of a photo-opportunity, a staged event that may link, for example, a perfume brand to a tropical island or a politician to a cause. But the viewer of the picture is aware that the picture is the product of a temporary marriage of convenience between two free-floating signifiers, which will soon go their separate ways. Ultimately, the perfume, the tropical island, the politician and the cause lose any meaning, outside the photograph. Like photographs, other consumer goods cease to express meanings and they too become self-referential. The gift is no longer the material proof of Christmas, nor is the wedding ring the material proof of the wedding. Both become opportunistic carriers of ever-decreasing fragments of meaning. Christmas becomes *the* gift; its meaning apart from gifts, photo-opportunities, TV images, drink and food opportunities shrivels to almost nothing. What makes you a mother is not having had a baby but the fact that you shop at a specialist shop called Mothercare. The wedding ring and paraphernalia procured from a shop called Pronuptia become *the* marriage. Disneyland is the photographs and merchandise one brings back. Ultimately Christmas, marriages, Disneyland and the other institutions of postmodern society become photo-opportunities, object-opportunities, spending-opportunities and little else.

New-wave Advertising

The names adopted by rock bands, seemingly laden with meaning, yet ultimately completely meaningless, highlight Baudrillard's notion of the arbitrariness of the sign. They are entirely self-referential, making no attempt at signification or classification, their only point being to make a temporary impact on our consciousness, without getting lost in the general clamour of which they are but an infinitesimal part. The same can be said of the postmodern advertisements that have become common since the 1980s. These advertisements, pioneered by a number of new advertising agencies that challenged the functional and pragmatic approaches of the older more traditional agencies, eschewed both hard-sell and soft-sell approaches in favour of images and compositions from which 'selling' is effectively banned (see Davidson, 1992; Lee, 1993a; Lury, 1994; Lury, 1996, 2004; Twitchell, 1999; Wernick, 1991). Instead of appealing to our reason or to our emotions, such advertising, along with other postmodern artefacts, celebrates visual images, 'decontextualising "great" works of art and established aesthetic conventions, raiding the iconographies of religious beliefs and political struggles, or incorporating the forms of other cultures into its own discursive frame and for its own ends' (Lee, 1993a: 149).

Many of these advertisements are intertextual, openly borrowing text or ideas from other advertisements and adding a twist. Alternatively, they are reflexive, being essentially advertisements about advertising. 'Aren't conventional ads a bore', they seem to say. 'Do they not treat consumers like dullards, presuming to manipulate their choices through silly images and naive stories. Now *we* know that *you* would not fall for such crude tricks, would you? In fact, we know that you cannot be manipulated at all. You are cool, sophisticated. So, let's forget about us selling you a product. Forget about the product altogether. Let's have some fun together.' Such is the message of this new generation of advertisements. Fun assumes the form of a joke, a pun, a parody of a competitor's advertisement or product, a puzzle, a guilty pleasure or the breaking of a taboo. Such fun undoubtedly creates a degree of solidarity between the advertiser and the reader/viewer based on a shared sense of non-conformism, cleverness, originality, rebelliousness. A conspiracy is sometimes orchestrated between clever advertiser and smart consumer at the expense of supposedly dull advertisers, dumb consumers, or even the very manufacturer who is paying for the commercial. Whether consumers are flattered by such treatment and whether they appropriate the positive qualities residing in the hyper-text are as questionable as whether such advertisements help sell products at all.

According to Davidson (1992), these advertisements tell no story about a product; their stories are at best about themselves and those who conceived them, at worst they would seem to have no story at all. They are pure signs without meaning, signs that almost coincidentally collide with 'products' (that are themselves but signs) only to destroy them, part of the 'hyper-real' world of the mass media, which in Baudrillard's later arguments completely defines the 'real' world. In the hyper-real world, everything mutates into everything else, all is image, appearance and simulation. The TV soap opera is more real than the viewers' own personal reality, the brand is more real than the product. In this hyper-real world, the consumer is no longer a communicator, nor are commodities sign-values. The consumer becomes a Pavlovian dog salivating mechanically at the sight of simple images, his or her emotions are conditioned responses to the sight of brands. Communication dissolves into seduction.

Baudrillard's insights unlock some of the mysteries and mystifications of modern advertising, mass media and communications, pointing at a very real crisis of meanings and signification. They highlight the fragility of systems of signification that are built around seemingly solid objects. They also act as a constant reminder that when we believe that we are most aware that we know what is going on, that we have objective, up-to-the-minute information from CNN, the BBC and other media organizations, we are in fact being transported in a world of special effects, simulations and virtual reality (see, for example, Baudrillard's discussions of the Gulf War as a consumer spectacle (Baudrillard and Gane, 1993)). At the same time, one cannot escape the impression that Baudrillard's views on the omnipotence of modern media, their ability to shift signs and signifiers, to define reality and to destroy meaning, these are the products of one fixated on the mass media, living through the media and ultimately becoming himself part of the hyper-real world which alone interests him. 'I live in the virtual. Send me into the real, and I don't know what to do' (Baudrillard and Gane, 1993: 188), was Baudrillard's response to an offer to go the Gulf and see for himself what was going on during that War.

Even if a good deal of modern consumption unfolds in the realm of virtual reality, simulations and make-believe, Baudrillard underestimates the consumers' ability to *alter* rather than just receive and carry messages. It may be quite true that everyday reality is cluttered by the noise of commodities, signs and images, yet most of us have learned to ignore much of this noise, screen it out and live with it, just as we can enjoy listening to music over the noise that surrounds it. We also learn to experiment with objects, to try them in different ways, and discover meanings in the *uses* we find for them. As de Certeau (1984) has argued, through makeshift arrangements and creative combinations of objects, we learn both to discard the spurious significations of the media and to redefine objects, replenishing them with meanings and significations. (See Chapter 8, 'The Consumer as Rebel'.) Advertising agencies today are only too aware how deft consumers have become at subverting some sign-values, ridiculing others or appropriating others for the 'wrong' purposes.

In addition, Baudrillard simply disregards those areas of consumption which are rooted in the functional qualities of goods. A washing-machine *is* after all a device for washing clothes, and one can hardly imagine doing without if one can afford it, sign-value or no sign-value. Many of the ordinary, unbranded, quiet, unobtrusive objects that surround us never seem to quit the mundane realms of the real for the fantasy world of simulations. And even when they become fantasy objects, they are just as likely to take on the robust cultural symbolic qualities highlighted by Douglas (a Valentine card stands for romantic love and roast turkey for Christmas) than the volatile, nervous and transient qualities of the hyper-real.

In Conclusion

Consumption as communication opens numerous windows into our relations to the physical objects that surround us and the ways we use these objects to express meanings, feelings and social distinctions. This approach can account for the seemingly endless and absurd variety of products that we seek and use, without resorting to tautologies regarding the use-values of such objects or reducing everything to greed. Once we recognize that goods tell stories, that these stories resonate with symbolism and express meanings that cannot be expressed effectively through language, consumption becomes strangely re-humanized. Even irrational, absurd consumption, can be seen as a muddled, ambiguous, contested but ultimately sensical activity, rather than a zombie-like delirium. This is part of being human. Consider the following example from everyday experience:

> I am looking at a kitchen-gadget, described on its package as an olive/cherry pip remover. It is a shining stainless steel contraption, a cousin to that other object which can be found in many kitchens, the garlic crusher. To describe this object as useful would be simply absurd. As a cooking implement, the object is an insult to my intelligence. As an object for which money was paid, it is an insult to my sense of thrift and economy. As an object for that natural resources were used up, to manufacture it, package it, transport it and display it, it is an affront to my 'green' conscience. As an object that clutters my already over-full kitchen drawers, it is a nuisance. Dear old Marcuse might have seen this object as evidence of the spiritual bankruptcy of modern culture and the alienation of the consumer. From most points of view, this is exactly the kind of object I abhor.
>
> Yet, my feelings towards it are tempered, once communication is brought into the picture. This olive/cherry pip remover was a present from a friend, who may have meant it as a joke (and a rather good one to someone who thinks he knows all there is to know about olives) or as a compliment of my cooking skills. Come to think about it, several friends have offered me kitchen gadgets over the years. It is possible that my friend might have been lured into buying this object by its claim to make a fine gift 'for the cook who has everything'; or more simply, my friend might have wanted to share a laugh with me at the expense of a plainly ridiculous object, whose uselessness is evident to all. In any event, the object resolved my friend's aporia, the difficulty of expressing something in words. It was not the perfect gift, I shall not be using it very much, nor will it become a permanent feature of my identity, but I do not reproach my friend for giving it me. I too have succumbed to the temptation of buying silly presents to friends, expecting a degree of clemency in their reading of them. A bit like a joke, which though not very funny, serves its purpose.

The point of this example is to show how objects can be useful as communicative devices. In this way, the idea of usefulness is brought very close to that of communicating meaning. For many objects, use has always involved communication. This applies not only to purely decorative objects with no proclaimed functional purposes or to objects that will serve as media in communication (such as telephones, television sets), but also to a class of largely functional objects whose mere display may forestall their physical use. Weapons, guard dogs and burglar alarms (including fake ones), for instance, can be useful without actually being used, for their deterrent effect, which is achieved through communication. In a similar way, the olive/cherry pip remover was useful as a gift, even if I can never envisage using it.

In spite of its remarkable ability to explain numerous aspects of consumption, the image of consumer as communicator presents only a partial picture of consumption. Gifts, status symbols, fashion and branded goods, designer products and goods that are self-consciously displayed, these are objects for which it seems tailor-made. For goods which are consumed without fuss, in privacy, it is less illuminating. The idea of self-gifts, which turns personal consumption into part of self-dialogue, seems more like an excuse or rationalization for behaviour rather than an explanation of it. The fact that an object can equally be a self-reward for success or a consolation for failure would support this scepticism. Unless we accept unconditionally Baudrillard's challenge and provocation, a hyper-real world of simulations and mirages, of fleeting signifiers and black holes of meaning, it is not clear from the idea of consumer as communicator why objects that require payment have such unique significance in our lives, what drives our desire for them and why we need excuses for purchasing them. Unlike myths, with which we argued commodities have much in common as carriers of symbolism, the resonance of most objects that were once desired and subsequently purchased fades away quickly. The image of consumer as communicator simply fails to account either for the kick we get when we acquire a new and much longed-for commodity or for the frequent disappointment we feel for yesterday's purchases. The portrait of the consumer we next move to, that which portrays the consumer as explorer, holds the promise of insights into these excitements and disappointments.

CHAPTER **4**

The Consumer as Explorer

When you start on your way to Ithaca,
then pray that the road is long,
full of adventure, full of knowledge.

...

Stop at Phoenician markets,
and purchase fine merchandise,
mother-of-pearl and corals, amber and ebony,
and delicious perfumes of all kinds.

...

And if you find her poor, Ithaca has not deceived you,
With the wisdom you have gained, with so much experience,
you have surely understood what Ithacas mean.

Kavafis, 'Ithaca'

CORE ARGUMENTS

Under the rule of consumerism, cities and countryside become dominated by cathedrals of consumption, such as theme parks, shopping malls, casinos, tourist resorts and attractions, sporting venues and museums. These are spaces that consumers are invited to explore for new products and new experiences, with which to create meaning in their lives. Different quests go on in these sites – quests for bargains, quests for difference and even quests for spiritual fulfilment. In the last decade, the Internet has become an additional vast arena for consumer explorations, turning the home into a temple of consumption in its own right.

Who could fail to experience the eternal fascination of exotic markets, their strange displays, their unfamiliar smells and sights, their mystifying rituals of coaxing, bargaining and bluffing? There are no signs anywhere around you, no empty Marlborough packets, no Coca-Cola logos on refrigerated displays. American Express is not known here. These markets are ageless, chance alone has taken you there. You are surrounded by unfamiliar things; or familiar things in unfamiliar guises, at unfamiliar prices. These are not generally friendly places. Excitement is mixed with danger. Are things what they appear to be? Is the amber real or might it be a clever plastic imitation? Would you be taken for a ride if you paid the asking price for a local wood-carving? And what would it look like back in your house, miles away from its siblings and forced to mix with your other valuable possessions? A good topic of conversation or an eyesore?

Now picture yourself in a shopping mall, not perhaps the one you visit regularly whose features you know well, but one slightly less familiar. It may have been purpose-built or it may be housed in an old canning factory or a converted and 'preserved' warehouse. This too is a place to explore, a place to discover, but it is certainly more user-friendly. This is a space that has been *designed* for exploration. An invisible hand has planned everything for your delectation. The reassuring quality of its anchor supermarket at one end, the familiar array of boutiques next to the intriguing shop selling Peruvian parrots and Colombian hammocks, the bars, the restaurants, the soft background music, the discreet lighting, the comfortable climatization, the instantly meaningful signs – this is a synthetic oasis, and none the less stimulating for being designed with people like you in mind. It is a clean, genial, graffiti-free space, where a cultural oxymoron can be acted out, relaxed exploration. There are no worries here, no pushy salesmen, no invisible pickpockets, goods have fixed price-tags and are covered by legislation aimed at protecting consumers. If you run short of cash, plastic money is welcome. To be sure, this is a fantasy world; it brings exotica to the consumer instead of taking the consumer to the exotic. Yet it is a space of exploration.

Exploring and shopping have become one. Bargain hunting, discovering new lines, new fashions, new 'product ideas' and new forms of fun; these are all part of the excitement of shopping. But exploration can begin before you leave your home; it can take place in a relaxed, poised manner, merely flicking the pages of glossy magazines, brimming with new ideas for entertaining guests, decorating your home or stimulating your partner (Barthes, 1973: 86). You can explore the lives of the rich and famous, study the interior of their houses and scrutinize every particle of their face. You can savour dream-like cuisine and be transported to magical places, hardly needing to leave your armchair or strain your purse. Tele-shopping hopes to bring the excitement of high-street exploration into your own home. The Internet has opened up unprecedented possibilities of exploration, not restricted to shopping. The 'Internet Explorer' is, of course, Microsoft's® aptly named web-browser, which promises to carry you into new worlds, converting a simple mouse click into the key that unlocks them.

Alternatively, you may join the armies of energetic explorers, travel to distant places and fill your bags with souvenirs and your camera with digital images. Or you may explore the latest changes in your own high street's array of shops, window displays, signs and street life. Whether we envisage the consumer browsing a magazine or touring, it is hard to imagine consumption without exploration or exploration without consumption.

This chapter looks at contemporary consumers as explorers of goods, market-places and signs. We examine the curiosity that is manifest in the act of shopping in all its diversity and the quest for novelty that drives some of our consuming behaviour. Some of the approaches we introduce may seem far-fetched and removed from the world of mundane day-to-day consumption. They lend them-selves to easy ridicule as hopelessly indulgent and middle-class, oblivious to the world of poverty and privation, as portrayed by analysts like Townsend (1993; Townsend and Gordon, 2002), Mack and Lansley (1985) and Seabrook (1985). Nevertheless, the image of the consumer as explorer was implicit in much of the work on consumption done by cultural theorists since the 1980s. It also inspired an entire generation of retailers and their designers, who sought to transform shopping areas, from hypermarkets to boutiques, into terrains of exploration. By making explicit what has hitherto been implicit, that is, the view of the consumer driven by insatiable curiosity, we seek to highlight both the strengths and, later, the serious deficiencies of these approaches.

Bargain Hunting

Exploration takes many forms. Bargain hunting is perhaps the most evident. Even unfamiliar foreign markets may contain goods that can easily be obtained 'back home', though perhaps at different prices. Prices exercise undoubtedly a strange fascination on consumers. How is it possible that exactly the same item of cloth-ing, the same bar of chocolate, the same shampoo, can cost different amounts in different shops? How is it possible that exactly the same train journey can incur dozens of different fares? How can the price of an electronic toy be halved in less than a year? Or for a pack of four DVDs to retail for less than a pack of three iden-tical DVDs on display in the same shop? Not for nothing did Marx argue in his concept of commodity fetishism that commodities assume mystical qualities, long before marketers adopted pricing as one of the four Ps (the others being product, place and people) of their *métier* and decided to make these things still more confusing.

In spite of the growth of non-utilitarian, esoteric advertising, words like 'free', 'extra', 'more', 'value', 'savings' and, above all, 'bargain' dominate numerous com-mercials. What is a bargain? Clearly a bargain is in the first place quality at low price; good value for money. But this cannot make bargains the subject of a hunt, or fuel the kind of fever that is generated by the sales of large department stores, let alone explain the joy and delight generated by the discovery of a bargain, which parallels that of discovering a secret or sharing a good joke. Dry beans may repre-sent excellent value for money, especially if value is defined in nutritional terms, though they could hardly be described as a bargain. Conversely, discovering a designer scarf at half its normal price may seem like a great bargain, even if the last thing you want is another scarf. A free bottle of champagne with every dozen you buy can look irresistible. Bargain hunting has little to do with sound management of household budgets and more to do with discovering a secret, which few may share, a secret of getting something for nothing, in a world where everything has to be paid for. For years immemorial, the secret of commerce has been spotting bar-gains, buying cheap and selling dear. Whole areas of trade, from antiques to houses, and from second-hand cars to coin or stamp collections are driven by the craving for bargains. The discovery of a bargain performs great services to our self-esteem. It is not uncommon for individuals to fashion their identities around their uncanny ability to spot bargains and take advantage of them. Their exploits are often recounted to others (who may feel bored to tears or, alternatively, envious at having missed an opportunity) and embroidered for greater effect, while the spoils of their adventures are displayed with considerable pride.

While much energy and money is spent by advertisers to inform consumers of the bargains on offer, it seems to us that, like secrets, bargains cannot be known to everybody. Nor can a shop or a retailer be perceived to make a living by always offering bargains, although particular shops may become well known as bargain-hunting terrains. A discounted Italian designer suit may be a bargain, a cheap suit is not. Looking for a bargain then, is not the same as looking for value for money. It is more like looking for opportunities to discover anomalies in the market and take advantage of them. The bargain spotter is akin to a trickster figure who exposes fissures in the system and triumphs against its dictates through cunning and opportunism. Bargain hunters are not always solitary creatures. Informal networks of information exist through which individuals can share their discoveries with friends and neighbours (Lang and Raven, 1994). Finding a bargain marks the triumph of opportunism, like scoring an undeserved goal, which is all the sweeter for being undeserved.

A Duty to Explore?

It is paradoxical that bargain hunting, which is central to value-for-money consumerism and to consumer advocacy (see Chapter 9, 'The Consumer as Activist'), has attracted limited attention in studies of consumption (Cox et al., 2005; Furnham and Okamura, 1999; Tatzel, 2002). Economists, in particular, have been reproached for ignoring *curiosity* as one of the consumer's motives. Scitovsky, one of the few economists who has introduced the concept of exploration in the discussion of modern consumption, has criticized other economists for failing to recognize

> that most important motive force of behavior, including consumer behavior – man's yearning for novelty, his desire to know the unknown. The yearning for new things and ideas is the source of all progress, all civilization; to ignore it as a source of satisfaction is surely wrong. (Scitovsky, 1976: 11)

By contrast, however, curiosity was a notion of considerable interest in cultural theory circles, coupled with the idea of difference. When applied to the study of consumption, these generated immense excitement: the consumers' quests for new pleasures, new meanings and even new identities, through tiny differences in what they purchased, through their sorties to the market, were endlessly probed. Today's Western consumer is constantly exhorted to savour new tastes, to discover new pleasures and to explore new worlds. As Baudrillard, a major figure in this trend, noted:

> the modern consumer, the modern citizen, cannot evade the constraint of happiness and pleasure, which in the new ethics is equivalent to the traditional constraint of labor and production. ... He must constantly be ready to actualize all of his potential, all of his capacity for consumption. If he forgets, he will be gently reminded that he has no right not to be happy. He is therefore not passive: he is engaged, and must be engaged, in continuous activity.

> Otherwise he runs the risk of being satisfied with what he has and of becoming asocial. A *universal curiosity* (a concept to be exploited) has as a consequence been reawakened in the areas of cuisine, culture, science, religion, sexuality etc. (Baudrillard, 1988b[1970]: 48)

Being true to oneself as a consumer means being eager to browse and to explore. A vast number of consumer products, ranging from books, magazines, DVDs and films, to holiday packages, have materialized arousing consumer curiosities, exciting them, nurturing them and satisfying them. Newspapers are filled with curiosity features, exotic places, exotic cuisines, exotic people, and so on 'I don't like travelling' is an instant conversation stopper at parties, just as 'I don't have a TV' can be an instant conversation starter! The local grocery store has been metamorphosed into the hypermarket, which may stock up to 40,000 different items. This jungle of consumption offers a bewildering array of goods, whose prices, packages, sizes, formats and names, to say nothing of contents, are constantly changing. Thus, shopping for groceries turns from a habit or a rational choice into an exploration (see Chapter 2, 'The Consumer as Chooser').

Consumer explorations are not searches into deep unknowns, inner or outer. Instead they are explorations of minute variations, of infinitesimal idiosyncrasies of style, products, brands, signs and meanings. This type of exploration is the discourse of *difference*, the discovery of difference, the establishing of difference and the appropriation of difference. Even modest bargain hunting is a quest of a certain type of difference (that is, to be the person who spots the bargain) and the reading of meaning into this difference.

The Quest for Difference

Images of consumers as explorers, restless and impatient, driven by insatiable curiosity, constantly looking for difference, underscore the ideas of numerous prominent cultural theorists, including Bourdieu, Bauman, Featherstone, McCracken and the early Baudrillard. Reekie argues:

> shopping appears to have undergone re-skilling, from a management task defined by the shopper's ability to select 'bargains' (or quality at low cost), to a creative task defined by the shopper's ability to locate unusual, unstandardized or personalized goods. (Reekie, 1992: 190)

Difference drives the modern consumer, argues Baudrillard, effectively obliterating the concept of *needs* that can be satisfied through material objects, since 'a need is not a need for a particular object as much as it is a "need" for difference (the *desire for social meaning*)' (Baudrillard, 1988b[1970]: 45).

Consumer explorations routinely assume this form of a quest for difference. It is not surprising, then, that even our local mall, our local supermarket and our local high street can be places of exploration, where the consumer pursues difference, just like the primitive huntsman pursues his prey (Ginzburg, 1980). And just like the primitive huntsman, the consumer/explorer is avidly and restlessly looking for tiny clues and disturbances for signs that a new fashion may be about to explode on the scene, that a new pleasure has been discovered or that a new signifier has been born.

The quest for difference has all the compulsive qualities of the 'Spot the Difference' game, something that manufacturers and advertisers have long appreciated. The consumer is presented with countless puzzles to unlock, countless catches to decode, countless knots to untie. Examples of semiotic puzzles include:

- misspelt words or brand-names;
- puns, word games, double entendres or innuendoes, especially in advertisements and corporate logos;
- unpronounceable words, especially in brand names;
- ambiguous newspaper headlines;
- advertisements that do not display the name of a brand or conceal the product in a collage of images.

The current trend among some car manufacturers, following BMW, of *not* marking their products with prestigious model signs is another play on difference. To the 'untrained' eye, two cars may seem identical, yet, to the connoisseur, tiny details of trim reveal enormous differences in price, specification and prestige. Such devices highlight the importance of the minuscule, heighten the consumer's state of alertness, provoke curiosity and reward perseverance.

Freud's concept of the 'narcissism of minor differences' captures well the symbolic and emotional importance of tiny details, especially when they distinguish social groups and individuals that are geographically and socially close to each other (Freud, 1985a[1921], 1985b[1930]). In such situations, group members are held together not by the force of shared ideals and powerful leadership, but rather through the signs that differentiate them from their immediate neighbours. It is to those little badges, emblems and colours that the group's and the individual's self-esteem become, as Freud would put it, condensed. Postmodern theorists would say that they act as metonymies for the group (Culler, 1981). Under the regime of the narcissism of minor differences, signs become essential differences and, therefore, essences. This is how small differences become big differences. Being able to read such differences is vital, since these differences become sources of in-group solidarity and out-group hostility. In this way, supporters of a football team reserve the highest hostility for supporters of the team based in a neighbouring part of the same town (Gabriel, 1999). Local accents, slang, anecdotes, badges, stories, myths and folklore can also provide similarly charged symbolic differences, as can consumer products. In this way, clothes, watches, CDs, shoes, cars, bikes and other visible products offer the symbolic means of self-identification through which individuals align themselves emotionally with those sharing their lifestyles, forming what Maffesoli aptly described as 'neo-tribes' (Maffesoli, 1995). These neo-tribes are transient and volatile, mutating and cross-fertilizing, but they are a reliable source of narcissistic satisfaction for their 'members'.

Being able to identify and decode what to others may be imperceptible differences between products, solving those semiotic puzzles that either defeat or escape others, gives people a sense of uniqueness. In this way, they can become sources of narcissistic pleasure, similar to the pleasures of people who solve the *New York Times* crossword puzzle before breakfast or hack their way into any secure computer for the thrill of unlocking what is seemingly impregnable. This may explain the compulsive puzzle-solving responses generated by unmarked products, cryptic advertisements, unorthodox hairstyles and other mildly unusual signs of difference. The ability to decipher such signs, as well as a selection of the signs themselves, are incorporated in the consumers' idealized images of themselves (what Freud calls 'egos-ideals' (Freud, 1985a[1921]) which fuel their further explorations. Being street-wise means being able to recognize instantly signs like those above.

If Freudian theory may indicate that narcissism is the fuel of the individual's quest for difference and compulsive puzzle-solving, Simmel's trickle-down hypothesis (see Chapter 3, 'The Consumer as Communicator') offers an interesting sociological parallel, linking these phenomena with the impersonal qualities of modern urban life and the decline of traditional fixed status markers. For Simmel (as indeed for Veblen), consumption turns into an arena for status explorations, where subordinate groups constantly seek to imitate the consumption patterns of superordinate groups, which, in turn, strive to differentiate themselves by adopting new fashions and generating new status markers. Imitation and differentiation act as a motor for social change. Discovering *difference*, becoming different and discovering ways of becoming different are all, in Simmel's view, responses to the pervasive *indifference* of urban cultures.

> This leads ultimately to the strangest eccentricities, to specifically metropolitan extravagances of self-distantiation, of caprice, of fastidiousness, the meaning of which is no longer to be found in the content of such activity itself but rather in its being a form of 'being different' – of making oneself noticeable. (Simmel, 1971[1903]: 331)

In this remarkable passage, which anticipates the concept of 'cool' as well as theories of free-floating signifiers, Simmel captures two important themes; first, that consumers set interpretative puzzles for each other so that manufacturers and advertisers may be seen merely as riding rather than causing this tendency; and, second, that difference is not a fact, but a way of looking. When consumers are looking for difference, they are in effect looking for different ways of looking. Whether or not two pairs of trousers are alike or different has less to do with the qualities of the trousers themselves than with the meanings attached to them by different groups. A pair of jeans may stand out from an ocean of grey suits; a pair of bleached jeans may stand out from a sea of jeans; a pair of torn and bleached jeans may stand out from the rest, ... only to the practised eye. In this way, 'decoding the minutiae of distinctions in dress, house, furnishing, leisure lifestyles and equipment' (Featherstone, quoted in Tomlinson, 1990: 21) turns into a compulsion for all of us. It is because we strive for difference that we become compulsive 'readers of signs', experimenting with different interpretations.

The shopping space becomes a jungle of signs and symbols where products and people alike seek to present themselves as, what the marketers would call, 'unique selling propositions'. Shoppers are at once explorers and explored. New shopping design incorporates the shoppers as part of the adventure, as they try different clothes, stare at themselves in mirrors, or simply display their enigmatic hairstyles, clothes or 'looks' (Nixon, 1992).

> Shopping is ... adventure, safari, carnival, and contains unexpected 'risks' in what you may find and who you may meet. It is a kind of self-discovery. And by its very nature it possesses theatricality: one dresses up to go out and one shops to acquire the new persona, to modify the old one or to perfect the setting in which one is seen and known. (Clammer, 1992: 203–4)

Consumption sites such as theme parks, cruise ships, casinos, tourist resorts, hotels, restaurants and, above all, shopping malls, are referred to as 'cathedrals of consumption' by George Ritzer to indicate their quasi-religious, enchanted qualities.

Ritzer (1999) views them as the core institutions of late modernity, which have redefined the nature of society. The great sociologists of modernity, including Weber and Durkheim, emphasized its rationalizing qualities that dissolve traditional elements, such as superstition, myth and folklore. Ritzer argues that where modernity led to a Weberian 'disenchantment of the world', a stripping away of myth, folklore and fantasy, late modernity reintroduces these into social life through 'hyper-consumption', mass festivals of consumption taking place in its spiritual homes, the cathedrals. Ritzer's central thesis is that contemporary management sets its eyes firmly not on the toiling worker, but on the fantasizing consumer. What management does is to furnish, in a highly rationalized manner, an endless stream of consumable fantasies inviting consumers to pick and choose, thus creating the possibility of re-enchanting a disenchanted world through mass festivals in the new cathedrals of consumption.

Ritzer offers prodigious illustrations of the ways in which consumption is constantly promoted, enhanced and controlled in these new settings, not so much through direct advertising, as through indirect means such as spatial arrangements, uses of language, festivals, simulations and extravaganzas, as well as the cross-fertilization ('implosion') of products and images. Above all, consumption gradually colonizes every public and private domain of social life, which become saturated with fantasizing, spending and discarding opportunities. Thus, schools, universities and hospitals are converted from sober, utilitarian institutions into main terrains of consumption, treating their constituents as customers, offering them a profusion of merchandise and indulging their fantasies and caprices. Hyper-consumption is a state of affairs where every social experience is mediated by market mechanisms.

Before Ritzer adopted it as the centre point of his argument, the first edition of this book described the term 'cathedral of consumption' as a hackneyed metaphor. Some have ridiculed the idea that shopping (and web-shopping) can be spiritual experiences akin to visiting a real cathedral. Given the arrant materialism of contemporary consumption, to describe it as a spiritual experience may indeed be stretching the meaning of words to the point of meaninglessness. All the same, we should not forget that places of worship have long been places of trade and that promises of spiritual salvation have often come at a material cost. Remember Christ wielding the whip as he drove the money changers from the temple and overturned their tables (John 2:14 & 15).

One particular cathedral of consumption with pronounced religious and spiritual qualities is the re-invented football stadium. Stadiums like Bernabeu, Neu Camp, San Siro, Old Trafford and Stanford Bridge have become sites where footballers are accorded demi-god status among delirious fans, where watching the intricacies of the game on the field assumes secondary importance to the spiritual union with other fans, especially in the presence of evil, embodied by the supporters of the opposing team (Edge, 1999; Eyre, 1997). Touching the players as they emerge from the tunnel or even appearing in a television shot with a player taking a corner kick becomes tantamount to coming close to god. At the same time, these spaces are very much spaces of consumption where a bewildering array of merchandise is available. Some of this, including a wide variety of clothes, shoes and trinkets, may be linked to the football team but others, such as food and drink, games, toys and so forth promote synergistic brands that are absorbed by association in the fans' spiritual experience.

Ritzer may be overstating the enchanted qualities of contemporary consumption, although if we view cathedrals as spaces of inner exploration as well as outer, as places, in other words, where novel experiences are to be had and new selves fashioned, the parallel between cathedrals of old and the consumption temples of today may not be far-fetched. Where the religious ascetics and visionaries may seek enlightenment in fasting, self-denial and faith, today's consumers may be seen as seeking to explore their own limits, physical, psychological and spiritual, through extreme experiences, induced by travel, drugs and spectacle. As Kyrtatas (2004) has suggested, spirituality today may be discovering new homes in tourist destinations, theme parks and all those earthly paradises that have replaced the great one in heaven.

Not that the theme parks, malls and redesigned department stores are the only spaces of consumer exploration and discovery. Browsing at 'exciting new titles' from academic book catalogues one notices that many of these 'titles' present little semiotic puzzles to be deciphered, such as puns, metaphors, paradoxes, oxymora, caricatures, or, most commonly, spoofs on famous titles. The books' covers are equally exciting and inviting. Collages, distorted photographs, parodies of famous images, decontextualized cuttings all help to create the feeling that not only is the catalogue a space to be explored, but each book is itself a little mystery, having an utterly unique and personal story to tell. It easy to regard these qualities as uniquely 1980s' consumption phenomena. They have in fact been the hallmark of consumerism since its early phase, whether in Parisian department stores (Williams, 1982), the Army and Navy stores throughout the British Empire or the famous Sears catalogue to US homesteaders since the turn of the century. Whether looking at goods directly or through their images in catalogues, contemporary consumers are constantly invited to become explorers of differences.

Goods and their Stories

Just like goods in the catalogue, so too do other consumer objects cry out loudly that they have their own personal stories to tell (see Chapter 3, 'The Consumer as Communicator'). The consumer as expert semiotician can disentangle the voices of the different objects, and quickly reads the clues about their stories in their appearance, their name, their packaging, their relationships and, unnoticed to postmodern thinkers, their prices. If, as Baudrillard argues, commodities are 'sign-values' rather than use-values, price is an important aspect of the story which they tell. For example:

- 'I am pricey, I know it and I invite you to find out for yourself if I am worth it.'
- 'I offer no-nonsense value for money; I may look plain, but if you choose me you will receive loyal and reliable service.'
- 'I am really inexpensive, but what do you lose by trying me?'
- 'I look pricey, but I am not really.'

Of course, price is by no means the only feature of goods which tells a story. The story told by a shampoo or a motor-cycle is fashioned by numerous other features as well: brand name, packaging, advertisers' images for the product, the images of people displaying or using the product, the images of those who eschew it, the images of other products with which it is associated or against which it competes. All these things and many others shape the stories told by a particular commodity. Consumers listen to these stories and make their own decisions about the products. Some goods are quickly discarded as boring, uncool, poor imitations of the 'real thing', sheep in wolves' clothes, phoney, unfashionable. Others, are appreciated as clever challenges, for example, a witty advertisement, an amusing package, a clever spoof on an existing product or an imaginative new *product idea*. Being phoney does not necessarily diminish a product in the eyes of today's consumer, if it can be interpreted as an imaginative, cheeky or defiant simulation rather than as an inferior copy, seeking to conceal its inferiority or the fact that it *is* a copy. Such products may generate a desire to acquire them, not because their stories are untold to the prospective purchaser, but because they can provide semiotic tests to others. Will *they* be able to 'read' them, or will they be fooled by them? We go exploring for such objects, which will serve as puzzles that we enjoy setting for others.

There is another category of objects that appear more reluctant to reveal their story to potential buyers. Such objects are either difficult to decode so long as they are not owned, or stimulate curiosity about, for example, the truthfulness of their claims. The resistance offered by these objects increases their aura and stimulates desire. They seem to cry out for further exploration, an exploration that cannot proceed unless the consumer can get them, either by paying for them, borrowing them or by 'liberating' them from their ownerless state (see discussion of shoplifting in Chapter 8 'The Consumer as Rebel'). A new arrival on a supermarket shelf or a sealed cartridge with a computer game act in this manner.

Such objects cannot be fully consumed, that is, tell their full story, unless the consumer can make them his or her own and appropriate them. Objects that require no payment seem hardly worth exploring; their value in the eyes of the consumer is reduced, the quality of the exploration is diminished in his or her own eyes. How unalluring are the various free newspapers that are dispensed through our letter-boxes; how unexciting the various experiences on offer 'for free'; how insipid the water that comes out of our taps when compared to the sparkling glamour that pours out of a delicately tinted bottle that we have paid for! Notice that 'something for free' is not at all the same as 'something for nothing' which, as we saw, is the trademark of the true bargain. If the bargain represents a little symbolic triumph at the expense of the system, free handouts carry many of the dreary marks of philanthropy, the dispensation of second-hand or second-rate goods with a symbolic or moral catch. Payment, then, is far from incidental to consumer explorations. Paying for a product signals the start of a new phase of exploration, the exploration of the owned object. Think of the excitement of bringing a new acquisition back from the shop or of receiving an order in the morning's mail. What will the new armchair look like in your sitting room? How will the new CD player perform with your amplifier? What will the new blouse look like with your green skirt?

The Careers of Objects

Once an object has been paid for, rented or stolen, safely tucked away inside a bag, it begins a new life as an object of consumer exploration; this life can assume several different twists. Many authors have commented on the tendency of objects to disappoint once they have been paid for and numerous explanations of this phenomenon have been offered (Baudrillard, 1988a[1968]; Bocock, 1993; Campbell, 1989; Galbraith, 1967; McCracken, 1988). In these instances, the consumer finds that the object has no story to tell, no secret to reveal. Like Kavafis's poem 'Ithaca' it has no special magic of its own. Its promise is the journey, not the final destination. Such objects lose their charm instantly and sink into an anonymous existence, forgotten at the bottom of a drawer or quickly discarded in a dustbin. Occasionally, they may be rediscovered, as gifts to someone who unaccountably values them, as items of kitsch value, as antiques or even as souvenirs of one's consumer follies. Many end up in charity shops and jumble sales, where they can be discovered as bargains and start new careers.

Consumers may or may not feel cheated at such inglorious turns of events (see Chapter 7, 'The Consumer as Victim'). What is interesting is the extent to which they are prepared to weather disappointments; after all, exploration is full of dead-ends, and if they paid good money for what turned out to be quite ordinary or a dud, so be it; perhaps the price was worth paying for the satisfaction of knowing that the product was quite ordinary. Sometimes disappointment is swift. There are instances, however, where the consumer stubbornly refuses to relinquish faith in a product, against considerable evidence to the contrary as illustrated by the following experience.

> I remember purchasing what had seemed like a marvellous Italian motor-car, much to the amusement of my friends and relatives who teased me endlessly about the car's poor reputation for reliability and its general 'tackiness'. No matter. Since my childhood this make of car, famous for its sweetly purring engine, had held an overwhelming fascination for me. It did not take long for me to realize that every allegation against the car was true, as hardly a week went by without the car needing garage attention. The story told by the car was very different from the one I was longing to hear. Yet, the car's aura refused to wane. Each time I took it to be repaired, I thought it would be the last visit, the one that would finally get the car back into full health. This was no love–hate relationship; it was straightforward love. I was prepared to forgive the car its every misbehaviour, as one forgives a pampered child. It took me fully 18 months before I was willing to recognize that the car was simply a fiasco. I employed every conceivable rationalization to defend the car, until I finally gave up and sold it. Yet, I felt no anger or disappointment for having bought it; I paid good money for what turned out to be a bad car. But I felt that I had owed it to myself to buy this car, and the money was spent to very good effect. It was like staking some money on a bet and losing. As a consumer-explorer, I was philosophical about losing money on bad bets.

In addition to objects that sooner or later disappoint, there are objects that stubbornly refuse to yield their full stories. How often is it that we discover that having purchased something, we may not obtain full advantage of it unless certain accessories are purchased, which in turn emerge as nothing but preambles for further purchases. We may suspect that such objects are mere entrapments, that they try to lure us into explorational impasses, yet, as in the case of the Italian car, the temptation to throw good money after bad is powerful. Explorers find it very difficult to turn full circle and return to base.

There is yet another class of products, those with which we develop a relationship of sorts. Some of them are quickly absorbed in our self-perceptions; they pose no further puzzles but offer the prospect of quiet contentment. A new track suit in which we feel comfortable, a trusted brand of virtually anything, a no-nonsense watch – such items do not challenge us, although in their quiet way they may be important parts of our identity. Then, there are objects which cannot be incorporated so easily: a 'loud' jacket, a flash car, an eye-catching hat, a suggestive T-shirt. They maybe need to be used at first in private before we feel confident to present them as part of our public persona. These things may make us self-conscious, they cannot be readily accommodated in our identity, which needs to stretch or adjust itself in order to absorb them. It is then that exploration of the world of objects initiates an exploration of identity, the quest for outer difference becomes a quest for inner meaning. This will be the main focus of the next chapter, which examines the consumer as identity-seeker.

Strengths and Weaknesses of the Image of the Consumer as Explorer

Few images capture the driven qualities of modern consumption, its excitements and disappointments, as vividly as that of the explorer. And yet, few figures can so easily be ridiculed and disparaged as the explorer who never left his or her back yard, the explorer who dreamed it all up. The worlds explored by modern consumers are certainly not natural worlds; the discoveries they make along the way are carefully orchestrated by producers, designers and retailers to greet them at the appropriate time in the appropriate place. Many surprises are premeditated, many wonders staged. Here lies one of the paradoxes of modern consumption – the experience of exploration can be genuine, even if the object is simulated and the subject knows that it is simulated, a theme that has fascinated Baudrillard (Baudrillard, 1983, 1988c). Why go looking for real alligators, unpredictable as they are, when you can catch a grand view of them in the theme park, where they are guaranteed to make an appearance? And why indeed go to the theme park, when you can put your face right inside the mouth of one through the lens of a camera or virtual reality?

Consumer 'explorations' easily end up in quotation marks, as simulated pseudo-explorations in the virtual pseudo-realities generated by the magicians of postmodern spectacle societies. Yet, even if theme parks, shopping malls, museums, galleries, tourist attractions and other sites are pre-arranged and man-made, does this disqualify them from being sites of exploration? Does the fact that others, sometimes thousands or even millions, have been there before, invalidate their experience of exploration, excitement and discovery? Hardly. It is perfectly possible to explore man-made artefacts, whether they be the pyramids of Egypt, a Gothic cathedral or a Doris Lessing novel. If it is possible to explore a novel, a symphony or a building, why not a CD, a suit or a shopping mall? Nor does the circumstance that many have been there before, diminish the experience of one who, for the first time, 'discovers' Mahler. With innocent eyes and ears, he or she may even discover a line of interpretation, a symbolic twist, a coded melodic reference that has not been noticed before. A young student discovered an extended quotation from Pergolesi in Mozart's Requiem, which had escaped the notice of experts, who had spent lifetimes studying the piece. Besides, leftovers by previous explorers can be fascinating in their own right; one may, for example, remember one's first forays into an area of literature through second-hand paper-backs, which have been read and underlined in different colours by several previous owners, each leaving their own comments on the margins. This can enhance one's experience of exploring.

In sum then, neither the artificial quality of the terrains of exploration, nor the presence of numerous fellow-explorers detract from the aptness of a metaphor of exploration, which captures admirably the restless, exciting, insatiable qualities of modern consumption, its endless fascination with tiny differences, and its obsession with puzzle-solving, interpretations, clues and signs. The metaphor highlights curiosity as a driving force of Western consumers, the desire to know the unknown and the yearning for innovation and change. In this sense, it accounts for the consumers' unique vulnerability to lucky draws, mystery presents, promises of exotic trips and other marketing gimmicks, which rely on our state of excited curiosity and our longing for the unknown as a leverage for sales. Curiosity, once aroused, makes us highly vulnerable to the merchandisers' tease 'Discover x', where x can range from Turkey to a new brand of lavatory cleaner, a new food product or a new sanitary towel.

What the perspective of the consumer-explorer fails to do is to illuminate what makes things or spaces worth exploring in the first place and at what point they lose their charm and are discarded in favour of new ones. Equally, it obscures the wide range of instances when consumers appear to strive after the familiar and the safe. Brand loyalty would seem incongruous from a perspective that stresses change, innovation and adventure. Surely one of the defining paradoxes of modern consumption is the consumer's need to mix the familiar with the unfamiliar, the simultaneous travel to exotic places with patronage of McDonald's and Holiday Inns (logo: 'No surprises'), the simultaneous capitulation to the comfort of habit and the pursuit of adventure. This is an instance of fragmentation in contemporary consumption that frequently goes unnoticed.

In general, the explorer metaphor presents a somewhat individualistic concept of consumption, underplaying its social character except for the interpretative puzzles that consumers set for each other, known as fashion. Even then, the metaphor is more successful at illuminating why individuals seek to decode and solve these puzzles than why they are inclined to set them for others. In these different ways, this metaphor draws attention to consumption in the first place as a range of relationships between people and things and only to a much lesser extent as relationships among people, consumers and producers or among consumers themselves (as highlighted in Chapter 3, 'The Consumer as Communicator').

All in all, it is a metaphor that creates rather too heroic an image of consumers. It is also too cheerful and, perhaps, frivolous an image. What if the driven qualities of modern consumption, instead of being a quest for novelty and adventure amount to little more than an attempt to escape reality, to find solace in fantasy and self-delusion? In any event, the sorrows, deprivations and frustrations of modern consumption are far from the sights of images of the consumer as explorer. The drudgery of routine shopping, the furtive sorties to shops between family and work commitments, the sacrifices necessitated by demanding children and social expectations, above all, the anxiety about making ends meet or stretching the family budget, these things have no place in the realms of consumers as explorers.

No other image of the consumer studied in this book is quite as firmly middle-class as that of the consumer-explorer. It is remarkable that in a period that spawned several important studies of poverty and deprivation (see, for example, Brandt, 1980; Mack and Lansley, 1992; Seabrook, 1985; Townsend, 1979, 1993) many commentaries on consumption simply chose to turn a blind eye on the hardships experienced by increasing numbers of consumers, both in developed countries and the Third World. Disregarding the difficulties involved in precise definitions and measurements of poverty in different parts of the world, one suspects that large numbers of people on the breadline would regard the idea of consumers as explorers as a cruel joke. One suspects that consumer-explorers, in their youthful enthusiasm and exuberance, their constant desire to experiment and try, their naive fascination with puzzles, signs and symbols and their obsession with difference, were a wish-fulfilling fantasy of glossy marketers and excitable semioticians in the 1980s. It is a fantasy on which, from time-to-time, some consumers became fellow-travellers.

CHAPTER 5

The Consumer as Identity-Seeker

That which is for me through the medium of *money* – that for which I can pay (that is, which money can buy) – that am *I*, the possessor of money. The extent of the power of money is the extent of my power. Money's properties are my properties and essential powers – the properties and powers of its possessor. Thus, what I *am* and *am capable* of is by no means determined by my individuality. I am ugly, but I can buy or myself the most *beautiful* of women. Therefore I am not *ugly*, for the effect of *ugliness* – its deterrent power – is nullified by money. I, in my character as an individual, am *lame*, but money furnishes me with twenty-four feet. Therefore I am not lame. I am bad, dishonest, unscrupulous, stupid; but money is honoured, and therefore so is its possessor.

Marx, 1972[1844]: 81

CORE ARGUMENTS

Identity has assumed centre-stage in discussions of contemporary politics, culture and consumption. Most commentators agree that psychological identity represents a difficult and precarious project for most people today, as established social categories of class, gender, occupation and so forth become eroded. Choice (of occupation, of partner, of sexual preference, of goods to consume and so forth) has opened up new possibilities of identity construction but also created new burdens. The material culture both supports and undermines efforts to create and maintain identities. On the one hand, many branded and unbranded goods become, at least, temporarily parts of an extended self, at least temporarily boosting identity, self-image and self-esteem. In this sense, consumer culture is tailor-made for the narcissistic strivings of contemporary society. Several authors, however, have commented on the addictive quality of consumption – while temporarily assuaging narcissism and bolstering identities, consumer culture creates long-term dissatisfaction, dependency and meaninglessness.

Debates on Western consumption rarely stay clear of the theme of identity for long. Identity is Rome to which all discussions of modern Western consumption lead, whether undertaken by Marxist critics or advertising executives, deconstructionists or liberal reformers, advocates of multi-culturalism or radical feminists. The consensus of otherwise irreconcilable perspectives appears to be that, in late capitalism, consumption is the area where personal and group identities are fought over, contested, precariously put together and licked into shape. As previous chapters have indicated, the Western consumer readily transfigures into an identity-seeker. Whether choosing goods, exploring them, buying them, displaying them, disfiguring them or giving them away, consumers are, above all, frequently presented as thirsting for identity and using commodities to quench this thirst. This chapter examines this popular image of the consumer as identity-seeker, highlighting some crucial ambiguities in the concept of identity.

Identity, like stress, is a concept whose currency and expedience belies its relatively recent pedigree in psychology. It is a concept that we all feel that we grasp intuitively and is given great explanatory weight in discussions of consumption. For these reasons, it is important to investigate how this idea achieved its privileged place in contemporary cultural discussions and then ask what it adds. We start by examining some of the ambiguities acquired by the concept of identity, as it migrated from objects onto people and as the quest of identity came to be regarded as the cause of most major social and individual problems. How did identity turn from a fact into a problem and what is its relevance to consumption? We will also indicate some of the ways in which the obsession with identity, brands and consumption among cultural theorists has hogged the limelight and obscured some other promising lines of study into the relationship between the individual, their sense of self and what they consume.

Fixed Identities: From People to Goods

Initially, the word 'identity', drawing on its Latin derivation, stood for the sameness, continuity and distinctiveness of things. It applied equally to humans, animals and material objects. Establishing the identity of a person, a flower or a mineral amounted to giving it a name and specifying its uniqueness and distinctiveness in terms of similarities with, and differences from, its relatives. Even in this early conception, identity is not merely a property of the object being identified; it is equally an expression of the interest of those who identify it. The identity of minerals or plants generally coincides with the name of their species – the particular specimen at hand generally requires no further identification to establish it as something singular and unique. This, however, is not the case with a famous diamond that has been given a name, such as the Koh-i-Noor; its identification, notably if stolen and recovered, is not complete unless confirmed to be the very specimen that is missing. Simply establishing the identity of a recovered gem as a diamond is not enough. It is immediately apparent that forensic investigations crucially depend on the identity of objects as absolutely unique items. And it is also apparent why identity cards have become an important issue in these days of vigilantly patrolled frontiers and stolen identities.

The identity of animals in many cases is adequately fixed by the species name alone, or species plus gender. Gardeners are quite happy to know the species of caterpillar that is ruining their crops without concerning themselves about the particular individuals that are most to blame. Knowing the species is enough to dictate the measures that may be taken against it. Likewise, bird spotters are generally content to establish the species and gender of a rare specimen that they catch sight of. Ornithologists, on the other hand, may be interested in knowing the habits and history of a particular specimen or pair; to do so, they may then seek to identify them through the use of coloured rings or other unique marks. Such marks would establish not just species identity, but individual identity and where they have been. In a similar way, family pets, race-horses or animal celebrities carry identities beyond their species and gender, names that establish them as unique individuals. As we shall see presently, the question of whether identity refers to species or specimen is not unconnected with the strivings of Western consumers.

People, too, are generally identified by names; but different people may have the same name, hence it is often necessary to specify the identities of the father and mother, the date of birth or some other feature to establish the identity of an individual. Identity, in this sense, is fixed. No matter what transformations are undergone by the individual, his or her identity cannot change. Nor is identity a matter of choice, will or desire; identity is the outcome of family lineage. Confusion over identity amounts to confusion over parenthood, confusion about facts not about meanings. This theme lies at the heart of drama, both in its tragic and comic senses. Establishing the identity of an individual, whether a person is accused of a crime, or is claiming to be somebody or to own something, is not always easy (especially before the discovery of DNA identification), but essentially it is a technical, forensic question. Odysseus, returning home after 20 years, had to prove his identity and establish that he was who he claimed he was. This he proceeded to do with the aid of signs – a scar on the knee as well as knowledge of several intimate secrets that no-one else could know (Homer, 1988).

Why is this important? As Ginzburg (1980) reminds us, the problem of identity was in the first place a *political* one, not an existential one, as consumer theorists have narrowed it down to. Claims to power and property depended crucially on establishing the identities of individuals making the claims. Equally importantly, the maintenance of criminal records and the administration of legal justice and discipline hinges on establishing the identity of people as unique individuals. This can be an immensely difficult problem if individuals are unwilling to co-operate. In a memorable scene from Kubrik's film *Spartacus*, the Romans ask the captured rebels which one of them is Spartacus; to protect their leader, each and every one of the rebels claims to be Spartacus, to great dramatic effect.

The branding of offenders was meant to establish their identity permanently, marking their criminal record, so to speak, on their bodies. Branding was not an option available to colonial administrators, though of course it was rediscovered by the Nazis in the 20th-century. A different type of branding has now assumed great importance as a way of marking a product on consumer consciousness. The problem of identity was especially pressing for the administrators of the British Empire, having to administer what they saw as justice, to 'natives' who seemed deceitful, disputatious and, to their Western eyes, all looked the same. Fingerprinting, introduced by Sir William Herschel in Bengal in the 1870s, seemed to provide a technical solution to the political problem of identity, a far more discreet but also more efficient solution than branding had been to the slave-owners. Each person carried permanently on their fingertips indelible evidence of their identity; no subjective claim or denial could thenceforth discredit the objective evidence of ink on paper. The fingerprint was proof of the person's identity. Thus a person's identity is, in the first place, part of a system of political practices that seek to classify, distinguish and differentiate each individual from others.

The political dimension of practices such as identity cards, fingerprinting, random identity checks or unobtrusive surveillance in shopping malls and elsewhere has led to endless controversy surrounding their introduction. We shall refer to this conceptualization of identity as 'forensic identity' to underline political nature, and to distinguish it in this chapter from the 'psychological' and 'group' identities. This discussion leads to two conclusions. First, we note that branding has shifted from being a mark to discriminate between people to being a device for according identity and individuality to products. Second, we note that forensic identity, unlike psychological identity, was a problem not for the individuals concerned, but for those who sought to control them. The importance of these ideas for the study of consumption will become apparent presently.

Identity as a Psychological and Sociological Concept

The migration of identity into psychology and sociology has maintained some of the qualities of forensic identity, reversed others, as well as introducing several new features of crucial relevance to consumption. It is interesting that psychoanalysis, which virtually invented the idea of psychological *identification*, did not seriously turn to identity until Erikson coined the expression 'identity crisis' (Erikson, 1959). He used this term to describe the condition of soldiers severely traumatized by the battlefield during the Second World War. These soldiers appeared to have lost their sense of sameness and continuity with their former selves. This suggested to Erikson the idea that psychological identity is not something given or fixed, but something that one achieves with the aid of others. Subsequently, Erikson developed his theory that identity crisis is a normal stage of ego development in late adolescence and early adulthood that may lead to different outcomes. Some individuals uncritically adopt identities derived from their parents, others endlessly experiment with different identities (a process Erikson refers to as 'moratorium'), at times failing to emerge with any coherent identity (a process he refers to as 'diffused identity'). The happiest conclusion of this process is the achievement of an identity in which the individual is both conscious of his or her uniqueness and which provides him or her with an anchoring into the here and now (Erikson, 1968). In these ways, self-esteem and self-image, as Erikson has acknowledged, are conceptually very close to ego identity.

Erikson's ideas of identity crisis and identity confusion and diffusion gained substantial popularity in the 1950s, when the search for identity came to preoccupy psychologists, especially American ones, very considerably. This led to a very different concept of identity from the fixed, stable and immutable forensic identity. The new concept was to serve psychologists intent on delivering the consumer as a manageable package to merchandisers very well. This identity is subjective; it is an individual's answer to questions such as 'Who am I?' and 'In what ways am I different from others?'. This is a changing, precarious and problematic entity, the product of an individual's perpetual adaptation to his or her environment. Uniqueness is not given, but is achieved; continuity can be undermined or ruptured. Psychological identity is the product of psychological work; it must be nurtured and defended, worked for and fought over. The importance of material objects to these processes was to prove seminal.

The sociological itineraries of identity took off from where psychological discussions left. Psychologists themselves had prepared the ground in their 'mass psychology', where it was argued that in crowds people lose their individual identities and become one with the mass, part of a collective mind, entirely derivative from it (Freud, 1985a[1921]; Fromm, 1966[1941]; Le Bon, 1985[1960]; Reich, 1970). The implicit assumption that identity is a free-flowing entity that pours from the collective to the individual characterizes much of the traditional sociological literature on the subject; by contrast, the pursuit of forensic identity has been to distinguish the individual from the masses. Thus, members of ethnic groups, sexual preference groups, political movements, occupational and professional groups are often seen as drawing their sense of identity from their group, sharing its ideals and aspirations. A group's identity, like personal identity, is problematic; it must be fought over and forged out of shared experiences and traditions; it must discard attributions imposed upon the group by others; it must discover and celebrate its own continuity with its past; it must choose who its friends and enemies are, where its boundaries lie, what its symbols are, and so on (Anthias, 1982; Hall, 1996; Hall and Du Gay, 1996; Omi and Winant, 1987). However, as groups shape their identities, their members' individual identity problems recede; individual identity derives from identification with the group. So long as the group is unique, uniqueness need no longer be part of the individual identity.

Modernity and Identity

Most cultural commentators agree that psychological and social identity is a uniquely modern problem. In a pre-modern society, psychological and group identities coincide with forensic identities, since they

> are easily recognizable, objectively and subjectively. Everybody knows who everybody else is and who he is himself. A knight *is* a knight and a peasant *is* a peasant. There is, therefore, no *problem* of identity. The question, 'Who am I?' is unlikely to arise in consciousness, since the socially predefined answer is massively real subjectively and consistently confirmed in all significant social interaction. (Berger and Luckman, 1967: 184)

Urban living, anonymous organizations, impersonal work, mass production, social and physical movement, the proliferation of choice; in short, modernity itself conspires against fixed identities. In late modernity, the media of mass communication assume extraordinary significance in shaping our perceptions of the world we inhabit, saturating our physical and mental spaces with images, yet producing a massive vacuum to the individual's question 'Who am I?'. With the possible exception of brief glimpses we may catch of ourselves on TV monitors in shopping malls or very rarely on a real television programme, our personal identities are emphatically denied by the world of simulations, where, as Baudrillard insists, only what appears on TV is regarded as real. One of us had maintained a totally impersonal relationship with his newsagent, until one morning the newsagent greeted him excitedly like a long lost-friend by saying: 'Dr Lang, Dr Lang, I saw you on TV last night!'. Appearing on TV had certainly made the author a real person in the eyes of the newsagent, whereas countless personal encounters had failed to elevate him above the status of 'another customer'.

Faced with a modern world that falls far short of providing the massive confirmation noted by Berger and Luckmann, identity becomes a major and continuous preoccupation of each individual. Unlike Erikson, who saw identity crisis as a temporary phase, eventually resolved and left behind, current cultural theory approaches identity as an interminable project, involving not only crucial life-choices and decisions but, equally, their translation into a narrative, a life-story. One of the clearest statements on identity has been offered by Giddens:

> In the post-traditional order of modernity, against the backdrop of new forms of mediated experience, self-identity becomes a reflexively organised endeavour. The reflexive project of the self, which consists in the sustaining of coherent, yet continuously revised, biographical narratives, takes place in the context of multiple choice as filtered through abstract systems. In modern social life, the notion of lifestyle takes on a particular significance. The more tradition loses its hold, and the more daily life is reconstituted in terms of the dialectical play of the local and the global, the more individuals are forced to negotiate lifestyle choices among a diversity of options. (Giddens, 1991: 5)

Identity, in this formulation, does not lie in any fixed attributes of personality or self, still less in certain fixed forms of behaviour. Nor can past achievements and glories form the basis of identity. As Schwartz reminds us, a '"has been" [is] somebody who once was somebody, but is no longer anybody' (Schwartz, 1990: 32). Instead, as Giddens states, identity lies now 'in the capacity *to keep a particular narrative going*' (Giddens, 1991: 54). Identity, then, can be seen as a story that a person writes and rewrites about him or herself, never reaching the end until they die, and always rewriting the earlier parts, so that the activity of writing becomes itself part of the story. In this sense, it is both reflexive and incomplete. Identity and identity-seeking are, at least in Western culture, essentially the same thing. In creating a story in which the author is a protagonist, the author creates himself or herself anew – author and protagonist co-create each other in an unending reflexive process.

Many authors believe that in our times, a variety of circumstances conspire to make the 'storying' of our lives particularly difficult. Thus Boje:

> Some *experiences* lack that linear sequence and are difficult to tell as a 'coherent' story. Telling stories that lack coherence is contrary to modernity. Yet, in the postmodern condition, stories are harder to tell because experience itself is so fragmented and full of *chaos* that fixing meaning or imagining coherence is fictive. (Boje, 2001: 7)

The theme that storying has become especially hard in our times is highly developed in Richard Sennett's work. He argues that new capitalism with its emphasis on flexibility, opportunism and the powerful illusions of choice and freedom fragment the continuity of today's life narratives, denying them the continuity and coherence enjoyed by the narratives of yesteryear (Sennett, 1998: 31). As Slater has noted, 'underlying such perspective is an ineradicable nostalgia or lamentation: consumer culture can never replace the world we have lost, or provide us with selves we can trust, or offer a culture in which we can be truly home' (Slater, 1997: 99).

Consumption and Identity

What then do individuals write in the precious life-stories that constitute their identities? How do they construct their selfhoods? What are the identity structures that distinguish late modernity from earlier periods? Various answers have been provided to these questions, although increasing emphasis is placed on consumption at the expense of personal and family histories, membership of occupational and professional groups, work and personal achievement, character and temperament, as the terrain in which identities are sought. Bauman (Bauman, 1988, 1992, 2001), has been one of the strongest champions of the view that the 'work ethic' has, at least in Western societies, been dislodged by a 'consumer ethic'. He argues:

> If in a life normatively motivated by the work ethic, material gains were deemed secondary and instrumental in relation to work itself (their importance consisting primarily of confirming the adequacy of the work effort), it is the other way round in a life guided by the 'consumer ethic'. Here, work is (at best) instrumental; it is in the material emoluments that one seeks, and finds, fulfilment, autonomy and freedom. (Bauman, 1988: 75)

Consumption, not only expands to fill the identity vacuum left by the decline of the work ethic, but it assumes the same structural significance that work enjoyed at the high noon of modernity.

> The same central role which was played by work, by job, occupation, profession, in modern society, is now performed in contemporary society, by consumer choice. ... The former was the lynch-pin which connected life-experience – the self-identity problem, life-work, life-business – on the one level; social integration on the second level; and systemic reproduction on the third level. ... Consumerism stands for production, distribution, desiring, obtaining and using, of symbolic goods. (Bauman, 1992: 223)

How do consumer choices fashion identity? At its simplest, the argument would suggest that individuals can buy identities off the peg, just as corporations can buy themselves new images, new brands and new identities by adopting new symbols, signs and other similar paraphernalia. Numerous commentators on consumption appear to regard this as self-evident, requiring little explanation or elaboration.

> Shopping is not merely the acquisition of things: it is the buying of identity. (Clammer, 1992: 195)

> The identity of the consumer is tied with the identity not only of the brand, but of the company that produces it. (Davidson, 1992: 178)

At their most mechanistic, such arguments suggest that images and qualities of products are simply transferred onto the consumer, either singly or in combinations. Identity is essentially a self-image resulting from the endless displacements and condensations of product images. 'Ours is a world in which it is our products that tell our stories for us', argues Davidson (Davidson, 1992: 15). The consumers' main preoccupation then is being able to afford those goods that they require to sustain their identities. This approach, however, disregards the reflexive qualities underlined earlier and only transposes the question 'Who am I?'. On what basis do individual consumers make their choices? Why are some objects liked and others disliked? Why do some objects easily blend with individual identity and others not? Why are some images convincing while others rejected as phoney? And if the qualities of objects are mechanically transferred onto their owners, such as branding for slaves, why does the project of identity remain uncompleted? What drives the consumers' desires for new products and new identities?

These questions can be foreclosed if we were to accept Baudrillard's argument that the *only* product image that today's consumers want is one that is perfectly unique, different from all others. Only this will make each consumer unique, forever standing out from the crowd. This is impossible, of course, though not merely because today's products are mass-produced and lack the required uniqueness. In a hyper-real world of self-devouring signifiers (see discussion of Clio and Nike in Chapter 3, 'The Consumer as Communicator'), where each new arrival on the scene consigns its predecessors to the undifferentiated state of also-rans, standing out from the crowd is an entirely futile project. Free-floating signifiers wreak havoc with our individual identities, which are ransacked by wave after wave of semiotic invaders. In this case, as Miller puts it, 'our identity has become synonymous with patterns of consumption which are determined elsewhere. Taken to its logical conclusion (and the advantage of Baudrillard is that he does just this), this view entails a denial of all signification' (Miller, 1987: 165). The project of identity, once it has been hijacked by hyper-real consumerism, is doomed. Uniqueness, continuity and value will forever elude it.

Many of the writers exploring the connection between consumption and identity in the 1980s and 1990s do not share Baudrillard's rather bleak view. Nor, however, do they take the view that identities can be constructed unproblematically by purchasing a particular set of images. Between the life-story that constitutes identity and the images of the consumer world, most of these authors seek to interpose human agency, a kind of creative *bricolage* whereby identities are fashioned through an active engagement with product images. This relationship between identity and the world of material objects will be the main focus of the rest of this chapter.

Objects and Extended Selves

The view that material objects are a vital feature of our identities, forensic, psychological and cultural, is neither novel nor particularly original. Owning a unique object, a sword or a crown, might have been as solid a proof of forensic identity as any branding or distinguishing mark. Furthermore, the qualities of material objects and their past history confers prestige and status onto their holders. Furthermore, there are categories of objects, such as family heirlooms or valued gifts, which may be so dear to us that we end up seeing them as parts of an extended self (Belk, 1988; Csikszentminhalyi and Rochberg-Halton, 1981; Dittmar, 1991; Lee, 1993a). Winnicott (1962, 1964) noted that in early childhood certain objects, like teddy bears or pieces of soft rag, acquire a great significance for children. These objects, which he calls 'transitional objects', are half-way between the infant's inner and outer realities, providing *bridges* between the internal and external worlds. Transitional objects are instrumental in the child's development and may be replaced later by other objects which have the same bridging function. From a very young age, we learn to look at such objects as extensions of ourselves. In the words of George, a 7-year-old boy to his dad:

> My owl collection is very valuable to me; it is part of me. It's like my hair. If you lose your hair you are sad, if I lost my owls I'd be sad.

In this way, some material objects can become central characters of our personal histories, without which our histories would be unthinkable. The quest for a particular object, whether it be the Holy Grail or another owl in George's collection, may be an important part of a person's life-story, and the finding of the object may confer fame and generate pride. In this way, the search for particular objects, the adventures encountered along the way, the glory and fame achieved by its discovery, these can all become part of an individual's identity.

As we saw in the Chapter 3 ('The Consumer as Communicator'), Levy-Bruhl (1966) noted that in pre-literate cultures, ornaments, clothes and tools, are seen as parts of the self. Over a century ago, William James (1961[1892]: 44) that a man's 'me' is made up of everything that he can call his, including his body and his mind, his clothes, his house, his wife, his children, his parents, his land, his yacht and his bank account. In all these instances, material objects become ensconced in our identity because of the closeness of our relationships with them, our physical and emotional *attachment* to them.

In contrast, however, to all these instances, Western consumption is unique in that identity becomes vitally and self-consciously enmeshed in stories that are read by consumers into innumerable, relatively mundane, mass-produced objects that they buy, use or own. These unexceptional objects are not so much carriers of meaning, as carriers of vivid and powerful *images*, enabling us to choose them consciously from among many similar ones, promising to act as the raw material out of which our individual identities may be fashioned. Unlike children who form attachments to their cuddly toys, Western consumers do not establish profound relationships with the majority of the goods they consume. Instead, they use them in opportunistic but highly visible ways, being very conscious of the inferences that others will draw from them and by the ways their image will be affected by them.

Children spontaneously like certain things and dislike others; they do not construct identities around them (Baumeister, 1986: 192). Yet by the time they reach school age, likes and dislikes lose their innocence. Liking unfashionable toys, making friends with unpopular children, wearing old-fashioned shoes, these things become tied to image and identity. By early adolescence, virtually every choice becomes tainted by image-consciousness. Smoking, drinking, eating, clothes, accents, hairstyles, friendships, music, sport and virtually every like and dislike become highly self-conscious matters. Whether this phenomenon exists in most cultures or not, it is beyond doubt exacerbated by the targeting of children as consumers (Barnet and Cavanagh, 1994: 137ff.).

For young people today, consumption appears as the key to entering adulthood. Abercrombie argues that 'young people will experiment with different identities, by ignoring the way in which class, gender and race construct the boundaries of identity' (Abercrombie, 1994: 51). Commodities, under consumer capitalism, rich in image, become young people's main accomplices in these attempts to reach adulthood (Lansley, 1994: 96–7). As Willis argues, adulthood 'is now achieved, it seems, by spending money in a certain way rather than "settling down" to a life of wedded bliss' (Willis, 1990: 137). Consumption becomes the core element in the rite of passage to adulthood. It is not enough for young people to be seen spending their own money on cigarettes, clothes, stereo and computer gear, and so on, although this in itself is not unimportant. What is more important is constructing out of these ingredients an individual style, a convincing image. Identity, then, does not mean the creation and projection of any image, but of one that commands respect and self-respect.

Shopping malls become the arenas for such explorations where young people try out different images and experiment with precarious selfhoods. Today's teenage identity-seekers are not a marginal social group; nor do they go through a temporary phase that will be overcome with triumphant entry into adulthood, as Erikson or anthropologists debating rites of passages might have envisaged. Instead, teenagers become pioneers of a new lifestyle revolving around TV and the mall, which emerges as the Gothic cathedral of today.

> Malling confirms consumption-based activities, lifestyles and identities; teenaged mall-rats and bunnies may be the prototypical group of amusement society. This is all the more the case as television, having hurried if not destroyed childhood, has created the grown-up child and immature adult as the whole of a life course is sandwiched between infancy and senility. (Langman, 1992: 58)

As Featherstone has argued, 'youth styles and lifestyles are migrating up the age scale and ... as the 1960s generation ages, they are taking some of the youth-orientated dispositions with them, and ... adults are being granted greater licence for childlike behaviour and vice versa' (1991: 100–1). This is especially noticeable when adults go on holiday or even on business trips, when, relieved of the hardened personas they assume at work and at home, they experiment with different styles, images and identities. They wear strange clothes, develop unusual mannerisms, let their hair down and feel free to explore pleasures that they would otherwise deny themselves. The transformation of airport and hotel lobbies into Meccas of consumption can be seen as testimony of the travelling consumers' thirst for experimentation with identity as well as of the loosening of their inhibitions towards spending. (See Chapter 4, 'The Consumer as Explorer'.)

Experimenting with identities and images of self can at times be seen to stretch into explorations of inner worlds, spiritual Ithacas and Idahos of the mind. Vast areas of the economy, including some of the so-called leisure industries, the hobby industry, the body industry, the personal growth industry, appear to be fuelled by the individuals' thirst for self-exploration (Lasch, 1984, 1991). Many of these explorations become quests for reaching one's own limits, whether in sport, art or learning. Occasionally buying or being given a new object, such as a trumpet, a tennis racket or a set of water-colours, may signal the opening of a new phase of selfhood. Yet, in truth, such inner explorations seldom go beyond ephemeral daydreams or the volatile fantasies. Compared to the explorations of the colourful world of objects and their images out there which many consumers pursue with skill and virtuosity, inner explorations seem murky, dull and not terribly productive.

Postmodern Identities, Images and Self-esteem

Images of the consumer as identity-seeker are compelling and feature centrally in postmodern theory. They account for the obsession with brands, the willingness to read stories into impersonal products, the fascination with difference, the preoccupation with signs, and above all the fetishism of images. They also account for the fragmented and precarious nature of selfhood, which has been a favourite theme of those writers who postulate a radical discontinuity between modernity and postmodernity, the phase of human history we are currently meant to be entering. One leading feature of this discontinuity concerns the final demise of the idea of a sovereign self, the managerial self that reflects, compares, decides, creates and takes responsibility. Following Freud, Mauss and Foucault, many postmodernists argue that this image of the sovereign self is an illusion reflecting the grand narratives of modernity – such as work, gender, happiness, healthy life, moral choice, and achievement – but fatally undermined by postmodernity. According to Firat, consumers of modernity fashioned their identities by purchasing products, whose stories and images echoed those grand narratives. By contrast:

> the consumers of postmodernity seem to be transcending these narratives, no longer seeking centered, unified characters, but increasingly seeking to 'feel good' in separate, different moments by acquiring self images that make them marketable, likeable and/or desirable in each moment. ... Thus occurs the fragmentation of the self. In postmodern culture, the self is not consistent, authentic, or centered. (Firat, 1992: 204)

Firat argues that fragmentation and discontinuity become themselves the dominant narratives of postmodernity, sweeping all in front of them and shattering the self into numerous self-images coming in and out of focus. If modern consumers could be seen as victims of self-delusions, their needs manipulated by image-makers, postmodern consumers suffer from no such self-delusions. They do not search for authentic, integrated, wholesome selves. They do not demand that product images should be authentic, integrated or wholesome. They are sophisticated enough to recognize that these images are only fleeting mirages, spawned in the imaginations of clever image-makers who want to sell them things. But they do not mind. They are content with diverse personas, all products of artifice, all inauthentic, often at odds with each other. Schizophrenia becomes a perennial condition for the postmodern consumer (Jameson, 1983).

Group identities, too, become fragmented. Groups themselves lose their boundaries, becoming transient, ephemeral and largely fictitious. Individuals will identify with each other through shared lifestyles or shared fantasies, their self-images temporarily shaped by memberships to imaginary clubs and societies, 'imagined communities' (Anderson, 1983), 'invented traditions' (Hobsbawn, 1983) or 'neo-tribes' (Bauman, 1992; Maffesoli, 1995). Some of these groups are the ephemeral result of converging identity projects, sharing imagined heritages, qualities or interests. Others exist purely in individual imaginations.

Some thinkers draw rather optimistic conclusions from images of consumers as identity-seekers. Bauman, one of the most insightful theorists of the intersection of consumption, identity and postmodernity, sees in consumer freedom the possibility of a healthy competition, which does not disintegrate into warfare and destruction:

In the game of consumer freedom all customers may be winners at the same time. Identities are not scarce goods. If anything their supply tends to be excessive, as the overabundance of any image is bound to detract from its value as a symbol of individual uniqueness. Devaluation of an image is never a disaster, however, as discarded images are immediately followed by new ones, as yet not too common, so that self-construction may start again, hopeful as ever to attain its purpose: the creation of unique selfhood. (Bauman, 1988: 63)

Can the idea of identity survive the many fragmentations and discontinuities celebrated by postmodern writers? Is the idea of the consumer as identity-seeker meaningful, when identity has turned into nothing more than a succession of mirages? And can Bauman talk plausibly of this succession of mirages as 'selfhood' (Warde, 1994)? The above extract illustrates well some of the paradoxical implications of postmodern thinking that at once obliterates unity, sameness, continuity, fixity, and independence, the features that defined identity as a concept, while at the same time giving it pride of place in cultural discussions. If, as Bauman, correctly points out, the overabundance of signifiers undermines their value, is it possible to view identities as non-scarce goods? While there may well be an over-abundance of *images*, we think that there is a scarcity of *value-laden images*, images that command respect. While identity, in the fragmented, anarchic postmodern sense may not be in short supply, the same could hardly be said of esteem and self-esteem. To individuals craving recognition and self-esteem, Bauman's pronouncement that 'identities are not scarce goods' sounds a bit like the sanctimonious preaching of conservative politicians to those living on state benefits. If uniqueness is so highly prized as a prerequisite for esteem and self-esteem, the notion that any image can be the basis of identity begins to sound like a cruel joke.

Postmodern thinking scorns to distinguish between identity and self-image, self-image and self-love; it also cheekily conflates image and self-image. If identity is treated as narrative pure and simple, not only is the issue of authenticity obviated (any story can be valid *as a story*), but also the traditional concerns of sociologists and psychologists regarding the differences between self-identity and presentation of self to others melts away. If self-image and image are only mirages, to ask whether they coincide becomes irrelevant. Yet, experience suggests that today's consumers are highly preoccupied both with the authenticity of their own identity and with the recognition of this authenticity by others. They spend much time scrutinizing each other for inauthentic personas, contrived styles, yesterday's fashion and false identities. To argue that in the postmodern carnival, every mask adds to the generalized delirium fails to recognize the high levels of policing and self-policing that governs styles, fashions, images and identities. The follies of those who assume images above their station, those who seek to deceive others with cheap imitations or those who deceive themselves with studied and affected lifestyles attract the same ridicule and censure today as they did in the age of the Molière's *Le Bourgeois gentilhomme*, the classic statement of a man who makes a fool of himself by seeking to give the appearance of one above his station. The struggle for identity is much less benign than Bauman envisages, and may indeed be ridden with malice, envy and contempt, clearly delineated by Veblen and Bourdieu (see Chapter 6, 'The Consumer: Hedonist or Artist?').

To summarize: if Western consumers are to be seen as identity-seekers as numerous postmodern theorists invite us to do, the craving for authenticity, unity and consistency must be seen as intrinsic features of their searches. Any image will simply not do. While today's consumers may be willing to adopt multiple personas in different circumstances, as Giddens has argued, lifestyles, are 'more or less *integrated*' sets of practices, through which self-identities are constituted (Giddens, 1991: 81). Cohesion cannot simply be wished away from identity, simply because it has become problematic. (Bourdieu's concept of 'habitus' is pointing in a similar direction.) Identity that does not command the respect of others and does not lead to self-love is quite pointless; even if image is in ample supply, the same can be said of neither respect nor self-love. Without these qualifications, the theme of fragmented identities and the figure of the consumer as identity-seeker threaten to collapse into meaningless, though fashionable, clichés. Identity, self, image, self-image and subjectivity threaten to become free-floating signifiers, easily substituting each other, merging and dividing up, losing their moorings and distinctiveness.

Identity, the Ego-ideal and Narcissism

Can money buy us identity? If identity were seen as pure image or as the respect of anonymous others, then, as Marx surmises in this chapter's opening extract, money would rule supreme. In spite of reservations expressed by theorists like Bourdieu, since the decline of the aristocratic ideal, matters such as taste, style, refinement, adventure and image are things that may be bought, if one is not born with them. In today's world, it is not unknown for rock stars to become country gentlemen. Identity should then not be a serious problem for the rich. Yet one searches in vain for confirmation of this view (see McCracken, 1988). Instead, we propose that to the extent that identity constitutes a 'problem' or a 'project', it must encompass not only image (which may be purchased) and narrative (which may be constructed) but, contrary to some postmodernist thinking, meaning and value as well. This is far more problematic, for rich and poor alike. It involves the fashioning of an image in which one may admire oneself and through which one may gain the respect of significant others. Identity is no mere life-story but a life-story that commands attention, respect and emotion. Extending Giddens' idea of identity as narrative, we would see identity not merely as the story of who we are, but also a fantasy of what we wish to be like. Identity is not only an embellished account of our adventures, accomplishments and tribulations, but also that vital web of truths, half-truths and wish-fulfilling fictions that sustain us. This accounts for identity being at once fragmented and discontinuous, as well as united and continuous; it also brings the project of identity surprisingly close to the psychoanalytic concept of the ego-ideal, an amalgam of idealized images, phantasies and wishes against which we measure our experiences.

The ego-ideal can be built around different themes, frequently drawing on cultural or organizational achievements, nostalgic recreations of a golden past or utopian visions of glorious futures (Gabriel, 1993; Schwartz, 1990). The ego-ideal represents an attempt to recreate, in later life, the condition of primary narcissism, the period of our infancy when we imagined ourselves the centre of a loving and admiring world. Our primary narcissism is doomed to receive numerous blows, starting with the realization that the world is generally not a loving place and that, contrary possibly to the impression created by mother, we are not its centre (Freud, 1984a[1914]; Schwartz, 1990: 17ff.). We may still cling to the fantasy that we are unique and special, but this too will receive a cruel blow during our first encounters with schools and other impersonal organizations, which consign us to the status of a number on a register or a face among unknowns. Thereafter, we discover that admiration is hard to come by and love even harder. For this reason, the fact that young children have little problem of identity is hardly surprising. With every injury to their narcissism, however, the need to erect an ego-ideal becomes more pressing. The ego-ideal, then, emerges as a wishful fantasy of ourselves as we wish to be in order to become once more the centre of an admiring and loving world.

> What man projects before him as his ideal is the substitute for the lost narcissism of his childhood in which he was his own ideal. ... To this ideal ego is now directed the self-love which the real ego enjoyed in childhood. The narcissism seems to be now displaced on to this new ideal ego, which, like the infantile ego, deems itself the possessor of all perfections. (Freud, 1984a[1914]: 94)

At times, our ego-ideal merges with our ego; these are moments of triumph and joy when admiration and love is lavished on us, either for our individual achievements or for the achievements of groups, organizations or cultures with which we identify. Traditional societies supported individual ideal-egos with cultural ideals, powerful role models and overbearing symbols. Members of religious or political sects, today, may derive total narcissistic fulfilment through their membership of these organizations, which promise them not only omnipotence and salvation but also immortality in one form or another.

Western culture not only exacerbates the need for an ego-ideal by inflicting numerous injuries to our narcissism, but it also places formidable obstacles to its formation. Gone are the days of sweeping cultural ideals and moral certainties. Gone are the powerful role-models, untouched by scandal and corruption. Gone are the stirring symbols. Gone, too, are the great cultural accomplishments, artistic, scientific or military, in which we may take unalloyed pride. In a world where heroes are forever cut to size and perfection remains elusive, the gleaming surfaces of material goods, their pristine packaging and virginal existence inevitably attract our attention, even before the image-makers get down to work. As Lasch (1980, 1984) has powerfully argued, the world of objects appears to hold the promise of delivery to our ailing narcissism. Consumerism promises to fill the void in our lives.

Lasch has provided vivid pictures of the narcissistic personality that he sees as dominating American culture. Today's Narcissus spends endless amounts of time looking at himself in mirrors, but is not lost in self-admiration. He is not happy with what he sees. He worries about growing old and ugly. He sets about busily constructing an ego-ideal around idealized qualities of commodities, aided and abetted by the propaganda of the makers of dreams. He pours money into anti-ageing cosmetics, plastic surgery, and every conceivable beauty aid. He yearns for admiration and recognition from others, striving for intimacy, yet he is unable to establish long-term relationships; after all his only interest lies in himself and his ego-ideal, forever elusive, yet forever appearing within reach. Although blemished, the narcissist always finds something to admire in himself; his life-story may not have been crowned with glory yet, but the happy end is within sight – if only he tries a little harder, gets a lucky break, or, above all, finds a bit more money.

The usefulness of material objects now becomes quite apparent – these objects hold the promise of bridging the distance between the actual and the ideal. The view of commodities as *bridges* has been developed by McCracken (1988), who regards them as instances of displaced meaning. 'If only I could buy that car I would be what I would ideally like to be'; the car becomes a phantasy bridging the actual and the ideal. The less accessible the car, the greater the promise it holds. As focal point of a phantasy, the longed-for car becomes a magnet for displaced meaning; the flawlessness of the paintwork, the power inside the bonnet, the overwhelming sense of perfection that it radiates, are thinly disguised narcissistic delusions trans-ferred onto the idealized object. Once acquired, the object may at least temporar-ily act as a powerful narcissistic booster. Grown-up men have been known to cry in the arms of their mothers, on seeing a tiny scratch on that gleaming bodywork. In such cases, the car is incorporated in the ego-ideal, its every affliction experienced as a personal calamity. In as much as it provides a reason for self-love and the respect of others, such an object can be said to support the consumer's identity quite effectively. Yet, as McCracken argues, once acquired, often at considerable sacrifice, the spell of the commodity is exposed to falsification:

> The possession of objects that serve as bridges to displaced meaning is perilous. Once possessed these objects can begin to collapse the distance between an individual and his or her ideals. When a 'bridge' is purchased, the owner has begun to run the risk of putting the displaced meaning to empirical test. (McCracken, 1988: 112)

Once the phantasy built around the product has accepted the test of reality, its value to the ego-ideal decreases; almost invariably, it is bound to be found lack-ing, not because the product is not good, but because such extraordinary expec-tations had been built on it. A new phantasy will already start to develop around some new product. It is this process that consumer capitalism thrives on.

Consumerism: Addiction or Choice?

In this chapter, we have argued that behind the consumer's ostensible quest for identity lurk more fundamental cravings for respect and self-love, born out of the injuries that modern life inflicts on us. These generate anxieties that cannot be allayed by image alone or narratives spun around commodities; they demand far more radical measures. These anxieties are the result of injuries sustained by our narcissism, whose healing requires nothing less than the formation of an idealized phantasy of the self, an ego-ideal, commanding admiration, respect and self-love. In a culture shorn of role models and ideals, consumerism throws up ephemeral images to identify with (pop-stars, sportspeople, TV celebrities) and a promise for boosting our ego-ideals, by proffering commodities around which phantasies of perfection, beauty and power may be built. These phantasies are wish-fulfilments that transform mundane everyday objects into highly charged symbols.

How successful is consumerism as the means of restoring our ailing narcis-sism? Cultural critics like Christopher Lasch are in no doubt that consumerism merely reinforces the discontents for which it promises consolations. Individuals become constantly more insecure and image-conscious, looking at themselves in mirrors.

> A culture organized around mass consumption encourages narcissism – which [we] can define, for the moment, as a disposition to see the world as a mirror, more particularly as a projection of one's own fears and desires – not because it makes people grasping and self-assertive but because it makes them weak and dependent. (Lasch, 1980: 33)

In the last resort, the self-illusions of uniqueness, power and beauty cannot be sustained in such a culture. As Horkheimer and Adorno put it in their memorable lament of lost individuality:

> What is individual is no more than the generalities' power to stamp so firmly that it is accepted as such. The defiant reserve or elegant appearance of the individual on show is mass produced like Yale locks, whose only difference can be measured in fractions of millimeters. The peculiarity of the self is a monopoly commodity determined by society. (Horkheimer and Adorno, 1997[1947]: 154)

In a more recent work, Lasch argues that Western consumerism, sustained by mass production and celebrated in the mass media, amounts to a mechanism of addiction.

> 'Shop till you drop.' Like exercise, it often seems to present itself as a form of therapy, designed to restore a sense of wholeness and well-being after long hours of unrewarding work. 'I feel like hell and I go out for a run, and before I know it, everything's OK.' Shopping serves the same purpose: 'It hardly matters what I buy, I just get a kick out of buying. It's like that first whiff of cocaine. It's euphoric and I just get higher and higher as I buy.' (Lasch, 1991: 521)

At this point, the consumer as identity-seeker turns into a victim, a willing victim, an unknowing victim perhaps, but a victim all the same. While the addictive qualities of consumption epitomized in the 'shopoholic' are widely recognized (Baudrillard, 1988a[1968], 1988b[1970]; Bocock, 1993; Campbell, 1989; Lebergott, 1993), Lasch's pessimism is not shared by everyone. A more equivocal picture emerges from the work of Bauman who argues that consumption is the new 'pioneer frontier' in which individuals may successfully assert themselves, with no insecurity and not harming others (Bauman, 1988c: 57). An earlier herald of the liberating potential of consumer freedom, Philip Rieff, argued:

> Confronted with the irrelevance of ascetic standards of conduct, the social reformer has retreated from nebulous doctrines attempting to state the desired quality of life to more substantial doctrines of quantity. The reformer asks only for more of everything – more goods, more housing, more leisure; in short, more life. This translation of quantity into quality states the algebra of our cultural revolution. Who will be stupid enough to lead a counter-revolution? (Rieff, 1966: 243)

Rieff's views are echoed by numerous less eloquent conservative theorists, who view consumerism, not only as offering delivery from the drudgery of self-reliance, but also as the begetter of genuine variety, choice, freedom and true individuality. Such enthusiasts dismiss the arguments of critics like Lasch as sanctimonious nonsense, flying in the face of all evidence. Lebergott (1993: 26–7) pours scorn on intellectuals who dismiss the choice presented by supermarkets while revering libraries full of unread tomes. The consumers' freedom to choose from 200 different beers, 600 different motor-cars or 160 different magazines is no less meaningful than the intellectuals' freedom to read or write what they please. Freedom of choice, in the view of conservative commentators, far from being empty or meaningless is the very foundation of our cultural identity, which has rejected apocalyptic messages and faith as the roads to the good life. The consumer garden of Eden, according to this view, with its limitless choice, endows us with narcissistic pride, even if its most alluring packages remain beyond our reach. A brief look at the images of poverty, warfare, hunger and suffering on our TV, or at the plight of those surviving on state benefits, deprived of the freedom of choice, suffices to convince us of the spiritual superiority of the culture of the mall, the supermarket and the gleaming surfaces. (See Chapter 2, 'The Consumer as Chooser'.)

In Conclusion

Our pursuit of the consumer as identity-seeker has brought us to a junction. In one direction, we can pursue the consumer exercising freedom, making choices, accepting satisfactions and set-backs, reaching compromises and, to a greater or lesser extent, succeeding in building an ego-ideal that commands the respect of others and inspires self-love; all this, through the act of consumption. In the other direction, we can pursue the consumer as an addict, unable to live without self-delusions, mediated by material goods, which ultimately aggravate his or her condition. Commodities represent nothing but a daily fix. Difficult questions now confront us. Is identity a project or a consolation? Are material objects bridges to an ideal or bridges to nowhere? Does everyone deal with the problem of identity through consumption in the same way?

The ambiguities of modern consumption are such that the face of the Western consumer is open to change. Like the images we examined earlier, it is hardly surprising that the consumer as identity-seeker has the tendency to metamorphose into something else. Like them, it tends to present too monochromatic a picture of the consumer. Some of us may and do, from time to time, seek identity by browsing in front of shop windows, purchasing goods and internalizing their images. These may prove disappointing or may provide considerable support to our ego-ideals and identities. At other times, however, our identities may be built around resistance to consumption and consumerism and the subversion of the symbolism carried by objects. Defying the slogans of advertisers and sneering at the propaganda of commodities may be as sound enough base for constructing an ego-ideal as the worship of the shopping mall. Alternatively, we can pursue our projects of identity by focusing our life-narratives elsewhere. At a time when workaholics compete with shopoholics, it seems premature to write off the work ethic. For many, work remains an arena (though of course not the only one) where identity is fashioned, as indeed is the family (single- or double-parent, extended or not) and other social networks that defy the neo-tribe sobriquet. And who would discount social class as a source of identity when practising marketers busily classify, monitor and target everyone in those terms? The organizations that we serve also nurture our ego-ideals, either by lending us some of their corporate aura (Schwartz, 1990) or by serving as objects of ridicule (Gabriel, 1999).

It seems premature, therefore, to conflate the pursuit of identity or the formation of an ego-ideal with compulsive shopping, the acquisition and display of commodities and their use to adorn bodies and souls. While the ascetic ideal may be gone for good, ostentatious spending can still rouse indignation, as shown by the roasting occasionally received by celebrities, when seen to go over the top in their profligacy. Image purchased at too high a cost, undermines esteem.

If the conflation of identity and consumerism is premature, might the conflation of self with identity be liable to exhaustion? Before closing this chapter, we may reflect briefly on the privileged position of 'identity' in contemporary discussions of selfhood. Is it not possible that identity has become itself a fashion, used to cover a multitude of sins? It certainly has some of the marks of a fashion: universal appeal, seeming inevitability, floating signifiers, a cottage industry of media pundits and image-makers sustaining it and a stream of celebrities embodying it. One thing is certain, that the prominence of identity since the 1980s has isolated cultural studies of consumption from addressing numerous types of consumer behaviour and action that have been of central importance to people ranging from financial analysts to consumer activists, to many consumers themselves. What if for a number of us, unaffected by this suggestive apparatus, identity simply does not exist as a problem or as a project or as anything else? This is how Lévi-Strauss has described his own experience of self:

> I never had, and still do not have, the perception of feeling my personal identity. I appear to myself as the place where something is going on, but there is no 'I', no 'me'. Each of us is a kind of crossroads where things happen. The crossroads is purely passive; something happens there. A different kind of thing, equally valid, happens elsewhere. There is no choice, it is just a matter of chance. (Lévi-Strauss, 1978: 3–4)

Read as a literal and honest description, rather than as a mischievous structuralist aphorism or an Olympian utterance by a sage who stands removed from mundane matters, this statement suggests that identity may not be such a universal preoccupation, after all. It is certainly possible to think of ourselves in ways that do not depend on the output of the identity industry. Could it be that identity, like other fashions, will eventually exhaust itself, its appeal shrinking to a niche market kept alive by nostalgia? Some of us may look forward to the day when identity sheds its psychosociological identity and returns to its forensic-political roots. But what a challenge that would pose to brands!

CHAPTER **6**

The Consumer: Hedonist or Artist?

I will offer one thousand golden pieces to any man who can show me a new pleasure.

Xerxes

C
O
ARGUMENTS
E

Most consumers claim to find pleasure in the goods and services they consume and economists have defended the view that higher living standards represent greater happiness. The pursuit of happiness and pleasure is ensconced in the American Constitution but may require more than just money. Different types of pleasure are identified, including pleasure that results from fulfilment of needs and pleasure that comes with heightened emotional experiences and fantasy. Aesthetic pleasure, deriving from the consumption of stylish, 'cool' products often comes at a cost to those who fail to match the pronouncements of style gurus, and 'tastes' can become an instrument of social ostracism and exclusion. In a narcissistic culture, pleasure deriving from fantasy all too easily becomes associated with domination and violence, assuming sadistic qualities that occasionally get acted out.

Pleasure lies at the heart of consumerism. It finds in consumerism a unique champion that promises to liberate it both from its bondage to sin, duty and morality as well as from its ties to faith, spirituality and redemption. Consumerism proclaims pleasure not merely as the right of every individual but also as every individual's obligation to him- or herself.

> The modern consumer, the modern citizen, cannot evade the constraint of happiness and pleasure, which in the new ethics is equivalent to the traditional constraint of labor and production. ... He must constantly be ready to actualize all of his potential, all of his capacity for consumption. If he forgets, he will be gently reminded that he has no right not to be happy. (Baudrillard, 1988b[1970]: 48–9)

Consumerism seeks to reclaim pleasure, not least physical, sensuous pleasure, from sanctimonious moralizing and the grim heritage of the Protestant ethic, which said 'Work! Work! Work!'. It celebrates the diversity of pleasures to be obtained from commodities, proposing such pleasures as realistic, attainable goals of everyday life. Enjoying life means consuming for pleasure, not consuming for survival or for need. If we fail to enjoy life, it may be that we are failing to look after ourselves, weighed down by self-inflicted hang-ups and inhibitions. The pursuit of pleasure, untarnished by guilt or shame, becomes the bedrock of a new moral philosophy, a new image of the good life. But how well does this image match the realities of contemporary consumption? How realistic is the project of attaining pleasure through material possessions? And to what extent do we, as consumers, answer the call of consumerism to enjoy ourselves? These are some of the issues that this chapter addresses.

The World of Commodities and the Pursuit of Pleasure

Western consumption, Bauman, Bourdieu, Baudrillard and countless other have argued, is a realm of *seduction* – alluring and glamorous. Few can escape its temptations, certainly not the poor whether they live in the First, the Second or the Third Worlds. Since the collapse of Eastern-style communism, consumerism has emerged as a global hegemonic idea, underpinning capitalist accumulation, free trade and the riotous commodification of everything (see 'Introduction: The Faces of the Consumer'). Consumer capitalism raises commodity fetishism to heights undreamed of by Marx. As goods leave the world of production to enter the sphere of display, circulation and consumption, they become objects of fantasy and instruments of pleasure. As Abercrombie has argued:

> Not only are the denizens of modern society consumers, they are also consumer*ist*. Their lives are organized around fantasies and daydreams about consuming; they are hedonists, primarily interested in pleasure, and sensual pleasure at that; they are individualists, largely pursuing their own ends and uncaring about others. (Abercrombie, 1994: 44)

In *The Cultural Contradictions of Capitalism*, Daniel Bell (1976) identified the central contradiction of late capitalism as one between the discipline, rationality and asceticism required in production and the spend-happy hedonism and waste of consumption. For Bauman (1988, 1992, 1997, 2001), a decade later, the contradiction has turned into symbiosis. Seduction becomes a mechanism of control;

the consumer's pursuit of pleasure enables him or her to endure the rigours of life under the capitalist reality principle, that is, alienating work, the threat of unemployment or worse. Pleasure, for so long the enemy of the capitalist project, against which no resource of puritanical morality was spared, is now mobilized to support the project. Pleasure and reality principles are at last reconciled.

> In the present consumer phase, the capitalist system deploys the *pleasure principle* for its own perpetuation. *Producers* moved by the pleasure principle would spell disaster to a profit-guided economy. Equally, if not more disastrous, would be *consumers* who are not moved by the same principle. ... For the consumer, reality is not the enemy of pleasure. The tragic moment has been removed from the insatiable drive to enjoyment. Reality, as the consumer experiences it, is a pursuit of pleasure. Freedom is about the choice between greater and lesser satisfactions, and rationality is about choosing the first over the second. (Bauman, 1992: 50)

In *Pursuing Happiness: American Consumers in the Twentieth Century*, Stanley Lebergott argues that 'in open societies, human consumption choices share one characteristic – they are made in pursuit of happiness' (Lebergott, 1993: 8). He then goes on to provide extensive economic documentation of the massive increases in US consumption since the end of the 19th-century, for example, an hour's work in 1990 earned on average six times more than it did in 1900. Lebergott dismisses the notions both that consumers are manipulated into purchasing items that do not afford them pleasure and that the variety and glamour of these items represent economic inefficiency and waste. Instead, he views the immense variety of commodities on display in shops as evidence that American consumers have never had it so good in terms of the quantity, quality and variety of things they consume and that American workers 'exchanged their labor hours for goods and services at a better rate than workers did in almost any other nation' (Lebergott, 1993: 68). Aware of their privileges in comparison with the rest of the world, US consumers are both proud of their consumerist culture and capable of taking advantage of it, he says. They make expert choices, refusing to be lured by unrealistic claims, contemptuously killing countless products that do not make it in the marketplace.

Lebergott, writing in the Reaganite 1980s, is especially scathing in his criticism of Tibor Scitovsky, an economist who in the 1970s had challenged (1) the economic assumption of consumer sovereignty, that is, that consumers choose whatever best satisfy their needs, and (2) the view that American consumers are either capable or willing to spend their money and even more importantly *their time* on things that give pleasure. Scitovsky (1976), for example, argued that Americans are far less concerned with the taste of the food they eat than its nutritional qualities and its convenience. To Scitovsky's idea that American consumers sacrifice pleasure for comfort, Lebergott counters:

> The United States does indeed lack an official corps of tasters and chewers, to decide which dinners are 'good, representative.' But what of the vast, untidy party of amateurs who exhort and instruct in newspaper food columns? And what of the best-sellers in US bookstores for decades – cookbooks? This record hardly demonstrates any 'lack of interest in the pleasures of food.' (Lebergott, 1993: 9)

Unlike Scitovsky, Lebergott scorns to distinguish between necessities and luxuries. One of the most interesting features of his argument is that 'necessities' make as big a contribution to the consumers' pursuit of pleasure as luxuries, since they free consumers from the drudgery of housework and extend their free time. Thus convenience foods, such as tinned peas, which for Scitovsky epitomize the Americans' indifference to the pleasures of the palate, are for Lebergott vehicles of pleasure – through them consumers free themselves from the drudgery of shopping for, cleaning, cutting up and preparing fresh vegetables. The greatest increases in consumer expenditure since 1900, he notes, went to those items 'that promised to extend lifetime hours of worthwhile experience,' for example, labour-saving devices, cars, convenience food, heating, lighting and more recently medicine (Lebergott, 1993: 36). He estimates that each American housewife spent 32 fewer hours weekly on meals and cleaning up between 1910 and 1975 (1993: 59).

One question that arises is how are consumers spending their 'free' time? In 'quality time' with their loved ones, in hobbies and other pleasure-imparting activities as Lebergott implies, or in increased travel times to and from work, shopping centres, and so on, or watching TV, as work by Gershuny (1992), Postman (1986) and others suggests? While Lebergott builds an impressive argument on the back of the grim picture of the labour-intensive domestic chores that filled most people's (especially women's) lives at the turn of the century, he fails to establish *pleasure* as the object of contemporary consumerism. True, the burden of doing the laundry or the washing up by hand, of fetching fuel and cleaning fireplaces, of baking bread and making and mending clothes, have been lightened. But can people today be said to be either happier or more pleasure-driven than their grandparents? Discomfort avoidance, curiosity and status thirst (the first two endorsed by Scitovsky) could replace 'happiness' in Lebergott's arguments without any loss of coherence. Buying a dishwasher may have little to do with the pleasurable activities that one may pursue while the machine gently washes away the grime, using up fossil fuel energy and polluting the world at the same time. Instead, one could see the purchase of a dishwasher as a discomfort-avoidance device, a status symbol or numerous other things.

Hedonism Old and New

Like many economists, Lebergott uses a quasi-democratic argument against arbiters of taste who distinguish between high-brow and low-brow pleasures, to defend the axiom that ordinary consumers, rather than aesthetes, academics, state planners, environmentalists, consumer activists and bureaucrats, or even producers, know best what pleases them. Lebergott's hedonism is axiomatic and, as a result, it adds little theoretical value, although it acts as a firm ideological support to enthusiasts of the free market. The axiom that what saves time is useful and what is useful is pleasurable is directly attacked by Campbell (1989), who has developed one of the most advanced positions of contemporary consumption as a unique and highly elaborate form of pleasure-seeking. Campbell's account of consumerism stands out from other commentaries in numerous respects. First, Campbell refuses to separate the sphere of consumption from that of production, each characterized by its own 'ethic'. Unlike Bell and even Bauman, he argues that the same psychocultural forces that drive a pleasure-orientated consumption also account for the broad range of work attitudes, normally subsumed under the Protestant work ethic label. Second, Campbell, almost alone among contemporary cultural theorists seriously explores the meaning of pleasure, both establishing its differences from utilitarian concepts such as need and satisfaction and identifying different modes of constructing and deriving pleasure. Third, Campbell provides a convincing and highly detailed picture of the original qualities of contemporary hedonism, which places it apart from traditional hedonism, yet maintains the centrality of pleasure. In this way, he provides an intriguing, though controversial, way of absorbing dissatisfaction, frustration and loss into an essentially hedonistic outlook on life.

The first of several astute distinctions made by Campbell is between pleasure and utility, conflated by utilitarianism and confused by economists. Like Baudrillard (1988b[1970]), Campbell criticizes the concept of utility by reviewing Galbraith's (1967) arguments. But while Baudrillard goes on to distinguish between use-values and sign-values of commodities, Campbell explores utility and pleasure as distinct motivational principles, the former deriving from need, the latter aiming at pleasure. Need represents the disturbance of a state of psychological equilibrium; it is based on absence, on lack, on necessity. By contrast, pleasure, argues Campbell, is 'not so much a state of being as a quality of experience' (Campbell, 1989: 60). Desire is triggered by the presence in one's environment of 'a recognized source of pleasure (1980: 60). Campbell's account of the pleasure principle could hardly be more different from that of Freud (1920, 1984b[1923]), who following Schopenhauer saw pleasure as essentially a negative phenomenon, a struggle to release oneself from unpleasure, pleasure being the lowering of tension that follows the gratification of an instinctual impulse. By contrast, the pursuit of pleasure, for Campbell, does not seek to restore an earlier state of disturbed equilibrium, but is a quest for a certain kind of stimulus that will bring about a pleasurable experience. Stimulation is therefore itself part of the pleasurable experience.

Both needs and desires drive consumption, although in modern societies desire assumes an ever-increasing role. Unlike Baudrillard, Campbell does not deny the continuing existence of needs or the merging of needs and desires. Hunger is paradigmatic of need, sexuality of desire. The two often operate in tandem; a meal may both yield pleasure and satisfy hunger. More importantly, however, guaranteed satisfaction saps the potential for pleasure. In the presence of guaranteed satisfaction by regular meals or routine sex, the pleasure-yielding potential of eating or sexual activities are moderated. Comfort undermines pleasure.

In spite of the fact that they may merge or oppose each other, needs and desires represent very different motivational principles. Needs are far more tied to specific means of satisfaction than desires. Hunger can only be met with food. Desire, by contrast, can be stimulated by a wide variety of objects and can migrate from one experience to another. More importantly, while needs are tied to objects, desires can wander into a world of fantasy and imagination; 'whilst only reality can provide satisfaction, both illusions and delusions can supply pleasure' (Campbell, 1989: 61).

Campbell now draws a second crucial distinction, between traditional and modern hedonism. Traditional hedonism is a hedonism of a multitude of pleasures, a hedonism of sensations attached to the senses, taste, smell, touch, sight and hearing. Modern hedonism, on the other hand, seeks pleasure not in sensation but in emotion accompanying all kinds of experiences, including what may be called sad or painful ones. Traditional hedonism is epitomized in the lives of luxury and opulence of potentates, princes and the super-rich. Their tables are spread with an abundance of exotic foods, their palaces decorated with artistic masterpieces. Musicians, comedians and entertainers are on call to offer finer and higher pleasures; harems, jugglers and fools to gratify lower ones. But, as Xerxes' heart-rending pronouncement at the opening to this chapter makes plain, 'guaranteed satisfaction' jades the senses. Pleasure becomes the ultimate scarce commodity for the traditional hedonist. Boredom and dissatisfaction set in.

When comfort kills pleasure, pleasure may be sought in new stimuli, less predictable, less comfortable, more dangerous. Comfort must yield to adventure. Few potentates have the courage or the latitude of doing so, without risking their power, wealth and status. Some may turn to hunting or to mixing incognito with lesser mortals as a means towards greater excitement; invading Greece seemed to provide Xerxes with the ultimate thrill in 480 BC. Such pursuits are certainly not consistent with comfort, yet it is only through exposing oneself to hardships and dangers that the project of hedonism can stay on course; hence, far from being the opposite to hedonism, adventure, hardship and privation become, for Campbell, its logical culmination. These 'adventurous' pursuits provide the bridge between traditional and modern hedonism. What sets modern hedonism apart from traditional hedonism is the emphasis on emotion and the submission of emotion to a special type of self-control that enables any emotion, including fear, pity, grief or nostalgia, to yield pleasure. This self-control disengages emotion from action and reinterprets it as a source of pleasure. Anger, for instance, can be greatly pleasurable if it can be stopped from turning into physical violence. Spectators of professional wrestling, for example, can be driven to paroxysms of rage by the orgy of evil unfolding in front of their eyes (Barthes, 1973). This is highly enjoyable for the spectators, so long as they do not join in on the mêlée, and even more so if the worst villains among the wrestlers meet with the most terrifying punishment. That terror itself can be highly thrilling is no more eloquently illustrated than by the successes of ever more frightening roller-coaster rides.

It can now be seen how important puritanism, with its emphasis on emotional control, was in promoting modern hedonism. By blocking feeling as a motive for action and replacing it with rational calculation, puritanism did not kill feeling; instead, it made it available to support a new mechanism of pleasure, one deriving not from the senses but from experience.

> Unlike traditional hedonism, however, [pleasure] is not gained solely, or even primarily, through the manipulation of objects and events in the world, but through a degree of control over their meaning. In addition, the modern hedonist possesses the very special power to conjure up stimuli in the absence of any externally generated sensations. This control is achieved through the power of imagination, and provides infinitely greater possibilities for the maximization of pleasurable experiences than was available under traditional, realistic hedonism to even the most powerful of potentates. This derives not merely from the fact that there are virtually no restrictions upon the faculty of imagination, but also from the fact that it is completely within the hedonist's own control. It is this highly rationalized form of self-illusory hedonism which characterizes modern pleasure-seeking. (Campbell, 1989: 76)

Consumerism and the New Hedonism

If the key to modern hedonism is the quest for pleasure via emotional experience rather than sensory stimulation, then modern consumption can be seen as an elaborate apparatus enabling individuals to *imagine* the dramas that afford them pleasure, to *dream* the scenarios that fulfil their desires. What commodities do is to act as props for the imagination, as stimulants for a reverie in which longing and fulfilment coincide.

> In modern, self-illusory hedonism, the individual is ... an artist of the imagination, someone who takes images from memory or the existing environment, and rearranges them or otherwise improves them in his mind in such a way that they become distinctly pleasing. No longer are they 'taken as given' from past experience, but crafted into unique products, pleasure being the guiding principle. In this sense, the contemporary hedonist is a dream artist, the special skills possessed by modern man making this possible. (Campbell, 1989: 79)

Consider the fashion of South American hammocks. The importation of hammocks from Peru, Bolivia and Paraguay is a curious reversal of the 19th-century, when hammocks mass-produced from Manchester wiped out South American production (Gott, 1993). Currently, hammocks are very popular with British workaholics, who evidently imagine themselves luxuriating in the sunshine, relaxing, at peace with themselves and with the world. The hammock becomes the stimulus for a longing reverie, at once unrealistic and unrealizable, frustrating and yet strangely fulfilling. If many of the hammocks sold are rarely used, and, if when they are used they fail to yield much relaxing time (since people who day-dream about hammocks are the very people unable to relax), these things hardly matter. To these people, the pleasure afforded by the hammock is at the level of fantasy, rather than as an object. The enjoyment of products as parts of fantasies and the fantasies about products are crucial feature of modern consumerism and may explain why window shopping or looking at magazines of unaffordable items can be enjoyable.

Modern consumption, according to Campbell, is built around day-dreaming, 'envisaged as an activity that mixes the pleasures of fantasy with those of reality' (Campbell, 1989: 85). Desire becomes itself subject to control, nurtured, encouraged, stimulated so long as it affords pleasure. Deferred gratification is no sacrifice of pleasure but a state of increased excitation, at once frustrating and enjoyable, endured in the interest of heightened pleasures ahead. Disillusionment in hedonism of this type is not the result of dulling of the senses, as it is with traditional hedonism, but the result of the fact that imagined pleasures are always greater than actual ones, that as the poet Keats said, 'heard melodies are sweet, those unheard are sweeter' (quoted in Campbell, 1989: 87). Dissatisfaction with reality, a generalized *tristesse*, becomes the back-cloth against which the consumer as a dream artist can embroider his or her fantasies. 'Thus the contemporary hedonist not only tends to welcome deferred gratification, but may also prematurely abandon a source of pleasure, as, by doing so, he maximizes the opportunities for indulging the emotions of grief, sorrow, nostalgia, and, of course, self-pity' (Campbell, 1989: 88).

Campbell's account of hedonism reveals consumer culture to be a space where a wide range of emotions can be experienced, through a combination of real and imagined stimuli. A bungee jump, a visit to one of the numerous terror attractions (Madame Tussaud's, the London Dungeons, and so on) or watching a horror movie are all experiences in terror; a visit at the Holocaust museum in Washington, DC becomes an experience in grief; the purchase of a gift for a loved one becomes an experience in romantic love and so on. Experiences fade with repetition, hence self-illusory hedonism is always seeking novelty, uniqueness and adventure, while at all times seeking to maintain control over the intensity of stimulation, balancing endurable longing with a kaleidoscopic survey of emotions and delectable morsels of pleasure.

> The cycle of desire – acquisition – use – disillusionment – renewed desire is a general feature of modern hedonism, and applies to romantic interpersonal relationships as much as the consumption of cultural products such as clothes and records. (Campbell, 1989: 90)

This type of hedonism finds its ideal in *romanticism*, which:

> had the effect of casting the individual of true virtue in the role of an opponent to 'society', whose conventions he must deny if only to secure proof of his genius and passion. At the same time, he becomes not merely a virtuoso in feeling but also in pleasure, something he must prove by creating cultural products which yield pleasure to others. Pleasure indeed becomes the crucial means of recognizing that ideal truth and beauty which imagination reveals – it is the 'grand elementary principle' in life – and thus becomes the means by which enlightenment and moral renewal can be achieved through art. (Campbell, 1989: 203)

Under the Romantic Ethic, the modern consumer fuses hedonism with an aesthetic attitude to life, seeking to emulate the artist in his or her pursuit of pleasures through the medium of imagination, repudiation of 'easy' pleasures or comforts in the interest of controlled stimulation and quest for a highly individual style. Here, Campbell joins an important tradition of consumer studies, which underlines the so-called aestheticization of everyday life, according to which everyday consumer objects are infected with aesthetic considerations, becoming signs of style and taste, and losing their functional qualities (see, for example, Ewen, 1990; Featherstone, 1991; Lury, 1996; Miller, 1987; Pountain and Robins, 2000; Slater, 1997; Willis, 1990). Western consumers will spend enormous amounts of time decorating their homes, choosing their clothes, food and other goods, planning their holidays, forever mixing ingredients, as if they were trying not merely to create works of art but to discover a uniquely individual style. To do so, commodities must appear forgetful of being use-values, and must appear exclusively as objects of pure taste. This, according to Bourdieu:

> asserts the *absolute primacy of form over function*, of the mode of representation over the object represented, [and] *categorically* demands a purely aesthetic disposition which earlier art demanded only conditionally. The demiurgic ambition of the artist, capable of applying to *any* object the pure intention of an artistic effort which is an end in itself, calls for unlimited repetitiveness on the part of the aesthete capable of applying the specifically aesthetic intention to any object, whether or not it has been produced with aesthetic intention. (Bourdieu, 1984: 30)

The corollary of the aestheticization of everyday life is the de-aestheticization of art. Surrealist painting initiated the project of stripping objects of art of their transcendental qualities and mystique, either by parodying well-known masterpieces (Dali adding a moustache to the Mona Lisa) or by presenting everyday objects as artwork. Many museums today routinely display 'ordinary' objects of everyday life, inviting the visitor to turn them into artistic works through the use of imagination.

The great advantage of Campbell's account over most others highlighting the artistic qualities of modern consumption is that it keeps both pleasure and dissatisfaction in the picture, built as it is on a sophisticated theory of desire and stimulation. Tastes and aesthetic preferences are not arbitrary social constructions, but are derivative of romantic sensibilities pursuing pleasure. Trivial objects of everyday life become charged with aestheticism, not because of Veblenesque status concerns, nor because individuals are influenced by taste-makers or 'new cultural intermediaries' working in the media, design, fashion, advertising and information (Bourdieu, 1984), but because they become objects of emotion activating pleasurable reveries. Furthermore, Campbell offers strong arguments for why dissatisfaction, inextricably linked with the pursuit of pleasure, drives innovation. His hedonist-consumers are inexorably drawn to exploration and experimentation. Above all, Campbell offers one of the few plausible explanations of why consumers may be pursuing horror, fright, anger, sadness, and even pain as part of the pursuit of pleasure.

The relative weaknesses in Campbell's account of modern consumption are paradoxically linked to his success in elucidating pleasure. His account of the pleasure principle is, as we saw, rich in insights, more dynamic and in some ways more convincing than the psychoanalytic account of the same concept, which is connected to homoeostasis and the reduction of tension. Yet, where Freud saw the world conspiring against individual pleasure, Campbell sees no such limitations. For Freud, the pleasure principle must be continuously modified, compromised and deflected according to the demands of reality:

> What decides the purpose of life is simply the programme of the pleasure principle. This principle dominates the operation of the mental apparatus from the start. There can be no doubt about its efficacy, and yet its programme is at loggerheads with the whole world, with the macrocosm as much as the microcosm. There is no possibility at all of its being carried through; all the regulations of the universe run counter to it. (Freud, 1985b[1930]: 76)

Unlike the psychoanalytic account of libido forever torn between pleasure and social bonding, forever frustrated by necessity, Campbell's pleasure principle rules supreme:

> Modern hedonism presents all individuals with the possibility of being their own despot, exercising total control over the stimuli they experience, and hence the pleasure they receive. (Campbell, 1989: 76)

The main limitations on pleasure entertained by Campbell appear to be those originating in the nature of pleasure, the dulling effects of comfort and the diminishing intensity of pleasure itself. This view does not explain what happens when one individual's pleasure inhibits the pleasure of somebody else. Nor what happens when one individual's pleasure runs counter to the broader institutions of morality, religion or law. Finally, it seems that Campbell's individual can pursue his Quixotic adventures, oblivious to the necessities and hardships of life or any other external demands.

While much of Campbell's discussion occurs at the level of macro-social and cultural trends across several centuries, the picture he paints of the modern consumer is highly individualistic. The pleasure principle, as he conceives it, operates across classes, races, genders, ages and all other social and cultural distinctions. Unlike Douglas and Isherwood (1978), who view the solitary consumer as a fiction, consumers emerge from Campbell's discussions as solitary creatures, individually pursuing pleasure, absorbed in their reveries, more or less oblivious of each other. Campbell's severe criticism of Veblen, his contemptuous dismissal of Packard's (1981[1957]) thesis of consumer manipulation, his steadfast refusal to relate fantasy with escapism or substitute gratification and his indifference to the social, political and communicative dimensions of consumption all underline his uncompromising commitment to pleasure as the totalizing principle at the heart of modern consumption. His account, however, serves as a warning of some of the absurdity that one ends up with, when seeing contemporary consumption through a single prism. It would be bizarre to envisage a single mother shopping for her weekly groceries as lost in a reverie of pleasure.

Social Hedonism

To Campbell's uncompromisingly solipsistic hedonism, it is interesting to juxtapose Bourdieu's social hedonism. Bourdieu's book *Distinction: A Social Critique of the Judgement of Taste* (1984) caused quite a substantial public debate when first published in France, partly because it was seen as debunking the concept of taste (notably 'high-brow taste') by re-integrating aesthetic consumption with ordinary everyday consumption. Bourdieu combines an emphasis on hedonism with an insistence that consumption is a set of practices establishing social differences, viewing consumers both as pleasure-seeking (like Campbell) and as hungry for distinction (like Douglas and Isherwood). Tastes, according to Bourdieu, emerge at once as avenues towards pleasure and as a class phenomenon, as a form of cultural capital and as an instrument of oppression.

Bourdieu's arguments draw on two extensive surveys on consumer tastes and lifestyles carried out in France in the 1960s. Judged on their own merit, these surveys are both outdated and methodologically mechanistic, suffering from all the familiar shortcomings of attempting to capture a person's lifestyle, tastes and meanings through standardized inflexible questions. Nevertheless, these surveys enable Bourdieu to argue that there are important differences in how different social classes, or even class factions, derive pleasure. The food and the drinks they consume, the films and TV programmes they watch, the cars they drive and the ways they furnish and decorate their homes are not merely governed by different tastes but reveal fundamentally different modes of deriving pleasure, different aesthetics, different pleasure principles.

The key to these differences is what he calls the 'Kantian aesthetic', which is central to middle-class lifestyles, yet entirely absent from working-class lifestyles. For Kant, the aesthetic experience occupies a position between morality and sensuousness and centres on the faculty of judgement. Judgement mediates between theoretical reason and practical reason, through the feeling of pleasure; its realm is art. Aesthetic experience rejects immediate sensuous pleasures in favour of abstract appreciation of the artistic, which comes through the faculty of imagination. Beauty, according to this view, is neither floating freely in an external world, nor the direct corollary of sensuous pleasure, but is creatively constituted through the work of imagination. Thus beauty can be discovered in an object's form as well as in the mode of its representation, if the object can be approached in a detached, disinterested manner that completely disregards its use or material composition. Even objects that could be classed as 'ugly', can therefore become beautiful.

A photograph of rotting vegetables, a painting of an ugly man or a grotesque inter-
lude in the midst of a symphony can all afford great aesthetic pleasure if the object
can be released from its bondage to both pleasure and usage and turned into a 'free'
being, signifying nothing but itself, through the free play of imagination.

Bourdieu rejects the Kantian theory as a theory of aesthetic judgement (respect-
ful parodying in the title of his book Kant's *Critique of Judgement*) but accepts it as a
description of bourgeois aesthetics. He regards the detached, aloof disposition of
the Kantian aesthetic not as a mental faculty, but as an orientation concomitant to
the affluence of today's bourgeoisie and an instrument of social distinctions. The
crux of his argument is that while the middle-class embrace the Kantian aesthetic,
cultivating tastes for the abstract, the working-class aesthetic is that of popular
culture, dictated by necessity and tied to both function and sensuous pleasure. This
fundamental difference cuts across every aspect of taste. The working-class invariably seeks direct gratification while the middle-class seeks 'style'.

Bourdieu provides numerous illustrations of this dichotomy, ranging from food
and drink to photography, from music to home decoration. A couple of his examples will suffice. Working people like food, plentiful in protein, nutritious, what
Orwell in *The Road to Wigan Pier* described as 'a little bit "tasty"'. (Orwell, 1962: 803)
Pleasure is synonymous to an 'honest' and unfussy but abundant assortment of
'strong' food, which ultimately reflects the value of virility, rooted in physical work.
By contrast middle-class tastes weigh heavily towards elaborately prepared food,
sauces, and so on, the uses of exotic ingredients (like rare mushrooms), or, towards
the extreme simplicity of nouvelle cuisine. These emphasize the 'higher and finer'
qualities inherent in preparation and presentation and, in the extreme, seem to
deny that food is anything quite as vulgar as nourishment.

Similar illustrations are offered by Bourdieu from music (working-class prefer
music with strong melodic and rhythmic content, middle-class prefer avant-garde),
photography (working-class prefer pictures of garish sunsets or innocent children
at first communion, middle-class prefer pictures of dissected cabbages or car
crashes) and others. In Bourdieu's account the aestheticization of everyday life is a
middle-class affliction, rather than a totalizing principle of late capitalism as for
some postmodern thinkers. If middle-class consumers approach their clothing,
eating and home furnishing with an anti-functional, detached outlook, this is not the
same for working-class lifestyles. 'Nothing is more alien to working-class women
than the typically bourgeois idea of making each object in the home the occasion
for an aesthetic choice' (Bourdieu, 1984: 47). For Bourdieu, even where the same
commodity is consumed by different social classes, its meaning will vary. Where
some movie-goers watch a 'Western starring Burt Lancaster', others have watched
'the latest Sam Peckinpah'; these are vastly different ways of seeing the same film,
at once reflecting different tastes, generating different pleasures and producing
social distinctions (Bourdieu, 1984: 28).

Consumers' tastes, for Bourdieu, have darker, less innocent qualities than they do
for Campbell or indeed economists. Aesthetic judgements act as a form of thought
terrorism (a favourite term of Bourdieu's) cutting across social classes and fractions.

> Terrorism [lies] in the peremptory verdicts which, in the name of taste, condemn to ridicule,
> indignity, shame, silence (here one could give examples, taken from everyone's familiar uni-
> verse), men and women who simply fall short, in the eyes of their judges, of the right way of

being and doing; it [lies] in the symbolic violence through which the dominant groups endeavour to impose their own life-style, and which abounds in the glossy weekly magazines: 'Conforama is the Guy Lux of furniture', says *Le Nouvel Observateur*, which will never tell you that the *Nouvel Obs* is the Club Méditeraneé of culture. There is terrorism in all such remarks, flashes of self-interested lucidity sparked off by class hatred and contempt. (Bourdieu, 1984: 511)

Insults rarely hurt more than when aimed at the adversary's 'taken for granted preferences'; few types of social humiliation can match the dismissal of someone's tastes. 'You like X? Oh dear, it's so passé/common!' where X can be anything from digital watches, dried tomatoes to yesterday's music idol or theories of Althusser or Baudrillard. Conversely, argues Bourdieu, a transgression of the aesthetic decrees of 'high culture' will outrage the bourgeois more effectively than the breach of a moral code. An improperly dressed person, for example, will incur more hostility than a sexual deviant. In this way, aesthetics becomes a major terrain of contest between social classes and fractions, a contest where much pleasure is derived from terrorizing the adversaries, either by passing judgements on their tastes or by violating aesthetic codes. If Campbell's hedonist-consumer is naturally driven towards the image of the consumer-explorer, Bourdieu's consumer tends to modulate from an aesthete into a snob, a sadist or a rebel, pleasure becoming linked, not to discovery and innovation, but to class violence and aggression. Bourdieu's account of the different classes' aesthetics has been criticized from both the left and the right; the left have accused him of diminishing the working-class lifestyle to a caricature, while the right have feigned horror at his questioning of their aesthetic taboos (see Jenkins, 1992 for an overview). Yet he does not seek to evaluate these aesthetics, since he rejects any transcendental aesthetic qualities. Ultimately, all tastes are socially constructed, as are their 'high' or 'low' qualities, that is, distinctions between tastes. To be sure, the middle-classes may sneer at the vulgarity and 'cheapness' of common culture, just as the working-class may, less blatantly, belittle the airs and affectations of the high-brows. But for Bourdieu, the two represent fundamentally different aesthetics. From the two, various social fractions and intermediate or marginal groups seek to mould their own aesthetics, for example, artlessly aspiring at high-brow or affectedly 'opting' for rustic simplicity. However the mechanisms for deriving pleasure are essentially different. Working-class lifestyle is one of a 'realistic (but not resigned) hedonism' (Bourdieu, 1984: 49), while the middle-class lifestyle becomes ever more closely aligned to the Kantian aesthetic, concerned with style, form and distinction.

Bourdieu's account of consumerism is one that combines a discussion of pleasure with a class analysis of tastes and patterns of consumption. In its emphasis on class differences in consumption, it is only matched by Douglas and Isherwood's analysis. Many commentators, however, have found Bourdieu's class analysis, not only inaccurate but also patronizing. Jenkins (1992) and Douglas (Douglas and Isherwood, 1978) herself have argued that style and cultivated/inane tastes are every bit as important for working-class people as they are for the middle-classes. Numerous British commentators have established the importance of style, fashion and fantasy in consumption patterns of young working-class people, whose preferred tastes in music may be as perplexing to middle-aged, middle-class people as any avant-garde may be to a working-class audience (Featherstone, 1991; Fiske, 1989; Pountain and Robins, 2000; Willis, 1990). In sum, one suspects that the class dimension in Bourdieu's argument is at least outdated or more alarmingly a projection of his own middle-class presumptions.

Comparing Bourdieu's and Campbell's hedonistic accounts of modern consumption, one may be tempted to discern an equivalence between the two mechanisms of pleasure they each describe. Bourdieu's Kantian ethic and Campbell's modern hedonism hinge on the imagination and on deferred pleasure. Bourdieu's realistic hedonism and Campbell's traditional hedonism are both associated with instant sensuous pleasure. The former present the consumer as artist or aesthete, the latter as hedonist. This similarity, however, could be somewhat misleading. For Bourdieu, taste, culture and pleasure are not only class experiences but historically constructed ones. An individual *learns to enjoy* a wide range of objects and activities, from coffee to frogs' legs, from Chinese opera to heavy metal music, from jogging to foxhunting on rainy days. Many of these may appear curious to those 'uneducated' in these pleasures, yet membership of a social group and induction into its social tastes substantially determines an individual's '*habitus*', which Bourdieu sees as the range of tastes from which he or she will derive a personal repertoire. This contrasts with Campbell's far more individualistic account, where individuals must discover pleasure for themselves, their aesthetic responses being a matter of individual psycho-history rather than class or group membership.

Hedonism and Sadism

For all their limitations, images of consumers as hedonists or artists that emerge from Campbell's and Bourdieu's works have a compelling quality. As we stare at the clothes in a shop window, at the CDs in a record store, at the motor-boats in our leisure magazine, at the mouth-watering dishes pictured in our Sunday newspapers or at our neighbour's smart new car, we experience a feeling that can only be described as desire, a desire that is at once sweet and frustrating, a desire capable at times of convulsing our physical being as though it were purely sexual. Such objects seduce us as though they were sexual objects, sparking off strings of fantasies, which continue to prosper the longer the object remains inaccessible. As Freud (1985a[1921]) realized in his theory of the relationship between sexual gratification and romantic love, the denial of consummation enhances the idealization of the inaccessible object, just as in courtly love the longing was all the sweeter, the more aloof and unresponsive was the object of the lover's languor.

The accounts that we have explored in this chapter put pleasure at the centre of modern consumption and more generally as the central ethic of Western cultures. Happiness is increasingly defined not in terms of achievement or success, but in broadly hedonistic or aesthetic terms reflected in the 'quality of life' both at and outside the workplace. Happiness is seen neither as a reward for effort or virtue, nor as the result of fortune. Instead, as Rieff (1959) has brutally put it, human happiness is a question of the *management of pleasure* and, therefore, a *duty* to oneself. So long as one is not excluded from the seductive world of commodities by being dependent on the state for survival, being unhappy is inexcusable. It can only be due to one's ineptness at managing pleasure.

Neither Campbell nor Bourdieu would seek to vindicate such a position as an ethical hedonism, the true road to the good life, if such a thing exists. They both believe that consumers are deluding themselves in their espousal of the pleasure principle (in any guise), and their determination to pretend that the grey world of necessity has melted away. The very shrinking of individual women and men to the status of consumers, the willingness to define oneself and others through their standing as consumers is indicative of this self-delusion. Yet, neither Campbell nor Bourdieu are remotely willing to entertain the notion that modern hedonism, though its roots lie in delusion, is a form of compensation for the greyness of life under the reality principle or an escapist form of substitute gratification. Consumerist fantasies may be detached from reality but the pleasure they afford is real. This is a position that has been criticized with considerable eloquence by Christopher Lasch. Lasch has argued over many years that the pleasures of consumerism are neither innocent in their origins nor in their implications.

> Commodity production and consumerism alter perceptions not just of the self but of the world outside the self. They create a world of mirrors, insubstantial images, illusions increasingly indistinguishable from reality. The mirror effect makes the subject an object; at the same time, it makes the world of objects an extension or projection of the self. It is misleading to characterize the culture of consumption as a culture dominated by things. The consumer lives surrounded not so much by things as by fantasies. He lives in a world that has no objective or independent existence and seems to exist only to gratify or thwart his desires. (Lasch, 1984: 30)

At the heart of this critique lies the connection between hedonism and narcissism, a link widely discussed in psychoanalytic literature (for example, Gabriel, 1999; Lasch, 1984). The modern narcissist is the individual who, unable to love and unwilling to be loved, constantly seeks to derive pleasure from his or her own image. This he tries to do by embellishing his ego through the consumption of material and human objects, which become objects of fantasy and desire. Contemporary hedonism erects a massive edifice of substitute gratifications which, instead of obliterating, compounds the narcissism and lovelessness of modern life. As objects of desire, commodities and people are indistinguishable – they are objects to be used, abused and manipulated for one's personal enhancement.

> Contemporary hedonism ... originates not in the pursuit of pleasure but in the war of all against all, in which even the most intimate encounters become a form of mutual exploitation. ... This hedonism is a fraud; the pursuit of pleasure disguises a struggle for power. (Lasch, 1980: 66)

Lasch tries to show the extent to which pleasure in our culture has become co-extensive with aggression; sex and violence become irredeemably intertwined in language, in fantasy and in reality. If individuals derive pleasure, aesthetic or otherwise, from violence or products associated with violence, this is not as Campbell might have argued because violence just happened to provide a springboard for pleasurable fantasies, in the same way that tenderness, love or romance might have done. Violence becomes one with pleasure, when pleasure becomes life's only business, detached from morality or order. If Bourdieu, following Veblen, clearly envisages the sadistic delights of both snobbery and aesthetic transgression, Lasch goes a step further. In the Marquis de Sade's explosive utopia, where sexual pleasure leads to every humiliation of the other imaginable, even as far as mutilation, hacking, tearing, cutting and killing, Lasch finds both the prototype and terminus of modern hedonism, seeing no distinction between objects and people as instruments of pleasure. De Sade's message, coming at the outset of the French republican era was that uncompromised hedonism, far from leading to an emotional polytheism, can only lead to one thing, unbridled aggression. Once moral restraints have been removed, the pursuit of pleasure quickly turns into violence.

> In a society that has reduced reason to mere calculation, reason can impose no limits on the pursuit of pleasure – on the immediate gratification of every desire no matter how perverse, insane, criminal, or merely immoral. For the standards that would condemn cruelty derive from religion, compassion, or the kind of reason that rejects purely instrumental applications; and none of these outmoded forms of thought or feeling has any logical place in a society based on commodity production. (Lasch, 1980: 69)

To be sure, de Sade's vision has not become reality 200 years later. Nevertheless, aggression has assumed a central position in every aspect of Western life, including the predatory nature of personal relationships, the pitiless abuse of nature in pursuit of ever-higher standards of living, the use of commodities as weapons in a Veblenesque combat for status and the savagery of modern spectacles.

The fantasies of consumer culture, pleasurable though they may be, have little of the day-dreaming, bitter-sweet qualities envisaged by Campbell. The material or human object's resistance to being possessed, far from heightening the delights of yearning, spawn murderous fantasies of rape, pillage and destruction. These occasionally get a chance to be acted out as the dreadful photographs of sexual abuse of prisoners at the Abu Ghraib prison camp in Iraq have shown. Sexuality becomes the basis of torture and humiliation, performed ceremonially in front of the photographic lens. If a narcissist cannot have something, whether it be the goods in a shop window, the neighbour's car or the object of his sexual interest, far from gently dreaming of acquiring it by seduction or payment, he dreams of smashing it, breaking it or destroying it. Any residual pleasure in the object rests in its annihilation. Vandalism and destruction are the flip side of consumer hedonism, something that often goes unnoticed among those who preach both the worship of commodities and respect for human values.

In Conclusion

This bleak picture contrasts sharply with the more upbeat depictions of Western consumers as pleasure-seekers. But, like them, Lasch sees individuals today as much more likely to associate happiness with pleasure than with achievement, success or virtue. They are likely to envisage pleasure as residing in those objects that attract desire, and in doing so they may treat commodities or people in a similar manner, as stimulants for fantasies. Life assumes the character of an erotic simmer, a never-ending process of seduction, maintaining a constant level of desire that migrates from object to object as they each assume the spotlight in our fantasies.

Different accounts of consumer hedonism take different views on the nature of pleasure and the extent to which it differs across social classes and other groups. Nevertheless, there is wide agreement that consumer pleasure lies not so much in physical sensation as in total emotional experience, pleasure lies in the meaning of this experience. While this experience may be fantastic or delusory, the pleasure is not delusory at all. Thus the pleasure derived from a 'designer' ashtray lies in its imaginary qualities, which lift it above the mundane realities of its function, its substance, its price or its future uses. The object is idealized in much the same way as any object of infatuation is. It seduces us in exactly the same way that a person might.

Bourdieu and Campbell go some way towards providing an explanation for the thesis that everyday reality in Western cultures becomes aestheticized, with objects and activities assuming the qualities of art and losing their functional and material bearings. Style becomes more important than utility, which acquires a vulgar, common hue. The consumer as hedonist must be able to derive pleasure from every item with which he or she comes into contact and everything must be orientated to that end.

Starting with Lasch, our view is that consumer hedonism is neither playful nor innocent. Instead it is the outcome of a culture in which the market becomes the dominant institution regulating relations among individuals and tastes reign supreme, with little restraint from loyalty, morality, duty or love. Pleasure derived from material and symbolic manipulation of people and objects entails a substantial amount of aggression and the pursuit of this type of pleasure may be ultimately futile. The consumer becomes an addict capable of inflicting any amount of pain on others in order to obtain what he or she believes will satisfy his or her desires. Consumer hedonism can lead to a complete dead end, reinforcing the very discontents that drive it. Few have expressed this idea with the force and clarity of an old militant, interviewed by Seabrook:

> People aren't satisfied, only they don't seem to know why they're not. The only chance of satisfaction we can imagine is getting more of what we've already got now. But it's what we've got now that makes everybody dissatisfied. So what will more of it do, make us more satisfied, or more dissatisfied? (Seabrook, 1978: 132)

Whether today's consumers are locked in a vicious circle of dependency, frustration and hate or whether they enjoy in a limited but vital way the satisfactions available to them, in practice or fantasy, this remains a vital question at the heart of the debate on today's consumerism.

Hedonism is an idea that accounts for certain qualities of contemporary consumption; the thrill we get when we acquire an object we like, our insistence on what we like and what we do not like, and our ability to derive pleasure, thrills and fun out of seemingly disagreeable experiences. It also can elucidate different ways in which different social classes, including the very poorest, derive pleasure out of material objects. The underside of this is that hedonism is neither the only principle driving today's consumers, nor the liberating force celebrated by its apologists.

CHAPTER 7

The Consumer as Victim

[C]onsumers are being manipulated, defrauded, and injured not just by marginal businesses or fly-by-night hucksters but by the US blue-chip business firms ...

Ralph Nader (1968)

CORE ARGUMENTS

Victimhood is the flipside of consumer sovereignty. Even when most free, consumers are open to being defrauded, manipulated and short-changed. Victimhood, whether conscious or unconscious, has played a central role in Western debates about modern consumption. Even the strongest proponents of consumer choice recognize the potential for consumers to be exploited. However, there are splits between those who argue that the law is needed to protect consumers from abuse and those who see the market as being able to provide its own correction. For the former group, the notion of fairness and use of state power to determine the level playing field is central. For marketeers, the key issue is information as the means for oiling the commercial mechanism. In their view, consumer scares have to be kept in proportion and are not grounds for mass hypochondria. The organized consumer movement, however, has argued that only strong advocacy can ultimately protect and educate consumers. This is particularly pertinent in the new era of globalization, which has brought increasing distance between producers and consumers as well as strains upon national traditions of consumer protection.

The idea that consumers are victims no longer enjoys quite the high profile it once did. While victimhood and empowerment are widely discussed in connection with particular social groups ranging from women to ethnic minorities or people with physical disabilities, the world of consumption is not the first to come to mind when thinking of people as seriously wronged. Is the image of the consumer as victim therefore a trifle excessive? Should it be used only for serious injustice, cases where consumption directly threatens life? We think not, although we recognize that most people think of victimhood as occurring where events are beyond their control, such as sexual harassment, political or social discrimination, and so on. Consumers can not only be victims of blatant exploitation and fraud but may equally create themselves as victims or collude in the victimization of others. Indeed, the notion that consumers may too easily be victims – be used, exploited, defrauded, done down – unless better organized and/or protected, is central to modern notions of what it is to be a consumer. As we show in Chapter 9, 'The Consumer as Activist', the experience or threat of victimhood can be a prime motivation for consumers getting organized.

Although victimhood is as old as any trading system, in the modern senses that we explore in this book, it was from the 1950s that the image of victimhood took a really central position in post-war cultural commentaries on Western consumption. Vance Packard's book, *The Hidden Persuaders*, was published in 1957 and created a stir with its revelations of consumer manipulation by new techniques of depth psychology and mass advertising (Packard, 1981[1957]). The consumer was seen not only as a victim of unscrupulous commercial interests but also as fodder for the sophisticated techniques of the emerging science of consumer psychology, drawing on the insights of Freud and their application in marketing (see 'Introduction: The Faces of the Consumer'). In *One Dimensional Man* (Marcuse, 1964), a book that like Packard's achieved cult status, Herbert Marcuse launched a powerful attack on late capitalism as compounding the alienation of the worker by turning people into one-dimensional beings solely preoccupied with consumption. This post-Second World War critical tradition lost some of its glamour and momentum in the 1980s when, under the influence of postmodernism, many cultural commentators began to celebrate consumption as an active pursuit rather than a passive escapist activity. A new generation of neo-Marxist commentators represented by the journal *Marxism Today* began to argue that consumption holds not only creative but liberating potential (Hall and Jacques, 1989). In spite of attempts by Lasch (1991), Sklair (1991) and others to underline the continuing addictive qualities of contemporary consumption (see Chapters 5 and 6), it would be fair to say that cultural studies lost interest in the notion of the consumer as victim. Instead, they have sought to present the consumer as an explorer, as a semiotic puzzle-solver, as a *bricoleur*, as an identity-seeker, or as we shall see in the Chapter 8, as a rebel.

Rejecting the view propounded by cultural theory, consumer advocates and a new wave of consumer organizations around the world have highlighted the increased vulnerabilities of consumers in the age of global consumer capitalism. In this chapter, we will explore some of these arguments and some of the instances that fuelled this new critique. In Chapter 9, 'The Consumer as Activist', we will place this in context as movements, developing new new types of campaigning, product assessment and use of media.

The Experience of being a Victim

Not so deep beneath the surface of any consumer's mind is a sense that he or she may be exploited. The act of consuming taps a deep well of experience from childhood onwards. Few childhoods have not experienced the excitement of the first meaningful purchase of a longed-for toy or sweet. As part of the preparation for this book's first edition, we interviewed consumer activists and employees of consumer organizations from several different countries. We asked some of them if they could remember their first significant purchase. After sometimes intense interviews discussing the complexities of consumer activism and the challenges ahead, their eyes would light up and smile as they told of a mother giving money to buy a sweet or some early excitement. One, brought up in an isolated, near self-sufficient community in a developing country, told of the awe of being allowed to buy a canned drink on a trip out to town, an unheard of luxury. To anticipate such pleasure on every occasion (explored in Chapter 6, 'The Consumer: Hedonist or Artist?') is an unrealistic expectation. One is bound to be disappointed. The excitement of the early experience of consumer power, such as buying your own toy, is counterbalanced by the bitterness or disappointment from a purchase that failed to live up to expectations – the toy that quickly fell apart, the sweet that looked nice but wasn't – or that went wrong. The consumer as victim is, in this respect, the other side of the coin of consumer as pleasure-seeker.

As people get older, they often get more pleasure from giving than receiving and few purchases maintain the sense of excitement; yet the notion of being a victim has taken psychological root. The common identification of consuming and shopping as a female preserve means that women's cultural experience of oppression transfers easily to their experience of consuming. Consuming makes one vulnerable, at risk, a potential victim. Is it accidental that many of those who work in consumer organizations are women? In the late 20th-century, however, consuming became much more a pleasure within conceptions of masculinity; to that extent the postmodernists reflected and voiced a transition. But this came fraught with difficulties for males, too; shopping failure can be a highly charged experience. Those who are accustomed to being powerful at work, in public places, let alone the home, can easily be a victim on the high street or in the shopping mall.

Anyone who has been in the first line of contact with the public as consumers, or who trains people to deal with the public, is familiar with instances when shopping, eating at a restaurant, queuing for service, can generate situations during which tempers can fray, emotions can be raw, and social dynamics can take off in all kinds of potentially uncontrollable directions. As a result, the shop assistant, the waiter, the check-out till operator are frequently expected to exhibit extraordinary patience in dealing with the frustrations and anger of consumers who feel that their rights have been violated. Front-line staff usually only survive psychologically in their dealings with the public if they adopt one consistent style of dealing with them; this may be a style of identifying with the customer or of remaining distant, cool and professional (Pines and Aronson, 1989). Hopping from 'being solicitous to the customer' to 'frozen indifference' puts tremendous strain on the employee. Assertiveness training both for customers and staff is sometimes presented as the way of overcoming victimhood and achieving one's rights, an assumption about how to engender successful outcomes of victimhood that has been absorbed by the currently fashionable rhetoric of empowerment.

The psycho-therapeutic language of empowerment and self-assertion has close associations with the social construct of consumers as victims. Empowerment suggests an evolution from 'whingeing' about failure, via knowing how to complain, to the pinnacle of self-assertion. The model is almost straight from the American so-called humanist or Third Force (neither Freudian nor behaviourist) psychologists Abraham Maslow (1970[1954]), or Carl Rogers (1951). In effect, empowerment through consumption is not always easy for consumers to accomplish; nor is it always possible to find their rights through recourse to the state, even when the state acknowledges them. In the last decades of the 20th-century, the dominant deregulatory ideology ensured that a reference to the need for protection could be countered by a gibe about the nanny state or spoon-feeding. When the US Federal Trade Commission proposed controls on TV advertising for sugared cereals for children, for instance, the *Washington Post* accused it of becoming a national nanny (Aaker and Day, 1982: 2). Over 20 years later, when there was worldwide attention on childhood obesity and, once again, attention of the mismatch between desirable dietary intake and what is advertised and targeted at children, the same argument was used by the food industry. 'Nanny state', 'unwarranted intrusion on liberties', the 'right to be unhealthy', all these notions were marshalled to attack health campaigners (Brownell and Horgen, 2004; Hastings et al., 2003; Nestle, 2002).

The notion of empowerment can be an excuse for ignoring the unequal terrain: knowledgeable company versus atomized, under-resourced and under-educated individual consumer and can enshrine an individualized notion of the consumer and his or her rights. Even before late 20th-century's unprecedented burst of consumption, the dream of Redfern, an early champion of consumers from within the Co-operative movement (arguably the first movement to take the risk of institutionalized victimhood seriously) was that consumers would unite co-operatively and organize politically. The only way, Redfern and his co-thinkers argued, for consumers to avoid victimhood is to foster a collective consumer experience (Redfern, 1920: 55). But who could do this organizing? The Co-operative movement said: consumers should combine and do it themselves, by owning the means of production. By the second half of the 20th-century, this model was on the wane, surviving more as 'light' rather than 'deep' co-operation. Vance Packard had unpicked why: the appeal was to own things oneself; consumption as private affair gave greatest pleasure. Yet victimhood remained a likely outcome. Complaints to the state, not just business, meant that recourse to compensation or 'getting one's rights' was necessary to retain trust in trading systems. In the UK, attempts to provide pre-shopping advice for consumers, such as the Consumer Advice Centres in the 1970s, were premised upon a welfare state notion of the relationship between consumer and the state, with the public sector acting on behalf of the consumer because sufficient redress could not be achieved without support from the state. These centres were designed to instil greater self-assertion into the consumer, but in practice most of their work was dealing with consumer complaints and in mediating on behalf of consumers (Cranston, 1979). In terms the early Fabians would have applauded, but Redfern would have been wary of – the Co-operative Consumer movement preferring autonomous consumer action

(Thompson, 1994) – the Consumer Advice Centres were the result of demands being made of the state, both nationally and locally, to support and protect the consumer. This innovation was cut short by the election of Mrs Thatcher's government in 1979 and there was a major reworking of the relationship between the state, supply chain and consumer (see Chapter 10, 'The Consumer as Citizen'). This is still unfolding. Under New Labour, the compact owed more to US philosopher John Rawls' focus on rights and responsibilities (Rawls, 1971) than to neo-liberalism's doctrinal conception of market relationships. The new 'social Europe' model is that business is to be encouraged but that consumers have rights too, particularly to safety and information. Both have responsibilities. Indeed, one source of neo-conservative distaste on both sides of the Atlantic for the European Union (EU) is that it is perceived as being the fount of too much meddling interference in the name of consumer protection and that there is excessive regulation on labelling, product standards, safety, recycling, competition and more.

Despite such political divides over how they define and approach the consumer as victim, all political ideologies concede that victimhood exists, a function of consumer society. No wonder, then, that consumer protection is a theme that unites all waves of consumer activist work, mainstream and fringe (Best, 1981; Nadel, 1971). The theme is built into laws and cultures worldwide for two reasons. First, even the most doctrinaire proponents of the advantages of market economics for consumers accept that there can be market failures due to the emergence of oligopolies (monopoly), imperfect information and barriers to entry. In addition, consumers can be disenfranchized due to poverty (not strictly a market failure) and poor access. To take one of these causes of market failure, monopoly, today's globalizing economy poses new challenges for consumer rights due to the emergence of hugely powerful corporations, which already have awesome market share and influence over relatively weak global institutions. As we shall see later, in the 20th-century there was a persistent thread of individual consumer action against corporations at the national level, but the track record of concerted consumer action on an international level has yet to emerge on a routine basis (for some exceptions see Smith (1990) and also the Chapters 8 and 9, 'The Consumer as Rebel' and 'The Consumer as Activist'). As we argue in the final chapter, the ramifications of the emerging global economy suggest new patterns as well as a new volatility in consumer behaviour – what we refer to as unmanageability. Already we can note that a culture of victimization can emerge with surprising speed and vengeance. In the UK, for instance, public outcry against 'excessive' profits and high pay and share remunerations for senior managers in newly privatized public utilities emerged in the mid 1990s and runs to this day, only a few years after there had been hardly a warning or thought of such consumer 'injustice' when the utilities were being sold off. The sell-off went through relatively quietly, to the pleasure of market ideologues, who were left perplexed by the U-turn in public mores a short space of time later. Even in commercial sectors famous for their market efficiency and consumer choice, such as food retailing, there can be concerns at the marginalization of large sections of consumers (Dowler et al., 2001; Raven et al., 1995). Victimization and volatility are new bedfellows.

The second reason consumer protection is so pervasive is that, as long as there have been commercial transactions, there has been the possibility of defrauding or harming the purchaser. Trading standards laws go back centuries; and in civilizations where there are no written rules, there is custom and practice to similar effect (Douglas and Isherwood, 1978; Evans-Pritchard, 1940). Today, defrauding the consumer may occur via products and in locations unimaginable even decades ago. With global supply chains and use of the Internet, the potential for far-away fraud or malpractice is considerable. But often the process that renders the consumer into a victim follows well-established patterns. Shopping is a complex process, involving considerable sums, let alone emotional investment, from the individual's point of view. The UK's Molony Committee, reporting in the 1960s, as the post-war consumer society got up to speed, recognized this new vulnerability for modern consumers in language that today sounds patronising:

> Whereas the consumer of fifty years ago needed only a reasonable modicum of skill and knowledge to recognise the composition of the goods on offer and their manner of production, and to assess their quality and fitness for his particular purpose, the consumer of today finds it difficult if not impossible to do. It is only in the laboratory that the fibre content of a piece of modern cloth can be determined with certainty. The range of timbers from which furniture is made (many of them unknown to the general public twenty years ago) has increased vastly, and the methods of furniture manufacture have been materially changed in a number of ways. The uppers of shoes may be cemented, instead of sewn to the soles, which in turn may be made of synthetic materials instead of leather. Properly utilised, these and a hundred other new materials and manufacturing method may be of great advantage; employed without regard to their limitations or placed in the hands of an ill-informed purchaser, they may prove worthless. (Board of Trade (UK), 1962: para. 41)

You buy a car, and find it was stolen; a food sold as pure turns out to be adulterated or contaminated; a washing machine advertised as a best buy breaks down; a medicine turns out to have hidden side-effects; a quiet package holiday in the Mediterranean turns out to be a noisy nightmare next to a disco; a warranty turns out to exclude most eventualities in the small print; a repair contract costs much and delivers little; and so on. The legal profession as well as media consumer programmes prosper on the back of such daily victimization (Ramsay, 1989).

Herrmann has argued that consumer movements since the late 19th-century have emerged always in reaction to:

> three persisting problem areas: (1) ill-considered applications of new technology which result in dangerous or unreliable products, (2) changing conceptions of the social responsibilities of business, and (3) the operations of a dishonest fringe and the occasional lapses of others in the business community. (Hermann, 1982: 31)

Organized consumer activism is thus often a reactive social force (see Chapter 9, 'The Consumer as Activist'). Consumers are thus inevitably on the defensive; they respond and react to events and changed circumstances where other interests dominate, whatever the rhetoric of the market. Specialist consumer research, as well as coverage of consumer affairs in the media, reinforces this view repeatedly. Consumer experience incorporates widespread victimhood, not just in faulty goods, but also service. Early in the formulation of its consumer protection policy, the EU's then Consumer Policy Service, for instance, commissioned a study of after-sales service and consumer guarantees. This study explored 800 consumer complaints in Germany, Spain, France, Italy, Greece, Ireland, Netherlands and Portugal and found that national laws gave consumers weak rights of redress if there was poor after-sales service (BEUC, 1994). Complaints included failure to get replacement goods if they were faulty, failure to accept guarantees and responsibility being passed from the retailer to manufacturers, and so on. Now, the EU has a whole Directorate-General (that is, ministry) dedicated to consumer affairs and health – DG SANCO. Consumer protection law is deemed often best set at European level, rather than by each member state on its own, because products are more rarely made completely from one country and certainly seek cross-border markets. This work ranges from labelling to contracts and compliance, setting structures that enable consumers to seek redress and minimise risks. Announcing an ambitious programme of work up to 2013, DG SANCO pronounced that its purpose was to 'protect citizens from risks and threats which are beyond the control of individuals and that cannot be effectively tackled by individual Member States [...] and to increase the ability of citizens to take better decisions about their health and consumer interests' (CEC, 2005: 3).

The goal is for consumers to achieve fairness within the marketplace, whether this be for products or health and well-being. The goal to curb illicit trade, unfair practices or substandard quality is usually widely supported by industry; no-one wants to be seen to be implicitly defrauding the consumer. But the impact of regulations that deliver those ideals tends to be more contentious, with business nervous about being targeted, whether the law's powers are proportionate to their impact, and whether self-regulation might not be better than regulation (Confederation of British Industry, 2002; DG SANCO, 2005).

If the European Commission (EC) was undergoing tortuous negotiations for years over consumer protection in Europe, this had in theory been introduced decades earlier in the USA. But the tensions were not similar. Mark Nadel's study of the political negotiations in Congress over US consumer protection suggests that often, but by no means always, new law has been introduced or tightened up only after a scandal, a whistle-blowing or an exposé, broken by a watchdog organization or journalist (Nadel, 1971: 143). Two of his three case studies were famous scandals – the thalidomide tragedy led to amendments to US food and drug law, as did the shoddy treatment of Ralph Nader, the consumer advocate, after he exposed General Motors on the safety of one of its models. The mass media thrive on such stories, which provide a perfect combination of personal interest, collective experience and the victim's humiliation or suffering. The story is often crowned with a happy outcome, if the programme researchers have done their work and can force a recalcitrant firm or official or institution to make amends while they are in turn publicly humiliated. Readers and viewers sigh to themselves, 'There but for the grace of God, go I.' This makes for perfect TV, but hardly changes the ground rules of consuming experience; if anything, it can accentuate the worry and victimization for consumers.

Companies are increasingly sophisticated in how to respond to such media exposé. The sugar still gets put into babies drinks and rots teeth, but a new 'sugar-free' drink is brought on to the market. In this way, a victim story has helped create a new niche product. It also places the responsibility on the consumer by making it his or her choice whether to purchase the old product. Blame is now placed squarely on the victim. 'If you care about your children's teeth, why did you not purchase our sugar-free brand?'

This pattern of exposé, followed by public outrage, legal intervention, modification by case law, cultural acceptance, has been witnessed in most affluent consumer societies. The attention and glamour in consumer circles centres on the exposé rather than the follow-up, which is where commerce can erode the gain, or side-step the motive behind the new legislation, setting up the conditions for new exposés, and so on. This dynamic has been common in most main product markets, from houses to cars to food. US legislation and public interest in food quality has been invigorated by endless best-selling books, since the publication of exposés like Upton Sinclair's *The Jungle* in the 1900s (Sinclair, 1985[1906]) and Kallet and Schlink's *100,000,000 Guinea Pigs* in the 1930s. Such exposes appeal to all social classes and fractions. In Britain, the struggle for consumer protection through legislation can be traced still further back. Frederick Accum prefaced his famous exposé of systematic food adulteration in 1820 with the observation that the practice of adulteration affected all classes, all people. The appeal to consensus did Accum little good, as he was ultimately hounded out of Britain, having made powerful enemies with his publications. His science was not disproven; instead his powerful enemies relished it when he was accused of stealing pages of books from the Royal Institution, though it was never clarified whether this happened. His departure just a year after his 1820 treatise set back the consumers' cause by three decades, until Thomas Wakley and Arthur Hassall and the journal *The Lancet* took up where Accum had been cut short (Coley, 2005).

In most mature capitalist societies, by the mid 20th-century a platform of consumer protection laws and services were in place. There is no shortage of provisions aimed at protecting the consumer, yet the effectiveness of these provisions at the structural level is highly variable. Why is this? In part, as we noted earlier in the case of the EU, this is because changes at the state level require different powers and responsibilities. In part, it is because innovations create new problems; this was the case with the arrival of e-commerce, the selling and buying of goods using the Internet. The law is always having to catch up. On top of these reasons, the individualized nature of modern consumption adds existential angst; the individual consumer's plight is his or her problem alone. Enabling consumers to apply their weight collectively is a challenge of Atlas-like proportions for the consumer movement. While one consumer may feel sympathy for another's plight, as shown on television, he or she is not likely to take up cudgels on their behalf unless there are exceptional circumstances. A major scandal, for example, broke out in the 1990s over the British pension industry; millions of consumers had been encouraged to opt out of established, relatively secure state schemes, which the government wanted to phase out, and to take out private pensions. There was little support from those unaffected when these private schemes did not live up to the promise. Whose responsibility was this? A report on private pensions in the UK by the Securities and Investment Board (SIB) in 1994 detailed the poor state of control over the self-regulated private pensions sales system (SIB, 1993). A decade on, the pensions mis-selling saga continued. In theory there was some redress, but in practice the entire edifice of contributions to private pensions had been weakened by turmoil in the world's stock exchanges. If pensions are invested in stocks, when these go down in value, there is a shortfall. What looked like being a 'bad apple' in the 1990s, looked more like being endemic rot in the 2000s. When such structural problems emerge, some turn to the state for protection. On the other hand, others argue that this abuses the functions of the state; the state should not bale out poor deals but stick to protecting people's rights in the marketplace. Not for the first or last time, consumers can be beautifully divided.

One occasion when public tolerance of the status quo was overcome and consumers were united was the international campaign to remove the residues of a particular pesticide from apple juice and apples in 1989. A combination of environmentalists and media stars formed alliances like Mothers and Others for Safe Food in the US and Parents for Safe Food in the UK and Australia and forced the withdrawal of the product almost everywhere in the world (Taylor and Taylor, 1990). This campaign was effective in part because it was short and its target defined and clear. With bigger goals such as raising the standard of living of Africa to enable its people to consume adequately, called for by the 'End Poverty Now' campaign – a combination of rock concerts and political lobbying of the G-8 meetings in July 2005 – the measurement of success is harder. Judgments divide about whether raising awareness works or whether such media festivals are the ultimate in consumerist spectacle.

Dimensions of Victimhood and Globalization

There is a qualitative difference between the harm done to individual consumers by inadequate or dangerous goods and the generalized damage inflicted on future generations and the planet by the wanton consumerism and pollution of their forebears. These represent different forms of victimhood. One is individual, the other is collective; one is short-term, the other is long-term. Nor do the problems confronted by consumers in the Third World, where old-style adulteration of food and the sale of products which have been banned in other countries pose continuing and, from a Western perspective, extra hazards, and those of the First World necessarily coincide. The problems of consumers in all three dimensions – personal/ collective; present/future; First World/ Third World – are exacerbated by the globalization of capital and the considerable difficulty of product regulation across international borders.

Until recently, in affluent economies, first, legal provisions in what the consumer can expect from a commercial transaction and second, fear of media exposé have curbed the worst excesses. Today, however, the mechanisms for legislation to counteract global fraud and the systematic long-term damage to the interests of consumers or the environment across national boundaries are vague or non-existent. Not only redress for individual victims, but collective measures to protect consumers internationally and the future are severely hampered. The new globalized economy constrains justice for consumers to the individual level, when often what is needed is action at the collective level. Take, for example, the failure of Enron in the USA in 2001 or the Bank of Credit and Commerce International (BCCI) in 1991, a bank with heavy investments and drawings by ethnic minorities in both the USA and UK (Bingham, 1992; McLean and Elkind, 2004). Both these enormous collapses exposed bribery, corruption, shady deals, false accounting, top-level complicity, and enquiries illustrated the short-comings of consumer protection across national boundaries. National systems of financial scrutiny were not up to the task of monitoring complex international financial transactions. As a result, the short-coming of regulatory controls and the inadequacies of consumer protection were exposed. Indeed, the long-established and standard consumer movement position on competition policy (John, 1994; Locke, 1994) which includes seeking better representation on regulatory, monitoring and advisory bodies (Whitworth, 1994) is probably inadequate for dealing with problems posed by the power and speed of global transactions in the new world order. In a global production and distribution system, the trader, rather than the consumer, is sovereign. Consumers International, the alliance of consumer organizations has understandably tried to balance the contradiction between being in favour of trade liberalization but wary about its downsides. This ambivalence came to a head in the heated debates over what line to take towards the GATT negotiations in the early 1990s (International Organization of Consumers' Unions, 1993; National Consumer Council (UK), 1993) Although generally supportive, Consumers International (CI) quickly recognized that it 'has strengthened the hand of the transnational corporation' in competition policy (Evans, 1990: 96). CI accepts market systems and seeks international agency collaboration to prevent worse excesses, but it worries that the 'power of transnational corporations (TNCs) threatens market diversity and competition by cramping domestic production, investment and innovation, particularly in developing countries' (Consumers International, 2005: 1).

Dissatisfaction, Victimization and Consumer Protection

In marketing terms, the notion of being a victim almost does not exist. Marketing is about putting information before the consumer; it does not make people consume. It certainly does not want to portray consumers as victims if it is simultaneously trying to sell to them the notion that they can choose. When and if things go wrong, there is always the language of consumer irrationality to fall back on. Business is rational, its customers unpredictable. The marketing task, therefore, is to plot the predictability of the unpredictable, and to lay down the rules of how to handle what might seem random (O'Shaughnessy, 1987: 83ff.). Shopping is an irrational pursuit that the business framework or home economist or consumer activist has to rationalize. To the marketer, there are just pre- and post-purchase satisfaction and dissatisfaction ratings. The entire model can be seen as elitist (Andreasen, 1982), but there is nothing callous about this categorization; far from it. The good firm knows that if it can get its dissatisfaction rating down, a repeat purchase is on the cards; this is why retailers and manufacturers invest in customer satisfaction and tracker polls. Retaining the customer generally is a cheap, but none-too-easy form of marketing, which is why in the USA car manufacturers await the 'Power Report', a regularly updated ranking of makes and models by users, with some trepidation. Founded in the 1960s, J.D. Power Associates began with consumer ratings of cars, but expanded to other products and services (Loudon and Della Bitta, 1993).

Those marketing texts that review 'postdecision regret' (Engel et al., 1990: 544) tend to rely upon a psychological model of the consumer as suffering from cognitive dissonance, a disequilibrium of attitude. More recently, marketing textbooks have adopted the language of risk assessment, whereby every purchase can be assessed for the risk it carries. Risk assessment is being used by today's corporations, particularly in high-profile areas such as agrochemicals and nuclear industries, to counter consumer claims that they have been turned into unwitting victims. They claim that the every form of consumption carries a risk. It quickly follows that consumers ought to be prepared to carry some risk. Risk assessment for today's management serves the same function that many psychological models from the 1950s did: it allows the enterprise to decide what is good (or bad) for the consumer while at the same time blaming the victim whenever things go wrong. It thus become easy to scorn the consumer who rejects an infinitesimal risk. Writing in the business magazine *Fortune*, Guzzardi scoffed at the 'mindless pursuit of safety':

> Now ascending among the many blessings that the citizenry expects of government in our society is that flower, safety. Popular demand for this latest entitlement has become practically a national frenzy, and the rush is on to give us full protection from those former-friends-turned-enemies, the myriad products and conveniences and adornments of the industrial age. (Guzzardi, 1982: 365)

This pursuit, he argued, was 'dangerous' (sic) and Guzzardi proceeded to launch an attack on the US Food and Drug Administration and the Federal Trade Commission. Rigid standards can be bad for business if imposed from outside and to unrealizable degrees, he argued, an appeal reiterated in defence of market power over the decades.

To the consumer, satisfaction and dissatisfaction are at two ends of a continuum measuring outcome compared to expectation. Yet whether people complain is not easily predicted from psychological models. They may be more or less passive, more or less direct to the maker and seller. Singh produced a typology of dissatisfaction response: passives, irates, voicers and activists (Singh, 1990). Complainers in the USA, as everywhere, tend to be people from higher socio-economic classes.

From the marketing perspective, publicized complaints are bad for brand image, but equally, retailers may use 'money back if dissatisfied' promises as an active part of their marketing strategy. Since brands add extra value to a product, complaints are tarnish, so the seller or maker is generally encouraged to clarify and tighten up procedures on the following: information to customers, guarantees, after-sales service and assistance, speed of response to complaints, and so on (Loudon and DellaBitta, 1993: 575ff.). But for the consumer, the welter of warranties can themselves become an additional burden. In the UK, for instance, homeowners constantly complain about being the victims of unscrupulous installation and repair tradesmen, Warranties to guarantee repairs can be expensive. The consumer can be duped when thinking she or he is doing the sensible thing.

In UK law, prior to amendments under EU law, consumers were protected when buying goods by the Sale of Goods Act 1979, which was elegant and simple. It stated that goods must be 'of satisfactory quality', that is, free from defects unless the purchasers have been informed about them (for example, the good is shop-soiled); be 'fit for the purpose', that is, the computer purchased was actually a computer not a toy; and 'as described', that is, if the shirt was advertised or labelled as cotton, it should be just that. The law required goods to be free from even minor defects and of an appearance and finish reasonably to be expected. For services, the law states that they should be done with reasonable care and skill, within a reasonable time and at a reasonable charge, if no price was fixed in advance (Office of Fair Trading (UK), 1994: 4–10). Other laws add to and strengthen this basic provision. The Supply of Goods and Services Act 1982, for instance, would give a consumer who had poor building repairs done more rights than a guarantee backed by insurance. For the complainant, however, to have to take recourse to law is an additional burden, and as was evidenced by the reviews of the Consumer Advice Centres operating in the 1970s, consumer grievance action was and is an overwhelmingly middle-class pursuit. The key issue here, note, is the difficulty any consumer would have to define what is or is not reasonable. No wonder many consumers feel that choosing a builder to repair their roof or a garage to fix their car or a plumber to unblock their drains is akin to entering a minefield. To counter this scepticism, a new legal framework was introduced, stemming from EU debates. In the UK, this became the 1987 Consumer Protection Act, which provided a definition of product liability and consumer safety protection, attempting to balance consumer rights with producer liabilities. But producers could avoid liability if they could prove that they had shown due diligence, that is had not knowingly sold unfit products. If, for example, a defect emerged after the product had been sold and the seller had sold it in good faith, there would be no liability (Department of Trade and Industry (UK), 2005).

US Protection

One of the paradoxes noted by many observers of contemporary consumer activism is that it appeals to the middle-classes individually, but can only be effective if practised collectively by a broad alliance of forces. As Nadel, the author of an early and still important study of US consumer protection, argued, the success of legislative pressure has depended on how well organized the forces are across public interest groups, the Executive and Congress. US consumer protection has its roots in social processes that began after the Civil War and patterns were set then that persist to this day (Nadel, 1971: 5–6). Farmers and railroad companies had united to promote 150 laws to facilitate railways between 1868 and 1887, but abuses, such as discriminatory pricing and excessive rates, led to a backlash and an Interstate Commerce Act of 1887 was enacted to ban such practices, becoming a landmark bill in the development of [US] consumer protection. The passage of the Pure Food and Drug Act of 1906, following the publication of Sinclair's book *The Jungle* (1985[1906]), symbolizes the beginnings of the emergence of consumers as a political force in the USA. This legislative advance came after years of campaigning for firmer consumer protection, as Nadel shows, from inside the state machinery by people like Dr Harvey Wiley, chief chemist for the US Department of Agriculture (a role later filled by Rexford Tugwell, Assistant Secretary at the USDA).

Sinclair's book, often and justly cited, in fact brought to a head years of bubbling and poorly articulated discontent (Tiemstra, 1992). Hermann shows that the 1906 Pure Food and Drug Act was enacted only after years of effort beforehand and strong pressure from a powerful President Theodore Roosevelt. Sinclair's book was the final catalyst (Hermann, 1982). The new law enshrined the case for inspectors to act in the interests of consumers, implicitly acknowledging the principle that individual consumers need protecting and that the market alone did not offer adequate safeguards. This principle was severely undermined by the end of the 20th-century under the onslaught of the New Right, which successfully promoted the argument that self-regulation and the market mechanism effectively ruled out the need for state intervention to protect the consumer, although still recognizing the case for anti-fraud laws. In general, the Right has argued, consumers can protect themselves through the market (Nadel, 1971: 6ff.). The culture to come was flagged by Reagan, the then Governor of California in the late 1960s, when he advised consumers to rely on manufacturers' handbooks rather the report of consumer organizations to guide their purchasing (Nadel, 1971: 238).

Consumer protection in the USA was thus a meeting point – Nadel calls it 'the lowest common denominator' – between different classes of people (Nadel, 1971: 15). As Reich argued, it came in three waves, 1887–1914, 1927–39 and 1962–78 (Reich, 1981). Tiemstra argues that, in every instance, these waves of regulation were driven by a 'long-standing and uniquely American suspicion of large, powerful institutions, whether economic or political', the belief that the little guy can be crushed (Tiemstra, 1992: 3). If the first regulation was promoted at the turn of the century by the Progressives, the middle phase was identified with Roosevelt's New Deal. This period instituted not inspectors, but boards and councils. Roosevelt created the Consumers' Advisory Board in the 1930s with the best intentions of protecting the consumer, but its purpose was undermined by the lack of any significant organized consumer movement to give it bite. The state processes and structures were well in advance of an effective, organized, articulate movement's capacity to use them, just as in the area of labour legislation, Roosevelt's Wagner Act was ahead of the labour movement's ability to take full advantage of its provisions (Millis and Brown, 1950).

By the 1960s, Nader and his Raiders argued that these state provisions had atrophied to such an extent that they criticized them as morally corrupt and against the citizen's interest (Gorey, 1975). The third new regulatory phase:

> grew from a view that there was a need to redress the imbalance in the marketplace between buyer and seller. It was manifested in John Kennedy's 1962 statement of consumer rights [...]; it was symbolized by the behavior of the nation's largest corporation (General Motors) toward an individual (Ralph Nader) sharply critical of that firm.

> Conditions were right for the [consumer] movement. The increased complexity of products, the broadening of service channels and depersonalization of shopping, the growth of consumer services (of which consumers have more difficulty in judging quality), the broader availability of the 'material things of life' to those with newly expanded discretionary buying power; and other factors – all combined to create strong 'consumer demand' for ideas and action that would help the public obtain a better deal in the marketplace. (Bloom and Greyser, 1981: 4)

Business, however, took a very different view of state provisions, especially of the most recent regulatory wave initiated in response to pressure from Nader and other consumer organizations. It argued that these provisions amounted to an infringement of its liberty to make and sell as it wanted. Fernstrom called this transition of US regulatory policy an evolution from *caveat emptor* (buyer beware) to *caveat vendor* (seller beware), and suggested that the evolution went to a point where business leaders felt 'government had totally usurped the consumer's responsibility to think for or protect himself' (Fernstrom, 1984: 1–3).

What, then, has been the effect of these phases of regulation designed to protect the consumer from falling into victimhood? Nadel's assessment is clear. In general, to be effective in preventing consumers becoming victims, there needs to be a combination of forces, inside and outside the legislature: well-briefed, 'on-side' journalists, individualists in Congress, public goodwill and well-researched activists (see Chapter 9, 'The Consumer as Activist'). Nadel found occasions when such combinations occurred, but often pioneering work was done despite the absence of this combination. The picture he paints for the USA is of consumers en masse as too disparate, too individualized; consumer professionals too small in number; and Congress more of a follower than an initiator. While 17 Acts were initiated in the 1962–68 period that he studied, most were the fruits of deter-mined individuals in and out of Congress. Nadel's analysis is sobering. Consumer protection is not so much a forward march halted, as a halting march forward.

Taking this three-phase model of US consumer protection, it could be argued that a new fourth phase is emerging. The USA, like other mature capitalist econo-mies, has entered new cross-border trading agreements – not just the GATT/ WTO (World Trade Organization), but also the North American Free Trade Agreement (NAFTA). There are moves to turn this into a pan-Americas free trade agreement. Consumer protection, to be effective, has to send messages back down the supply chain and to build in improvements at source. This becomes more complex – not impossible but more complex – in complicated supply chains. If control remains within one company, this can be managed, but retailers selling thousands of prod-ucts from many sources, themselves combining parts from others, are perhaps inevitably more exposed to product liability. This is why the business world is now focused on delivering traceability. Being able to track where a product, part, or fault comes from is essential to retain consumer confidence. A management goal – Efficient Consumer Response (ECR) – is in part driven by a desire to cut costs and increase efficiency, but it also raises exposure to consumer victimhood. The new traceability technologies that electronically tag products using radio frequency identification (RFID) is replacing decades-old but familiar bar-coding technology (Brown, 1997). But according to a 2004 survey by CapGemini, business consultants, consumers can be nervous about whom this serves and who is tracking what (O'Connor, 2005).

Can the Law Prevent Victims or is the Market Enough?

Experience suggests that in complex markets consumers find themselves in con-stant danger of becoming victims to unscrupulous traders. Two questions follow. First, is it possible for the consumers to be victims even if the traders stay within the limits of the law? Second, can any law by itself offer adequate protection to consumers? In developed countries, protection relies upon a combination of statutes and competition in the market. The crucial issue, as we have suggested throughout this book, is the balance of forces between consumer, state and com-panies. Reviews of the value of the law seem agreed that the law, however strong or weak in relation to consumers, cannot cover the infinite diversity of eventual-ities facing consumers in the marketplace (Best, 1981; Cranston, 1984: 399–407).

Legislative bodies have always been ambivalent on whether to offer protection to consumers or whether to allow the market mechanism itself to obviate all but the worst excesses. According to the latter view, the markets sooner or later will eliminate inferior, uncompetitive or inefficient traders who offer less value for money to consumers. The EU, for instance, did not take a stance on consumer protection until the Paris summit of 1972, when it set up the first consumer protection services, housed with both nuclear and environmental protection services. For a decade or so, these services attempted to institute common rules and standards to little effect, for instance spending years trying to determine a common position on food additives and the composition of jam. With the Single European Act 1986, which ushered in the end of barriers to trade between the 12 member states, the EC took an entirely different tack, which combined a permissive approach to business with a minimalist aim of 'the removal of fear' for consumers, designed to remove unnecessary risks (Lawlor, 1988). By this time, Europe was placing its faith increasingly on the market mechanism.

Ross Cranston, author of the classic treatise on UK consumer law, who later became UK Solicitor General, was scathing about this kind of approach. 'It is difficult to take seriously the argument that the market will further consumer protection', he concluded (Cranston, 1984: 399). He argued that consumer protection is too easily a rhetorical afterthought, and that consumers' interests need to be built into the regulatory framework from the start. Echoing Nadel's findings about the USA, we could note that no law on its own can fully protect consumers; it takes a culture. For Cranston, what was needed was a half-way house between total market laissez-faire, with its deregulation and lack of consumer protection, and total state *dirigisme*, with its heavy hand and inflexibility. While expressing opposition to deregulation at the hands of free traders, Cranston felt that some self-regulation in the form of codes of conduct can be useful, and to include these in law in every case would be cumbersome (Cranston, 1984: 40–1). The problems stem from those codes that patently do not work or that are highly contentious, such as the codes on advertising practice. Emotions run high when children are concerned, almost always. In these cases, Cranston argued, legal statute is a better alternative: clearer, enforceable and transparent (Cranston, 1984: 55–9).

Not all commentators agree with Cranston. Penz, for example, while recognizing that consumers are vulnerable in the marketplace, seeks to attribute this vulnerability to their own needs, wants and inadequate self-knowledge. Protection is therefore limited from the start, though consumer grievances may be exacerbated by factors like market inefficiencies, the power of the corporations and techniques of mass manipulation such as advertising (Penz, 1986: 79). Margolius has highlighted another factor that adds to consumer grievances in complex markets. Consumers are burdened by both not having enough information and having information overload (Margolius, 1982). Echoing Baudrillard, he argues that they are bombarded with information from morning to night and face considerable difficulty in discriminating between stimuli, between fact and fiction. A good illustration of the confusion caused by the modern media is the current use of so-called advertorials and infomercials, where the boundary between news and advertising or commercial propaganda is dissolved; sometimes this is made clear to the reader, for instance by the magazine writing 'Promotion' at the top of the page; sometimes not. The editorial process thereby becomes less an expression of the journalists' views or an account of facts than the painting of a company or a product in favourable light. This is now beginning to cause some concern, even among media enthusiasts (Parsons and Rotfeld, 1990).

Best conducted a review of 2419 unsatisfactory consumer purchases, 132 of which were studied in detail, for Nader's Center for Study of Responsive Law in the USA. His assessment started cryptically: 'Do Americans get value in the marketplace? Sometimes.' (Best, 1981: 3). In extreme cases, consumers were indeed victims, having been blatantly swindled, but even then Best had difficulty in ascertaining the facts. This was more pronounced when the problem was poor goods or services. He found that many consumers were very reluctant to report instances of victimization (Best, 1981: 31). This suggests that many consumers do not want to appear unstreetwise or foolish and therefore take the blame for bad service or goods on themselves; victimization is thus internalized. Ironically, while British commentators like Pirie, head of the Adam Smith Institute, see American consumers as highly vociferous in defence of their rights (Pirie, 1991), Americans too have been criticized for 'accepting low quality and unfair prices' and one commentator quoted by Best (1981: 32) looked fondly towards Europe, arguing that it harboured a healthier culture of bargaining, comparing and seeking the best brand!

Best's research, however, goes well beyond the consumers' blaming themselves. He found cases of intimidation, retaliation by sellers, poor access to the law, and a lack of support for consumer victims for which he put the responsibility firmly with business, with a legal system more interested in its own strictures than justice, and with a culture of victim blaming. This latter feature is a 'common business technique for rejecting consumer complaints' (Best, 1981: 74) and is commonly employed from humble transactions to serious matters of life and death. Best cites a man whose expensive shirts were lost by a laundry being told that he shouldn't have sent such good ones to it, and this classic: 'They cut the legs off my new sofa when they came to deliver it. They should have measured the front door better' (Best, 1981: 5).

Blaming the victim is a convenient smoke-screen for industry to distract responsibility for its own actions and occurs overtly and covertly (Crawford, 1977). The former occurs, for example, when food poisoning or a national epidemic is blamed on poor hygiene by consumers in their own homes. Covert victim blaming occurs when an explanation or even an apology offered by a company insinuates that the consumer played a part in his or her own downfall. Despite such processes of passing the buck, which inevitably leads to apprehension about the market and business, one much-quoted study found that consumers did not expect to get everything their own way, nor did they want business to be on the defensive; they wanted a balance of forces. Consumers generally operated a 'buyer beware' approach, learned from the 1960s and 1970s consumer activist campaigns, without becoming excessively paranoid (Greyser and Diamond, 1983).

All in all, therefore, most consumers are realistic that they can expect only a modest amount of protection from the law or the mechanism of the market, and that victimhood looms at every turn of consumption. This is a far cry from the position of the free marketers of the Chicago School, criticized by Cranston as failing 'to take adequate account of the severe deficiencies in the operation of the market and common law system. Based on questionable premises, the [Chicago School's] conclusions are demonstrably false' (Cranston, 1984: 23). He argues that the effectiveness of the law depends crucially on the consumer's knowledge of it and their capacity to resort to agencies with teeth, but unfortunately, this is far from the case. Consumers are often ignorant of their rights, enduring their victimhood and writing off their losses. Often they do not even know that they are subsidizing business by accepting sub-standard goods, or by making early payments, or accepting allowances that round off figures to the seller's advantage. Overcharging a small amount on a systematic basis can amount to significant extra profit. In spite of all these reservations, Cranston still proposes that 'social engineering within the system is worthwhile and can be achieved' (Cranston, 1984: 8). The function of the law is to lay out the framework of rules and obligations, sanctions and rights. This it may do admirably, but unless consumers know their rights, are prepared to fight for them and have suitable institutional backing, the law by itself can achieve little.

Consumers across National Boundaries

Cranston argues that there are two clusters of factors affecting consumer protection: structural ones, such as the law or government policy and individual factors such as information, income and position in the world. Third World consumers are particularly at risk from structural forces. To them, the market mechanism offers virtually no protection and their own governments almost as little. Cranston cites the massive international campaign to restrict the sale of powdered milk for babies in developing countries and points out that Papua New Guinea was a rare instance where legislative action was taken prohibiting advertisements that encouraged bottle feeding in 1977. The moral of the tale was that only national governments can control the actions of transnational corporations, yet they rarely do (Cranston, 1984: 9–10). Another study examining the position of consumers in the Third World reinforces this assessment, arguing that those consumers are especially at risk from pressures to consume, such as advertising associated with the lifestyle of developed countries (James, 1983: 159). They also suffer additional victimization when companies and states in developed countries act with double standards, setting tough rules for the home market but not for export. In this way, produce of uncertain standard is kept out, while hazardous products, such as pesticides banned at home, continue to be exported abroad (Bull, 1982; Dinham, 1993; Jacobs and Dinham, 2003). Twenty years ago, the concern of pesticides campaigners was that consumers in the developed countries might then get back residues of the pesticides when eating imported food. Today, the concern is that dual standard markets have emerged: high standards for produce grown or made to be exported to affluent consumer markets, with lower standards at home in developing country markets (Barling and Lang, 2005).

The case of pesticides underlines how the protection of the individual as a consumer (and therefore eater of hazardous products), as a producer (and therefore a worker with hazardous products) and as an inhabitant of an environment (where hazardous products are dumped) are overlapping issues (Lang and Clutterbuck, 1991). The ill-effects of pesticide application are disproportionately suffered by rural inhabitants of the South. In 1990, the World Health Organization (WHO) estimated that there were a minimum of 3 million acute cases of pesticide poisoning and 20,000 unintentional deaths a year, mostly in Third World countries (UN and UNEP, 1990). Many more millions suffer as a result of pesticide use each year (Jeyarraratnam, 1990). Fifteen years later, the UN estimated some improvement in the situation. The UN Environment Programme and Food and Agriculture Organization of the UN (FAO) estimated that one to five million cases of pesticide poisoning occur every year, with 'several thousand fatalities among agricultural workers'. Mostly, these were still in developing countries which use only 25% of global pesticide production [but] ... account for a staggering 99% of the related deaths (FAO, 2004).

Consumer protection measures vary from country to country, as does the overall culture regarding consumer rights. In Sweden, there has been a long tradition of the state siding with the consumers, on the basis that producers were strong enough to look after their own interests (Johansson, 1982). Sweden developed one of the most sophisticated systems of consumer protection laws and agencies, ranging from a Public Complaints Office to a National Price and Cartel Office, as well as the celebrated Scandinavian phenomenon of the Ombudsman. The role of these officials, initially meant to investigate citizens' complaints against the government, has now been expanded to investigating consumer grievances and to assisting in achievement of fair settlements. The Scandinavian model of consumer protection is probably the most divergent from the laissez-faire model that has prevailed in the USA and UK in the 1980s and 1990s. A statement like the following is inconceivable within a culture of consumer choice:

> If a particular brand of product X is judged as the one which best meets the real needs of the consumer it is unnecessary to have alternative brands on the market, particularly since they must be inferior. To paraphrase, if Volvos are best everyone who wants a car should drive a Volvo. (Johansson, 1982: 66)

Strange as this Swedish quote may seem to contemporary Anglo-Saxon eyes, the notion of restricting choice as a measure for protecting the consumer is not far-fetched. The Seikatsu Clubs, a successful system of consumer co-operatives in Japan formed in 1965, offer their members a product range of around 600 goods, on the argument that if they are the best products and meet consumers' needs, why offer a range of 15,000 as supermarket chains do? Shigeki Maruyama of the Seikatsu Club Union in Tokyo has stated: 'We refuse to handle products if they are detrimental to the health of our members or the health of the environment' (Seikatsu Club, 2005). This questioning of whether ever-expanding choice yields increase in happiness is now being voiced in the West, too (Layard, 2005; Levett et al., 2003). The Index of Sustainable Economic Welfare (ISEW) is an attempt to benchmark welfare in a more experiential as well as material way. Applied to eight countries so far, it breaks the conventional economists' automatic link between national gross domestic product (GDP) and assumed happiness. ISEW includes non-tangibles such as unpaid domestic work, income disparities and perceptions of well-being. In the UK, ISEW rose until the 1970s but then stagnated. The UK Treasury is at the time of writing committed to produce a new ISEW-influenced range of indicators.

Self Help?

Might the era of apparently endless consumer individualization be tempered, if not replaced, by a return of the principle of co-operation among consumers? Those researching finite resources needed for consumption – minerals, energy, materials, water – increasingly debate this question (Jackson and Michaelis, 2003). If there is not more sharing, there might eventually have to be caps on consumption – through shortage if not imposition. This ecologically driven possibility lurks at the edge of mainstream policy, which still pursues more efficient consumption rather than less or shared consumption.

The contemporary dominant paradigms, based on the 'sacrifice' of personal choice, are aimed at increasing trust as well economic muscle; ever clearer feedback between producer, seller and consumer. If the notion of there being limits to consumption is key to the sustainability paradigm, the need to woo the consumer on a combination of price and quality is key to the conventional paradigm. For both, information-flow is key, but the models imply a different role for information. In the co-operative model, instead of every consumer setting out to beat a path through the marketplace jungle by him- or herself, he or she draws on the judgement of a trusted representative who can advise him or her reliably and point out obvious dangers. As soon as consumers act collectively, it is no longer necessary for each and every one of them to duplicate the Herculean task of acquiring knowledge on all market options. Despite the hyperbole surrounding choice, there are interesting examples of where restricted choice is perceived to have advantage. In European cities, car-pools are emerging as one example. Why own a car, when one can share one? Large car-pools work on a locality basis. You share a car with others in your district and merely book when you want it. French restaurants are another example. Their fixed price menu system famously offers limited choice. The chef does the big choosing as to what to cook; she or he produces a limited range and the customer selects from that. We noted above the example of the Japanese Seikatsu clubs, pockets of co-operation within a culture known for its celebratory approach to consumerism and choice. The Mountain Equipment Co-op (MEC) in Canada is another interesting case. It is a retail consumer co-operative, member owned and directed, had 2.1 million members and a (Canadian) $178 million sales turnover in 2004. To purchase from its good range of products – in the outdoor clothes and pursuits market – the buyer has to sign up to become, in effect, a co-op owner by paying Canadian $5 for lifetime membership (the same price as at the first edition of this book!). You have to be a member to buy the company's products and this entitles the consumer to vote for the Board (MEC, 2005).

The exceptionality of such examples of more co-operative consumption appears to run contrary to the entire ethos of contemporary Western consumption. As every previous chapter of this book has shown, whether as chooser or as identity-seeker, whether as communicator or as aesthete, today's consumer accords the highest value to the right to be individual. So long as this ethic persists, consumers will continue to be vulnerable and the muscle that they can exercise in the marketplace will be limited.

What Happens if Things Go Wrong?

What practical measures can consumers resort to when things go wrong? A system of small claims courts, first advocated in the USA in 1913 by Roscoe Pound, was in place in eight states and 12 cities by the 1930s (Best, 1981: 167). Their purpose was to simplify and reduce the cost of consumer complaints, yet their effectiveness was limited. Despite this, similar courts were introduced in the

UK in 1970 after a government report 'Justice out of reach' (Cranston, 1984: 88–9). After decades of experience, the consumer potential to benefit from small claims courts has been tempered by experience. It can be argued that they have been usefully colonized by business as a cheap way of collecting business debts; and they are not particularly consumer-friendly, a problem exacerbated in England and Wales by their being 'bolted on' to the County Court, with no separate rules. Small claims may often still not be worth pursuing because the cost of gathering the award can be worth more than the claim. A 1980 study of 2000 complaints found that none had used the small claims procedures against a shop or supplier (National Consumer Council (UK), 1981). In Denmark and Norway, such measures have gone one step further in reducing legal complexity and cost since the 20th-century by setting conciliation tribunals that use lawyers.

Another measure to support the wronged consumer is a system of advice, such as the Consumer Advice Centres described earlier in this chapter. Not surprisingly, their effectiveness was found to vary enormously across socioeconomic classes, the heaviest users being middle-class consumers pursuing complaints; there was little use by lower socioeconomic classes and 'at-risk groups such as the elderly, divorced, widowed and separated' (National Consumer Council (UK), 1977: 26). Yet the study found that the average cost of handling was a very modest £3 (National Consumer Council (UK), 1977: 21).

In contrast to both the British and Scandinavian approaches, which have sought pragmatic, reasonable, conciliatory measures to resolve the conflict between consumer and producer, a popular US handbook in the early 1970s with the memorable title *Sue the Bastards* advocated a high conflict approach (Matthews, 1973). Through the demand for punitive compensation from recalcitrant firms, the object is to deter bad practice and to keep firms on their toes, redressing the inequality of power in favour of consumers. Echoing Voltaire in *Candide*, it punishes one to 'encourage the others'. In spite of some spectacular awards, consumer supporters on both sides of the Atlantic have expressed deep reservations about the effectiveness of this approach on the mass of the consumers (Best, 1981: 182–93; Cranston, 1984: 402).

Generalized hypochondria?

But do consumers need supporters at all? Is it not the case that billions of consumers go out into marketplaces daily and enjoy the fruits of consumerism, hardly ever coming to grief? As the *Economist* noted in its title for a survey of food, consumers are 'Spoilt for Choice' (*Economist*, 2003). Market optimists argue that a relatively few instances of victimization in consumption are the price worth paying for choice, surely inevitable as they are in every walk of life. There is no need to blow them out of all proportion. Focusing on failures may make gripping TV, just like crime, but like crime it creates unnecessary fear in the minds of the populace. Such criticisms disregard the fact that if the market is to function as a chastising mechanism, disadvantaging unprincipled or inefficient suppliers, it requires the activities of consumer activists, testing organizations and other bodies that disseminate information and ensure that the worst excesses will be brought to light. If these checks did not exist, the market mechanism would lose its effectiveness.

To push the point further, it could be argued that by confronting failures and championing the consumer victims, organized consumer groups and media programmes succeed in making good what 'pure' markets would leave bad. Highlighting the experience of consumer victims provides necessary feedback that suppliers would otherwise too easily dismiss or be ignorant of. It is thanks to the tireless activity of campaigning consumer organizations that firms have had to accept minimum standards of service, information and quality that they would not have had to concede otherwise. This is the rationale for states supporting consumer organizations. The EU, for instance, supports the Brussels-based EU-wide umbrella body Bureau des Unions de Consomateurs (BEUC). Initially regarded as irritating and anti-corporate, many companies now welcome consumer advocates. Some even welcome regulation on both environmental and consumer protection grounds, if only as safeguards of their own reputation. 'Due diligence' means that as long as the company has done its best to meet existing standards, it cannot be blamed if there are victims elsewhere. So long as they can show that they have tried to abide by these standards and as long as they are independently monitored, they can counter criticisms levelled at them. This, rather than improved consumer transparency, is the real driver behind the huge investment in traceability in the 2000s.

Another criticism levelled at consumers parading victimhood is that modern culture cannot deal with risk. Affluent societies, goes this argument, are risk-averse. They seek risk-free pleasure. If something hurts, someone elsewhere must be to blame. The view that consumers suffer from a kind of generalized hypochondria, where the slightest threat to their health or well-being is magnified out of all proportion, is, if anything, evidence of the overwhelming powerlessness that consumers can feel when confronted by the might and sophistication of vast organizations whose resources and techniques they cannot match. Far from being quick to complain, consumers in advanced capitalist societies have tended, if anything, to give corporations the benefit of the doubt, unless major infringements are exposed (Greyser and Diamond, 1983). Consumer advocates the world over lament that consumers tend to be too pliant and can be too easily be fobbed off by excuses and rationalizations offered by the public relations and the image-making machine of corporations (Barnet and Cavanagh, 1994; Klein, 2000).

A more serious limitation of the image of the consumer as victim could be raised on the basis of the current fashion for 'quality' and 'service' as core business values. At least since the publication of Peters and Waterman's management 'bible' *In Search of Excellence* (1982), few ideas have held as powerful a grip in management thinking. Businesses devote billions a year to training their staff, to raising product safety and improving their environmental records, in order to keep the loyalty of their customers and to out-perform their competitors. A single, well-publicized case of a dissatisfied customer, a dangerous sub-standard product or one environmental disaster can be enough to undo the hard work of years of product development and image-making. From this perspective, what more protection can consumers require than that companies themselves so assiduously offer them? The company's self-interest rather than any guarantee from a 'nanny state' or a self-appointed consumer busybody is the safest base for consumer protection.

These arguments, which carry resonances of Adam Smith's butcher, brewer and baker (see 'Introduction: The Faces of the Consumer'), and ignore the difference between a company's image and the reality of its products, service and methods.

Of course, companies are concerned to present a smiling face to their customer. Of course, they train their staff to give the impression that the customer is sovereign. But for all the outpourings on quality and corporate culture, profit and raising market share remain the overpowering objective of most companies. Why else are they in business? Necessary as customers are to ensure profits, the need to cut costs and corners, increase prices and reduce service poses a constant threat to consumers.

Systematic Victimhood?

A criticism from a different political quarter can argue that consumer activists have been incorporated into consumer capitalism; they merely oil its wheels. They have become agents of a system, reformists, concentrating their fire on extreme and untypical cases of victimhood and disregarding the massive and systematic alienation of modern consumerism by allowing themselves to be sucked into the relative triviality of product quality and environmental hazards, when the key issues are, first, the inequalities of power, second, the stagnant dis/satisfaction that Western consumerism fosters and third, the despoliation of the eco-sphere upon which spiralling consumption depends. Western consumers, according to this charge, are victims not only when they get a dud deal from a corporation or inadequate information from a government body, but also every time that they place their hopes for a better future in this commodity or that. Here, we rejoin the Marcusean critique of consumer capitalism, where the consumer as victim actively colludes in his or her own oppression. By wanting goods and by having such high expectations from them, life is impoverished. People become slaves to the goods, still more to ensuring that they get the best deal. In the very act of trying to improve our lives by consuming, we submit ourselves to the forces that exacerbate our alienation (Miller, 2001; Monbiot, 2000).

The above bleak and uncompromising view can lead to patronising and arrogant attitudes, where intellectuals or organizations pontificate to the public about what is good for them. It also may play into the hands of the those who seek to flatter consumers rather than paralyse them with tales of woe. This view may also underestimate the extent to which consumers can turn the tables on victimhood by becoming rebels. This is the focus of the next chapter.

CHAPTER 8

The Consumer as Rebel

People never rebel just because they have to carry a heavy load or
because of exploitation. They don't know life without exploitation,
they don't even know that such a life exists. How can they desire
what they cannot imagine? The people will rebel only when, in a
single movement, someone tries to throw a second burden, a second
heavy bag onto their backs. The peasant will fall face down in the
mud – and then spring up and grab an ax. He'll grab an ax, my
gracious sir, not simply because he can't sustain this new burden –
he could carry it – he will rise because he feels that, in throwing the
second burden onto his back suddenly and stealthily, you have tried
to cheat him, you have treated him like an unthinking animal, you
have trampled what remains of his already strangled dignity, taken
him for an idiot who doesn't see, feel, or understand. A man doesn't
seize an ax in defence of his wallet, but in defence of his dignity.

Kapuscinski, 1983: p. 97

CORE ARGUMENTS

People can use different commodities to indicate rejection of the status
quo. For a long time, counterculture signified its opposition to dominant
ideologies by adopting particular styles of consuming and totemic
objects, such as music, cars and clothes. It is not surprising, therefore,
that opposition to consumerism itself often assumes such forms. The
recipes offered by rebellious consumption include consume with more
style, consume less, consume differently and consume not at all.
Consumerism, for its part, seeks to accommodate and incorporate such
acts of resistance. Indeed, it can be argued that all consumption trend-
setting starts as a rebellion against the status quo. We assess how deep
or shallow these challenges are. What are such rebellions against? Is the
target affluence itself, the system or marginalization of others?

This image of humans being able to use objects to express opposition to the status quo and send signals to the perceived oppressor, suggested in the excerpt from Kapuscinski above, offers a stark picture. Consumers can rebel against the world of goods, either in part or whole, and can turn their backs on conventional consumption. Depending on circumstance, they can invent their own forms of consumption, full of meaning, but in revolting, they are not just against goods but also against a set of social relations. Rebelling against products implies rebellion against social processes. This double-edged interpretation has mostly been perceived as deeply threatening to the architects and missionaries of the Fordist Deal, as outlined in this book. If consumers don't consume, there is no demand and therefore a squeeze on work; progress slows. Therefore, goes the logic, it is the consumer's duty to consume.

In this chapter we explore this image of the consumer as rebel and its implications. It is an image with many layers. Taken at face value, the image of the consumer as rebel flies in the face of the age-old wisdom, summed up in the Ancient Roman writer Juvenal's dismissive view of the Roman populace:

> They are only seriously bothered about two things – bread and circuses. (Juvenal, 1999 (AD 110–30): x, i,80)

Consumption, he was arguing, buys peace; he was writing from the point of view of rulers, of course, but he was articulating a cynical view that people will take the short-term pleasures of consumption and put them above 'higher' morals. People can be bought. Against this, there is a counterview – loudly articulated since the 1960s by one strand of Western anti-consumerism – that consumers can and should resist consumption. Consumption equals incorporation; it ties one to mainstream culture. Thus, if possessing goods from this culture signifies acceptance, it is more desirable to identify with other categories of goods, which lack the undesirable connotations. A dichotomy of 'good' versus 'bad' goods underpins rebellious consumption.

This juxtaposition – rejection versus acceptance, good versus bad – engenders rich discussions about the meaning of consumption, particularly the equation of rebellion with youth culture, youth being equated with the new. In *The Conquest of Cool*, Thomas Frank argued that what starts as resistance can easily and quickly be incorporated into consumerism:

> ... rebel youth culture remains the cultural mode of the corporate moment, used to promote not only specific products but the general idea of life in the cyber-revolution. Commercial fantasies of rebellion, liberation, and outright 'revolution' against the stultifying demands of mass society are commonplace almost to the point of invisibility in advertising, movies, and television programming. (Frank 1997: 11)

This insight that rebellion can be incorporated into consumer capitalism has been profitably explored by armies of psychologists, not least those working in and for advertising, marketing, and product development analysts. These professions have retained, and often burnished, the notion that consumption can be rebellious, but have tamed its supposed dangers. 'Come buy me; express opposition to [parents/society/school/peer group] by owning me and being seen to own me.' Rebellious consumption is 'cool'. But this message has to steer a delicate dividing line between outright rebellion and partial or quasi-rebellion, conveying some threat but not too much. If what starts as rebellious and cool becomes mass, then its radical chic can easily be lost. The function of marketing therefore is to retain the edge, to keep products that are in fact standardized looking and desired as rebellious. According to this analysis, consumer rebellion is a kind of endless round of identity rebellion, with every street cultural invention or rejection quickly picked up and turned mainstream.

In their book, *The Rebel Sell*, Joseph Heath and Andrew Potter, reject this account of consumption as rebellion (Heath and Potter, 2005; Marcuse, 1969). Far from being threatening from the outside and needing to be tamed before they can be incorporated, modern North American consumer rebels – from the 1960s hippie US counterculture to the 1990s Canadian Adbusters group, which wittily confronted the advertising industry with anti-ads or 'culture jamming' – have actually reinvigorated consumer capitalism. They are not peripheral but fundamental to consumerism. 'Culture jammers are not the first to try to break the system through consumer revolt. Countercultural rebels have been playing the same game for over forty years, and it obviously doesn't work. The counterculture was, from its very inception, intensely entrepreneurial' (www.harpercanada.com/rs/excerpt.asp). Rebellion, in Heath and Potter's account, is actually the lifeblood of consumerism. Far from being a threat, resistance is itself consumerist in that it expresses and breeds new ideas, products and ways of being. Far from the counterculture 'selling out', a diagnosis that the Frankfurt school analysis of 'incorporation' suggested, the acts of rebellion by the 1960s generation actually enabled a new wave of consumption.

> With the hippies, nothing symbolized their rejection of the 'consumerism' of American society more than love beads, Birkenstocks and the VW Beetle. Yet during the '80s, the same generation that had 'tuned in, turned on and dropped out' presided over the most significant resurgence of conspicuous consumption in American history. The hippies became yuppies. [...]
>
> The crucial point is that (contrary to rumor) the hippies did not sell out. Hippie ideology and yuppie ideology are one and the same. There simply never was any tension between the countercultural ideas that informed the '60s rebellion and the ideological requirements of the capitalist system. While there is no doubt that a cultural conflict developed between the members of the counterculture and the defenders of the older American Protestant establishment, there never was any tension between the values of the counterculture and the functional requirements of the capitalist economic system. (Heath and Potter, 2005)

Conscious or Unconscious Resistance?

Before the arrival of postmodernism, a whole generation of social critics in the 1960s and 1970s battled against consumerism, which they blamed for the disappearance of revolutionary ardour among the working-classes of Western societies. Consumerism, as the bourgeois ideology of material possessions, was readily absorbed within the Marxist view of alienated consciousness, a consciousness alienated not only in the course of commodity production, but equally by the state, the machinery of mass media and other ideological apparatuses. For Marcuse, consumerism penetrates into the unconscious mental structures, becoming the basis for a 'biological' second nature:

> The so-called consumer society and the politics of corporate capitalism have created a second nature of man which ties him libidinally and aggressively to the commodity form. The need for possessing, consuming, handling, and constantly renewing the gadgets, devices, instruments, engines, offered to and imposed upon the people, for using these wares even at the danger of one's own destruction, has become a 'biological' need ... The second nature of man thus militates against any change that would disrupt and perhaps even abolish this dependence of man on a market ever more densely filled with merchandise – abolish his existence as a consumer consuming himself in buying and selling. The needs generated by this system are thus eminently stabilizing, conservative needs: the counter-revolution anchored in the instinctual structure. (Marcuse, 1969: 11)

That generation of social critics would have found images of the consumer prevalent in the 1980s highly problematic. For them, consumers were massively manipulated, passive hostages to the capitalist logic of production; mass consumption was frequently seen (as in the quote above) as a smoke-screen, a euphemism for mass production and mass alienation (Williams, 1976).

Throughout the 1980s, an entirely new set of images of the consumer started to appear; these images grew out of a rejection of earlier critiques of modern consumption and all its paraphernalia, its luxuries and absurdities, its emphasis on style, its seeming unconcern with the origins of the commodities on offer, its obsession with difference and its domination by mass advertising and marketing. In place of the managed, manipulated and duped images of consumers of old, the new images became brighter, more active, more creative. Heroic qualities started to creep into images of consumers as explorers of new worlds or as artists. No image, however, captures these heroic qualities as vividly as that of the consumer-rebel.

Symbols of Rebellion

The view that social groups can find and express oppositional meanings in particular activities or objects is hardly new or original. Smoking, for example, can be a gesture of defiance, particularly in at a time when the evidence of its health impact is so strong (Doll, et al., 2004; Surgeon-General of the United States, 2004). To smoke in defiance of the evidence is the ultimate rebellion, an act of willful self-sacrifice:

> Smoking is not an addiction, but a form of rebellion – and much preferable to lobbing missiles at Heathrow. This has always been clearest in the case of women. From the beginning, smoke issuing from a lipstick-painted mouth was taken as a sign of sluthood. Thus millions of women took up the habit in solidarity with sluts and in hopes of being mistaken for one. ... The other great smoking rebels are, of course, blue-collar males. Once smoking was a bonding ritual performed by men of all classes, but when the suits turned to Perrier and jogging, it became a mark of proletarian pride ... [and] defiance. Confronted with the

> capitalists' homicidal abuses of the indoor and outdoor environment, who would not prefer
> to die gallantly by one's own hand? (Ehrenreich, 1994: 9)

Particular ways of looking, talking or walking, hairstyles, Camel cigarettes, Harley Davidson motorbikes, bleached jeans, Dr. Martens shoes, can all function as icons of disaffection and defiance. But are such tokens of modern anti-consumption, the adoption of branded commodities by the alienated or the rebellious to convey rejection of the system, really the acts of consumers-in-rebellion? Such groups do not rebel *against* commodities, but use commodities to express protest. According to this view, Dr. Martens, tough looks apart, are not even an instrument of rebellion (like the axe in the hands of Kapuscinski's rebel) but a symbol, which incidentally happens to be a branded commodity. In similar ways, punks used safety pins and razor blades as jewellery, signalling their protest through the use of cheap and unbranded items of everyday life. And Naomi Klein's *No Logo* (2000) and Adbusters' 'Culture-jamming', at first critiques, quickly became brands themselves; in 2004 Adbusters even produced its own brand of running shoes. The transition from opposition to becoming a brand was complete within two decades (Heath and Potter, 2005).

Symbols of disaffection, whether expensive branded items or cheap everyday ones, may be dismissed as tokens of youthful rebelliousness accompanied by submission to the rule of commodities. But on the other hand, is not this argument in danger of implying that the cynicism of the observer(s) is shared by the consumers? Not only disaffected young people, but many if not all consumers in industrialized societies of the North use commodities to rebel against the commoditization of everyday life. What unites the 1970s' use of safety pins as earrings with the 1980s' fashion of wearing torn jeans – the more frayed the better – as symbols of defiance is the discovery of *uses* for objects distinctly different from those assigned to them by manufacturers and merchandisers. This constitutes a rebellion against:

> the authority of the producer [which] lies in the capacity to define the meaning of that which
> is consumed. Producers have more authority to the extent that the meaning or value of an
> object or service is defined by how the producer understands, interprets, [and] judges it.
> (Abercrombie, 1994: 51)

According to this view, unorthodox uses of standardized objects are not seen as merely semiotic games (see Chapter 4, 'The Consumer as Explorer'), but as genuine acts of rebellion against the authority of the producer.

This acceptance of the consumer's act of rebellion as real, heartfelt and potentially dangerous is the starting point in Michel de Certeau's *The Practice of Everyday Life* (1984), which seeks to loosen the connection between a commodity and its sign-value, defined by some omnipotent Baudrillardian code. It is wrong, argues de Certeau, to equate consumption with the purchase of a particular item, its physical expenditure or the appropriation of its (given) sign-value. Instead he argues that consumers can resist the dominant economic order even as they consume its outputs, its commodities and its images. This is done not by active resistance (such as consumer boycotts, discussed later) or by passively refusing to buy its products and images, but by using them in ways that are foreign or antagonistic to those intended by manufacturers, advertisers, and so on. In this way, consumers may challenge the hegemonic order by rejecting the legitimacy of its claims, even if they do not reject its products.

Two interrelated metaphors are central to de Certeau's thinking: anti-colonization and guerrilla warfare. Native Americans resisted the religious, political and legal practices and representations imposed on them by Spanish colonialism, 'not by rejecting them or transforming them (though that occurred as well), but by many different ways of using them in the service of rules, customs or convictions foreign to the colonization which they could not escape' (de Certeau, 1984). Like those native Americans, consumers operate in an occupied territory; like the native Americans, they appear to accept passively what they receive. Yet in practice, they transform it, distort it, undermine it, twist it, and laugh at it. De Certeau uses the French anthropologist Claude Lévi-Strauss' idea of *bricolage*, a mixture of creative makeshift, improvisation, cunning and guileful ruses, to describe how consumers experiment with latent symbolic properties of commodities and images, fashioning new and unexpected entities out of mass marketed components. This act is both creative and oppositional.

De Certeau criticizes those radical and conservative critics of consumption who regard the consumer as victim or at least passive recipient of standardized, glamorized products:

> In reality, a rationalized, expansionist, centralist, spectacular and clamorous production is confronted by an entirely different kind of production, called 'consumption' and characterized by its ruses, its fragmentation (the result of the circumstances), its poaching, its clandestine nature, its tireless but quiet activity, in short its quasi-invisibility, since it shows itself not in its own products (where would it place them?) but in an art of using products imposed on it. (de Certeau, 1984: 32)

In this conception, consumption emerges as guerrilla fighting in an occupied territory. The powerful define and construct 'places' like shopping streets and malls, houses, cars, schools and factories that they seek to control and rule, using strategies and plans. The weak, for their part, are forced to operate in these places, but are constantly seeking to convert them into their own 'spaces', using ruse, guile and deception and relying on suddenness and surprise. To the strategies of the powerful, the weak proffer tactics, operating in isolated actions, forever discovering cracks in the system and opportunities for gain. The joy of consumption, then, comes not from the temporary sating of an addiction or from the fulfilment of greed, but from outwitting a more powerful opponent who has stacked the cards:

> Innumerable ways of playing and foiling the other's game, that is, the space instituted by others, characterize the subtle, stubborn, resistant activity of groups which, since they lack their own space, have to get along in a network of already established forces and representations. People have to make do with what they have. In these combatants' stratagems, there is a certain art of placing one's blows, a pleasure in getting around the rules of a constraining space. We see tactical and joyful dexterity of the mastery of a technique. Scapin and Figaro are only literary echoes of this art. (de Certeau, 1984: 31)

Torn Jeans

Fiske takes de Certeau's arguments a step further, arguing that 'consumption is a tactical raid on the system' (Fiske, 1989: 35). Consumption is neither passive nor purely individual, but is part of a 'popular culture [which] is made by the people, not by the culture industry. All the culture industries can do is produce a repertoire of texts or cultural resources for the various formations of the people to use or reject in the on-going process of producing their popular culture' (Fiske, 1989: 24). Meanings and pleasures, argues Fiske, are not conjured up by merchandisers of culture, trend-setters and other hirelings of capital; nor do meanings and pleasures reside in the texts themselves, whether they be TV programmes (Fiske, 1987), shopping malls, designer clothes or advertisements. Instead, the meaning and the pleasure emerge from the consumers' active engagement with such texts and frequent attempts to undermine them and subvert them. Fiske does not deny that today's cultural commodities:

> bear the forces that we can call centralizing, disciplinary, hegemonic, massifying, commodifying. Opposing these forces, however, are the cultural needs of the people, this shifting matrix of social allegiances that transgress categories of the individual, or class or gender or race or any category that is stable within the social order. These popular forces transform the cultural commodity into a cultural resource, pluralize the meanings and pleasures it offers, evade or resist its disciplinary efforts, fracture its homogeneity and coherence, raid or poach upon its terrain. All popular culture is a process of struggle, of struggle over the meanings of social experience, of one's personhood and its relations to the social order and of the texts and commodities of that order. (Fiske, 1989: 28)

In contrast to de Certeau's consumer-guerrillas who, judging by the examples he provides in the latter parts of his book, seem engaged in rather timid and esoteric practices, Fiske's consumer-guerrillas sneer, jeer and shout. They despoil the landscapes of capital, with graffiti, rubbish and noise; they tear, they break, they steal (or 'shop-lift'). They challenge ceaselessly capital's attempts to define the meanings of things and discover pleasure in destroying the pleasures that capital ostentatiously offers. In this argument, Fiske taps an important tradition within Anglo-American criminology, which through a series of studies of working-class youth culture generated the idea that what mainline sociology defined as deviance amounted to symbolic rebellion (Matza, 1964; Robins and Cohen, 1978; Taylor et al., 1973). A dominant theme of this tradition was that what seemed like hoodlum or nihilism was in fact a statement, at times poorly, at times well articulated, against the values of respectable society, including those of respectable working-class.

Fiske transposes some of these ideas from the area of crime to the area of consumption. His discussion the 'Jeaning of America', highlights the force of these arguments. Far from lamenting the hegemony of blue-jeans in American campuses as a sign of students willingly putting themselves in mass uniforms, while deluding themselves with images of youthful vigour and glamour (as Marcuse might have done), Fiske sees jeans as a cultural resource on which students set busily to work. Blue-jeans are a text on which students can write and read their own meanings. By disfiguring their jeans in particular ways, that is, by bleaching them, tie-dying them or, especially, tearing them, students can express oppositional meanings to those intended by manufacturers and advertisers. Thus, wearing torn jeans is 'an example of a user not simply consuming a commodity but reworking it, treating it not as a completed object to be accepted passively, but as a cultural resource to be used' (Fiske, 1989: 10). This is no idle fiddling, but 'a refusal of commodification and an assertion of one's right to generate one's own culture' (Fiske, 1989: 15).

Unlike de Certeau's cheerful *bricoleurs*, Fiske's rebels are angry, conscious and self-conscious; their tactics are not limited to semiotic games, jokes and fantasies, but extend into action. In Fiske's view, shop-lifting is true guerrilla infiltration into enemy terrain. It affords the thrill and excitement of rebelling against a system in which everything has to be paid for, and, when successfully accomplished, it marks a temporary victory of cunning against the strategies of capital, its electronic eyes and surveillance apparatuses.

> Shop-lifting is not a guerrilla raid just upon the store owners themselves, but upon the power block in general. The store owners are merely metonyms for their allies in power – parents, teachers, security guards, the legal system, and all agents of social discipline or repression. (Fiske, 1989: 39)

Fiske's position today seems dated. Over the last 20 years, even as he was writing, jeans had their designer make-over. They moved from being personally adorned to being factory adorned, with tears, designs, logos, bleach and colour effects factored in at source. And the market fragmented, with astonishingly cheap jeans being sold by discount retailers and own-label supermarkets, alongside others that were astonishingly expensive but superficially nearly identical being sold by upmarket fashion houses (Mintel, 2005). Behind the differences and nuances that could be instantly appraised by the cognoscenti, lies a rapidly changed world of production, now organized on global lines, with global chains of command (Icon Group International, 2002).

So is Fiske's narrative of shop-lifting and other raw acts of consumer rebellion to be rejected? We think not. At its most extreme, when there is media coverage of serious calamities such as earthquakes, power-cuts, uprisings or civil disturbances, it is noticeable how there is often property plunder. In societies marked by extreme poverty and disparities of wealth, social dislocation may be an opportunity. From this perspective, if individual shop-lifters may be seen as a free-shooters or guerrilla snipers at consumer capitalism, urban rioters represent mass consumer rebellion, a by-passing of the cash nexus, an opportunity to be oppportunistic. TV screens conveying images of people plundering electrical stores and supermarkets may be an indication that consumption can, as Fiske proposed, be the focal point of social struggle and rebellion, as it was at the time of the food riots of two centuries ago (Rudé, 1959; Thompson, 1993[1971]).

Tactics of Consumer Rebellion

Perhaps the quintessence of images of consumers as rebels is the joy-rider, who steals a smart car, drives it at tremendous speed, performs outrageous manoeuvres, causes as much havoc along the way as possible, and outsmarts attempts by police to stop him; the joy-rider is rarely 'her'. In some corners of society, such figures are celebrated, becoming quasi-folk heroes among disaffected youth, in spite of the havoc they wreak and the real suffering that they cause when their escapades take them in the path of pedestrians or, to their families, when they die or are maimed themselves. Joy-riders are as daring as they are unpredictable. They can enjoy the ultimate offering of consumer society, the fast car, not only without paying for it, but without being restrained by the responsibilities and burdens that such cars impose on their legitimate owners; alternatively, they may choose slow, ugly and battered old cars to pit against the police, before wrecking them or torching them. In all cases, they literally take over a piece of the road, rebelling against and re-writing its rules and meanings (Light et al., 1993; McCarney, 1981; Parker, 1974). To be sure, their victories may be short-lived as are those of most rebels, but they are none the sweeter for it. They also create victims out of other consumers.

Another archetype is perhaps the ram-raid, in which a powerful vehicle drives at speed into the window of a shop or any outlet with cash, usually late at night; the raiders empty as much of the contents of the shop into the van as they can and leave, while bystanders idly watch the spectacle or even cheer the ram-raiders. At one ram-raid in genteel Bath in the early 1990s, the bystanders physically stopped a policeman who tried in vain to arrest a group of ram-raiders (Ryle, 1993). This upsurge generated a moral panic for some in that city (local newspaper headline: 'A City Centre Held to Ransom'), whereas for others they became a weekly spectator sport (Pook, 1993). Ram-raiding is a worldwide phenomenon, with ram-raiders seeming to take literally the advertisers' message 'Come and get me', ignoring, as advertisers do, the other part of the bargain, the obligation to pay. Like joy-rides and shop-lifting, ram-raids feed property-owning paranoias and are demonized by respectable society, which endlessly seeks to criminalize and control them. Yet, the difficulty of controlling such guerrilla tactics reveals how well the tactics are chosen both to highlight the weakest points of the system and to take advantage of them. What starts off as shocking becomes part of the normality of culture; not desirable but normal.

A rather different type of rebellion against commodities has been identified by Susie Orbach and feminist analysts of obesity (Lang and Rayner, 2005). For her, not only fat and over-eating, but also anorexia and related eating 'disorders' are forms of protest against consumer society; both over-eating and starving are rejections of the social roles that define women in industrialized societies (Orbach, 1978, 1986). If fat is a rebellion against being an object of adornment and pleasure, anorexia is a symbolic rejection of the fruit of consumer society, a refusal of the poisoned chalice. Anorexia, like a hunger strike, is a political gesture, observes Orbach. Like shop-lifting, joy-riding and ram-raiding, eating disorders can be interpreted as rebellions against the edicts of consumerism, rebellions that do not always seek to destroy the objects of consumption but to redefine them, reclaim them and re-appropriate them.

One tactic of rebellion is 'subvertising', the deliberate and organized addition of adding graffiti to existing advertisements to subvert their meaning and destroy their appeal as consumerist icons (ECRA, 1994). The advertising industry is sensitive to accusations of infringing norms of decency, yet it also plays with the boundaries, knowing that to shock is to attract attention; and attention is a key measure of advertising's effectiveness. Subvertising therefore takes the subtlety and starkly confronts the disguised exploitation. The subvertising tactic is to be witty, pithy and daring and to expose social degradation. Sexism and health have been two key areas of action. Early targets were ads that equated ownership of cars with ownership or control of women. But today, the 1980s campaign to confront and disfigure sexist advertisements of Fiat's Panda cars might seem quaint; surely no-one could take seriously sure crude advertisements? Well, they did actually. And today, despite images of women as stronger and more active, advertisements still rely upon sexuality to sell. Despite self-regulation and self-policing, the boundaries of acceptable use of sexuality to sell products has been pushed back. The sex might be presented more subtly (perhaps), with women not in such submissive roles, but sex is being used nonetheless. The Australian campaign BUGA-UP (Billboard Utilizing Graffitists Against Unhealthy Promotions) was another 1980s act of rebellion, set up by a group of health professionals who systematically disfigured cigarette advertisements (Chesterfield Evans, 1987). They were incensed by the huge budgets of anti-health forces of the giant tobacco companies and decided that wit and despoliation were warranted. When such tactics assume organized forms, they are referred to as demarketing, as when campaign groups sponsor advertisements calling on consumers not to consume a specific product (Matsu, 1994). A long-standing exponent is the campaign to curtail use of animal fur waged by animal welfare organizations such as that by PETA, the People for Ethical Treatment of Animals, since 1980.

Rebels?

It would be easy but short-sighted to dismiss such rebellions as marginal or inconsequential. This is precisely what the strategies of hegemony would dictate, just as occupying forces dismiss every act of resistance, sabotage and vandalism against their rule as the product of a few trouble-makers and agitators. In 1934 in the UK – the first year they were recorded – there were nearly 13,000 cases of shop-lifters being apprehended; this rose to 300,000 by 2003–04 (Home Office (UK), 2004). Most are male rather than female, and most events occur in the run-up to Christmas. According to the 11th British Retail Crime Survey, in 2003, theft by customers cost the retail sector £410 million, and theft by staff themselves another £282 million. Burglaries on retail sites was far less, valuing goods taken at £111 million. 'Old-fashioned' crime like till snatches amounted to just over £1 million (British Retail Consortium, 2004). The British Retail Consortium, which represents most British retailers, estimates that, after years of steadily rising, shop-lifting costs to retailers dropped in the early 2000s to total of £2 billion. Enormous resources in equipment (CCTV, alarms, electronic tagging, and so on), manpower, management systems, plans and strategies are devoted to its curtailment and control, in a permanent and well-rehearsed cycle of action and reaction.

In a paradoxical way, the tactical raids on the system reinforce the rule of commodities and consumerism; for they are primarily rebellions against a system that denies its bounty to those who cannot afford it, but they seldom challenge the value of the bounty or the companies that produce it. On the contrary, the ram-raiders who display a preference for Benneton, just like the joy-rider who favours BMWs, reinforce the iconic allure of these products. In this modern drama, the suicide bomber in the public shopping space is the final nihilist, denying both themselves and others the chance to consume, an act of control and rebellion.

This extreme example apart, the adoption of particular brands as symbols of oppositional ideologies reinforces the rule of brands. To be sure, torn jeans, unfiltered Camels and Harley Davidsons may act as potent signs of nihilistic dissaffection, but offer only a limited challenge to those in power. Rave parties, ram-raids, joy-rides and even shop-lifting ultimately are tactics of symbolic protest, causing annoyance and paranoia, but are hardly likely to cause the merest tremor in the world's stock exchanges. On the contrary, many rebellious tactics merely fuel new areas of commodity production. This is not only manifested in the burgeoning growth of the security industry, but equally in the appropriation and subsequent emasculation by manufacturers of the symbols of rebellion. Do manufacturers care if youngsters bleach their jeans, if they want different brands or celebrate multi-cultural diversity, so long as they keep buying the products? (Rieff, 1993).

No sooner does a product become an icon of opposition than manufacturers seek to capitalize on it, by mass-producing it, raising its price or discovering a niche for it. The experience of jeans, discussed by Fiske, is instructive. As soon as manufacturers discovered that jeans were no longer a uniform icon of youth, independence and freedom, they adapted their products accordingly. Macy's, the large US department store, eagerly started selling jeans that were already shrunk, bleached or torn. In this way, the big retailing outlet affects to become an accomplice to rebel-images of disfigured jeans, thereby compromising them and neutralizing them. To be sure, as Fiske argues, new marks and new distinctions are produced by consumers, for example, between 'really rugged jeans' and 'mock rugged' jeans. Yet, one suspects that rebellions that end up consumed with such minutiae, only reinforce a system that prospers on diversity and difference. These rebels, whether joyful or angry, may divert themselves and others with their creative *bricolage* and occasional raids on the system. They may be celebrated as triumphant tricksters who poke fun at the system, but ultimately they lack the moral indignation, the single-mindedness and the destructive fury of true rebels.

Rebels with Causes

A system that can institutionalize rebelliousness by channelling it into unorthodox uses of its staples, blue-jeans, motorbikes or cigarettes, it could be argued, commodifies rebelliousness itself. As steady stream of books from Vance Packard to Heath and Potter have noted, consumer capitalism has an extraordinary capacity to take what first directly threatens it and, after a deep intake of breath, convert it into a marketing opportunity (Heath and Potter, 2005; Packard, 1981[1957]). Instead of destruction and retribution, rebels vent their anger and frustration into commodities, buying them, stealing them, disfiguring them and investing them with meaning. In such ways, they become entrapped in the very mechanism from which they seek to escape.

Consumer boycotts

Not all forms of consumer rebellion are quite as easily accommodated. If the tearing of jeans leaves the power block largely untroubled, the mere suggestion of consumer boycotts or sabotage of its products can, if not seriously damage a company's stock (except in dire circumstances), at least threaten its reputation and cause executives troubled nights. The term 'vigilante consumer' was coined to describe the activities of those organized or semi-organized consumers who take a serious interest in companies' ethical and environmental standards and lead public opinion against those companies that are found wanting (Dickenson, 1993). The UK magazine, *Ethical Consumer* has tracked consumer boycotts in UK since the 1990s. These range from boycotts against banks for their involvement in Third World debt to supermarkets for building on green field sites, to cosmetic manufacturers for animal testing, to chemical companies for continuing production of CFC gases. Entire countries have been singled out for boycotts – Botswana for forcing bushmen out of national parks, Barbados as a tourist destination for the export of monkeys for animal experimentation, Israel for 'decades of refusing to abide by UN resolutions', Norway for its commercial whaling, Taiwan for continuing to import rhino horn. The list on the website (www.ethicalconsumer.org/boycotts/boycotts_list.htm) is long, but, given the existence of such boycotts in many free societies, it is reasonable to ask about their effectiveness and impact.

Many of these boycotts attract limited media attention, although they may be significant enough to affect corporate policies (*Ethical Consumer*, 1994; Harrison et al., 2005). The threat of possible damage – to sales, reputation, staff morale, brand image – may be enough to generate change. In the 1990s, Neutrogena, manufacturers of the Norwegian Formula hand cream, moved its production to France and declared that it was 'adamantly opposed to whaling' as a result of the anti-whaling campaign. All major supermarket chains in Britain either stopped buying Faroese fish or declared its origin on the label, in response to a campaign to protect the pilot whale. The cosmetics manufacturer, L'Oréal, succeeded in having a consumer boycott of its products lifted, by signing an agreement with PETA, a US animal rights organization, to stop animal testing on its products.

Against such success stories for consumer boycotts, it could be argued that there are too many boycott calls and that collectively they are often too parochial ('single issue') or too restricted to the fringes of consumption to have a serious effect. The majority of consumers, overloaded by moral causes and saturated by information, signs and messages, ends up resigned, confused, impotent or unprepared to bother. The latest boycott, if it does gain attention, quickly fuses with numerous other messages and images, and may vanish as meaningless noise rather than as a lasting call to action. Yet neither companies nor the masses of consumers can ignore the critical commentary on commodities sustained by continuing, mutating and merging consumer boycotts. Baudrillard's flying signifiers (Baudrillard,

1988c) do not merely migrate from commodity to commodity as objects of desire, but also as objects of rejection and avoidance. So it does not matter so much what countries, companies or commodities are objects of current boycotts, as that a succession of boycotts constantly mobilizes consumers to remind manufacturers, merchandisers and retailers that they have moral and environmental responsibilities. The boycott tactic invites consumers to act in their individual capacity to a broader social end. Their effectiveness depends crucially on how well organized they are and how much media coverage they generate (Friedman, 1985; Hermann, 1993; Smith, 1990), issues that we shall pick up in Chapter 9.

'Alternative' consumption – pop festivals

If consumer boycotts and vigilante consumers express a concern for the environment and ethics, they hardly undermine the deeper foundation of consumerism, that good life is synonymous to rising living standards, better and bigger consumption. Alternative forms of consumption represent a different type of rebellion, one that repudiates products and practices of big capital, not because they happen to be ethically questionable and environmentally damaging, but because they are products and practices of a system that is ethically moribund and environmentally calamitous. Such rebellions are not expressed in unorthodox uses of products (although this may be part of it) nor in the rejection of targeted products as in boycotts. These rebellions reject all Western-style consumption and seek to supplant it with a radically different type of consumption, which encompasses a number of principles:

1   Consume less.
2   Consume local products.
3   Avoid products produced and merchandised by big capital.
4   Avoid cash and use alternative modes of economic transactions.

The last two of these principles are graphically portrayed by Hetherington in his description of the Stonehenge pop festivals and New Age travellers, who have sought to recreate in the 1990s something of the ethos of the 1960s hippies.

> Almost anything could be bought at Stonehenge: drugs, New Age paraphernalia, health remedies, old bits of tat, scrap, vehicle parts, food, services; one person used to provide hot baths in an old tub in the middle of the field (surrounded by a screen), somebody even had the enterprising idea of selling people breakfast in bed, strawberries and Champagne if it was your birthday, otherwise fried-egg sandwiches! ... Consumption at Stonehenge when related to festival is highly ambivalent. It is both spontaneous and organized, monetary but with a strong emphasis on gift exchange; it is removed from all associations with rational consumption (licensed, taxed and regulated) but the sense of reciprocity is strong. (Hetherington, 1992: 86–7)

Hetherington provides vivid descriptions of consumer-rebels who take over the places of the powerful and at least temporarily make them their own. What could be more symbolic than taking over Stonehenge, the archetypical heritage site turned consumerist theme park, and reducing it to a no-go area for respectable visitors, police and big capital. In this way, it becomes a shrine of alternative consumption, waste and excess. Noisy, extravagant, unrestrained – pop festivals represent one challenge to the strategies of modern consumerism. They too, however, can be compromised and hijacked by the cash nexus, as was illustrated when the recreation of the Woodstock free festival in 1994, 25 years after the original, turned into an all-ticket consumerist orgy. The Glastonbury festival in the UK set out from its inception in 1970 to raise money for good causes. It combined 'alternative' consumption with the mainstream. The initial charge for the first festival was £1; it was attended by 1500 people. By 2005, the ticket cost £125 plus £4 booking fee and £4 for postage and packing; 112,000 people attended (www.efestivals. co.uk/festivals/glastonbury/2005/tickets.shtml).

LETS

There are, however, quieter, more organized and down-to-earth challenges to consumer capitalism. One such challenge is the LETS, or Local Exchange Trading System. This is a form of cashless local economy in which people trade with each other on a bartering basis. LETS provides a network of members, often computerized, who offer their services and goods in exchange for units of a notional currency. This notional currency is not convertible to cash, but can be used to buy goods and services from other LETS members. The services range widely from gardening and baby-sitting to legal advice and car maintenance, from music lessons to accountancy, and from leasing of equipment (computers, lawn-mowers, washing-machines) to architectural design. The first LETS experiments took place in a cash-starved area of British Columbia in 1982; since then the system has spread into the USA, New Zealand, Australia and elsewhere. In the UK, by 1996, there were over 40,000 people involved in schemes in 450 local currency systems. Most had been formed since 1991, when LETSLINK-UK, a national development agency was set up (LETSLINK-UK, 2005). The membership of individual LETS may vary from about 10 (the number required to set up a new system) to 500 and interest in the scheme increased rapidly as a response to structural unemployment.

LETS is not merely a trading system at the margins of mainstream economy, devoid of ideology or a sense of mission. On the contrary, many of LETS' members regard it as a way of strengthening community links undermined by the cash nexus, and of regenerating local economies without relying on conventional capital. LETSLINK declares:

> Capital flight deprives an area of a means to trade within itself. Many low-income areas, however, still possess skills, human energy and potential, and all kinds of material resources. All the components of real wealth are there, locked away, alongside a myriad of unmet needs. All that is missing, essentially, is a medium of exchange. We simply need a communications system, linking supply and demand. (LETSLINK-UK, 1994)

LETS enables those with limited cash resources to become involved actively in their local economies and communities. Everyone, including the poorest people, has something to offer; everyone, including the richest, has a need to be met. Many of those who joined LETS report that they joined for ideological reasons, but they discover that it makes good economic sense, especially in a period of recession when the number of transactions increases considerably, if they accept payment in the local LETS currency. Some local traders, like grocers, opticians or clothing stores, have opted to accept part of the payment in cash and part in local currency and have reported much increased trade (Kellaway, 1993).

One issue that divides LETS schemes is whether their members should all charge the same basic unit for their time or whether they should be allowed to charge depending on the demand for their products and services. Some local economies uphold two LETS schemes, one in each category. Predictably, this has a divisive effect, since higher-status occupations tend to favour the differential system, while lower-status occupations favour the uniform rate. At the moment, it is not clear which system will predominate or whether the two can co-exist side by side. In any case, LETS systems have provided a radical alternative to conventional consumption, in several different ways. First, they focus on unbranded, unadvertised and unmediated goods and services (advertising is limited to internal bulletins). They re-affirm the value of hand-made, home-made products and regenerate arts and crafts, ranging from organic farming to woodland management, cheese-making, spinning and weaving, which are swept aside by big capital. Second, they bring together the person as a producer and seller of goods and services with the person as buyer and consumer. In this way, they replace an impersonal cash-nexus with a visible, personal relationship between consumer and producer. Third, they enable individuals and groups whose lack of cash would exclude them both from the local economy and from involvement in the community. Fourth, they bring together people of different social classes in relations of mutuality that cross social boundaries and encourage accountability and responsibility. Fifth, they keep capital local. Finally, they find a legitimate way of generating economic activity that evades taxation and by-passes the legislative and other apparatuses of the state.

The Ultimate Consumer-rebel: 'Consume Less'?

In all the ways described above, LETS schemes represent a highly organized and promising alternative to mainstream consumption, challenging its ethos and breaking some of its taboos. It is a mild rebellion, a well-tempered rebellion. It even goes as far as to challenge the ultimate taboo against which few dare to express themselves – the equation of better life with more consumption (Durning, 1992). The ascetic line, once such a prominent element of the Protestant work ethic and later a central value of hippie lifestyles, seems to have disappeared from the public discourses of the mass media and mainstream political debate. TV, press, magazines, dependent as they are on advertising revenue, have warmly espoused the concerns of activist-consumers or even ethical consumers, but they shy away from any direct assault on the premise of consumerism. It is only in the last 30 years that some progressive environmental and ethical consumer groups have started to discuss seriously a frontal assault on the religion of 'Shop 'til you drop, spend 'til the end, buy 'til you die'. In the words of Ignacio Peon Escalante, a Mexican consumer/citizen activist:

> Our vision is that we should live a more austere life, but also a better quality life; less quantity and more quality. Mexicans believe that if they want to be modern, they must imitate the Americans, aspire to their living standards. They confuse development with materialism,

they think that being 'modern' means having instead of being. Consumerism is an absurd form of materialism; this is true of the Third World as well as of the First World. (Interview with the authors for first edition, 1994)

'Consume less' is the focal point of these discussions – is it a recipe for political suicide, as the British Greens discovered when they seriously raised the issue as part of their electoral campaign in 1992, or is it an outlandish slogan today that will emerge as the commonsense of the future? Calls to consume less are all too frequently ridiculed, especially if those who make them can be seen sporting anything more ostentatious than sackcloth and ashes (Lansley, 1994; Sklair, 2002). Yet the earth's finite resources and its finite tolerance for abuse and neglect are no longer what Lasch called the 'forbidden topic' (Lasch, 1991). While the Northern countries maintain their 'riotous consumption standards', they have limited moral authority to pontificate to the ravished and exploited countries of the Third World on the needs to respect the environment and to preserve the earth's natural resources (Korten, 2001; Stiglitz, 2002).

'Consume less' may become the final frontier of the consumer-rebel, the consumer who does not merely seek living space within the present system or use the products of the system to express disaffection and protest, but decides that 'enough is enough'; anything less than a frontal assault on the core assumption of consumerism is inadequate. Such an assault would, of course, transcend the limits of rebellion and would amount to a major moral and political challenge to capitalist hegemony. As Sklair (1991) has eloquently argued, capitalism throughout the world has become so dependent on consumerism for its legitimation and reproduction that any threat to the equation of 'more' with 'better' would be deeply subversive:

> The control of ideas in the interests of consumerism is almost total. The ideas that are anta-gonistic to the global capitalist project can be reduced to one central counter-hegemonic idea, the rejection of the culture-ideology of consumerism itself. Without consumerism, the rationale for continuous capitalist accumulation dissolves. It is the capacity to commodify all ideas and material products in which they adhere, television images, advertisements, newsprint, books, tapes, films and so on, not the ideas themselves, that capitalism strives to appropriate. (1991: 82)

Beyond Rebellion

Images of consumers as rebels that started to emerge in the 1980s grew out of a rejection of images of consumers as passive objects of manipulation, as victims. Yet these are precisely the images that have fuelled not only the anger, but also the tireless activity of self-confessed consumer advocates over the last two centuries (see Chapter 9, 'The Consumer as Activist'). In this chapter, two different forms of rebellion have emerged. On the one hand, we examined the rebellion of those consumers who challenge the authority of producers, not by completely rejecting their wares, but by rejecting, first, the meanings assigned to them, second, the methods of acquiring them, third, the methods of using them, fourth, the meth-ods and costs, cultural and environmental, of their production. On the other hand, we looked at the rebellion of those who reject everything about consump-tion in the First World, its products, its meanings, its suppliers and its glamoriz-ers and who are beginning to map out a radical new vision:

We are reaching the end of the line in terms of that kind of existence, materialism and consumerism. People have not enough time in their lives to live. They work for long hours for
less pay. How do we move beyond consumerism and materialism? It is not enough to preach
and critique.

The only way away from materialism and consumerism is an alternative economic and social
framework with which people can identify. People will have less time at work and more on
alternative things. What do you do the rest of the time? You can spend it sitting in front of
a TV and get packaged entertainment and remain a bloated consumer society, or there is a
possibility that we can entice each other to become part of what I call the intimate society.
This is a volunteer economy, in which there is no market coercive relationships which transform people into things, but on service and gift giving. The bottom line is that the more people identify themselves with a serving capacity or a stewardship capacity, the less they define
themselves by the material things. I know that people who volunteer for work have less and
less time for their possessions and are less possessed by their possessions. They are serving,
they are giving, they are participating in a real way. Having said that I realize that you cannot have true participatory democracy in a market economy. Worker-run companies have
absolutely no way of invigorating principles of democracy based on volunteer work, so long
as they have to survive in a market economy. (Jeremy Rifkin, in an interview with the authors,
1994)

The future of consumption, according to this vision, lies neither in rebellion, nor
in activism limited to the area of consumption. The consumer must act beyond
his or her interests as consumer, in short he or she must once again act as a citizen, taking responsibility for the future.

In Conclusion

How convincing are images of consumers as rebels? As a corrective to images of
consumers as infinitely malleable, seducible and manageable, the phenomena
studied in this chapter are of considerable importance. De Certeau, Fiske, Abercrombie, Hermann and others have drawn attention to the unexpected, creative
and unmanageable aspects of modern consumption. Their contributions parallel
arguments concerning the resistance of workers to management's strategies of
control. Just as organizations may contain an unmanaged terrain in which individuals evade management controls through play, jokes, stories and fantasies
(Gabriel, 1995), contemporary consumption entails a large unmanaged dimension,
vividly portrayed by these writers. The unmanaged dimensions of consumption
lie not so much in the rejection of consumer products, let alone in the rejection
of consumption itself, but in unorthodox appropriation and uses of these products, especially in ways that express protest.

Finding heroic qualities in these activities seems more problematic. Teenagers
enjoying fast rides in stolen cars may be romantically envisioned as rebels against
a system that denies each man his own fast car. Anorexic women can be seen as
hunger strikers, heroic in their defiance and self-sacrifice. Shop-lifters may be conjured as tricksters scoring victories at the expense of omnipresent electronic eyes.
Young people piercing or tattooing their skins or (more temperately) disfiguring
their blue-jeans may be seen as revolting against the values of respectable society.
Yet, such constructions may reveal more about the omnipotence of consumerism

than challenges to it. Not only does consumer rebellion become automatically channelled into the world of commodities where it can be compromised and appropriated, but it automatically becomes commodified itself. Far from rejecting consumerism, one can become a rebel (and appropriate the heroic qualities of this image) simply by engaging in the appropriate type of consumption. Why pick up an axe (like Kapuscinski's rebel) when you can be a rebel merely by tearing up your blue-jeans or having a stud passed through your nose? Camus was one of the first to signal that rebellion can quickly degenerate into style, the rebel turning into a dandy or an aesthete:

> Romanticism demonstrates, in fact, that rebellion is part and parcel of dandyism: one of its objectives is outward appearances. ... Dandyism inaugurates an aesthetic which is still valid in our world, an aesthetic of solitary creators, who are obstinate rivals of a God they condemn. (Camus, 1971: 49)

Camus was not reluctant to castigate the sterility of this attitude, which accommodates, eviscerates and commodifies rebellion. By comparison to aesthetic rebels of this genre, who denounce the god of consumerism without denying him, the rebels who preach alternative consumption, organize consumer boycotts or set up a local LETS are far less romantic figures. Hollywood makes few films about them and postmodern theorists seem not to notice them at all. Their tireless and largely unpaid work goes mostly unnoticed, unless they can rouse enough people against the building of a nuclear power station or the sale of powdered breastmilk substitutes to the Third World so as to put a spanner in the plans of capital. Yet, it is these largely invisible rebels who may in the long run provide the greater, if not the only, challenge to consumerism. By saying 'No' or 'Less' or 'Do it differently', they may force a questioning of the core assumptions of consumerism and open up a range of choices that are currently if not invisible, at least submerged.

CHAPTER 9

The Consumer as Activist

Consumption and leisure are not substitutes for power.

Lester Thurow, 1993: 121

CORE ARGUMENTS

There is a long tradition of consumer activism in many different countries. The Irish gave the name to the boycott, but the Americans had practised it much earlier against the British when pressing for independence, as indeed did the Indians under Gandhi much later. But consumer activism assumes many different formats: campaigns, legal cases, education, individual and collective acts, whistle-blowing and other forms of direct action. We identify four waves and types of consumer activism, each with its own characteristics: the co-operative movement, which argued that consumers must take control of production; the value-for-money movement, which argued for scientific testing of products to provide information on best value; Naderism, which proposed that consumer activists must fight against corporate greed; and a new wave of alternative or political activism, which seeks to completely restructure and redefine consumption on more ethical and ecological grounds. While there are tensions between these waves of activism, elements of all four waves can be found to co-exist in many of today's initiatives.

In this chapter we reflect and build on the analysis we offered in the first edition on what we called the active consumer: those people and movements setting out to promote the rights, consciousness and interests of either all or particular groups of consumers. In the first edition of this book, we offered an historical and sociological analysis of consumer movements as 'active consumerism'. We depicted this as emerging in four waves. We posited that each wave proposed not only new forms of organizing, but different ways of looking at consumption. All of these waves have left traces that are still visible in the world of consumer organizations today throughout the world. This chapter outlines those four waves of consumer activism and asks what, if anything, has changed in the decade since we outlined our theory. We conclude that some interesting realignments are underway within and across the 'waves' of consumer activism, suggesting considerable dynamism and inventiveness.

Consumer activists have been high profile in most reasonably affluent societies for decades – appearing on the media, writing reports, appealing for support, giving government or companies a hard time. The range of their demands is extensive, ranging from calls for better products and to new ways of producing and selling. Responding to these protests and demands has had to be factored into corporate strategy. Gone are the days when suppliers had to deal with consumerists only in time of crisis. Today, being aware of and anticipating consumer complaints almost before the activists have articulated them is routine corporate behaviour. Of course, public relations in the pejorative sense of 'spin' and playing with appearances happens, but even there rhetoric can belie significant change. Companies don't just want to anticipate or respond to criticism from active consumers, for instance for better goods or more socially just or less exploitative processes. They also want to be seen to be doing so. This tussle between companies, the state as regulator and overseer of commerce and active consumerists is old, so it is perhaps surprising, as Winward suggested, that consumer activism 'has always been under-theorised' (Winward, 1994: 77). Reading the academic and historical literature for the first edition, we too noted the relative dearth of plausible analyses of active consumerism. Happily, since we wrote the first edition, there have been a few good, new studies that followed our call both to study and engage with active consumerists (Harrison et al., 2005). None of these leads us to question the value of the four models of active consumerism we proposed.

When consumer activists meet socially or in consumer congresses, there is no shortage of reflection or analysis. Partly, this is due to the high calibre of people attracted to work in such organizations. Partly, it is due to demanding work; arguing a case for consumers requires constant attention to detail, the 'opposition' and strategies. And partly, this is a reflection of the values to which activists subscribe. They want to make things better for others, for not just some but all consumers. Back in 1995, we judged that the consumer movement tended to do its most searing analysis in private, thereby leaving the theoretical terrain to academics. And we were underwhelmed with what we read. How different the situation is over a decade on. There has been a rush of interest in studying and debating the shape and role of consumer activism and academics have come out as engaged in some serious analysis of, with and for consumer groups.

This growth of interest is particularly pronounced in Europe and is probably not unrelated to the growth of 'single issue' activism in Europe, replacing more conventional party politics. But it is also a reflection, perhaps, of a shift within the social sciences, which a decade or so ago were dominated by the idealist debates associated with postmodernism (Trentmann, 2005). In the 1980s and early 1990s, academic approaches did appear to be dominated by cultural relativists looking at meanings, cultures and signs of markets rather than their material realities. This created a language divide with the more engaged activists who just 'get on with it'. This is no longer so. New studies, happily, are breaking down this schism. In the UK, for instance, around a half of the 25 projects funded by the £5 million 2002–07 Cultures of Consumption programme of the national Economic and Social Research Council had a dimension looking at different models of consumerism in one form or another. In particular, as we prophesied, there is interest in the harder end of consumer activism, those who push against market realities. And here, as we will see later, what were fringe consumer actions have become mainstream. Notions of fair trade and global justice were deemed very marginal actions indeed in the mid 1990s. In 2005, G-8 discussions and global rock concerts such as Live 8 linked hunger, justice and arcane issues of tariffs and market access to millions of 'ordinary' consumers. The fringe had become trendy.

Active Consumers and Campaigners

Boycotts have long had a seminal role in consumer activism because they symbolize a rejection of negative aspects of consumption and are the consumer-activists' act of defiance. They have 'bite' not just heart. Named after Captain Boycott, an Irish land agent against whom landless Irish peasants organized in 1880, the tactic now known as boycotts dates from earlier. Solidarity action against particular products were known before, as Witowski's study of the American non-importation movement in the late 18th-century shows (Witkowski, 1989). In the 20th-century, Gandhi's *ahimsa* or non-violent direct action included the organization of consumer boycotts of British cloth and salt. Boycotts range from local to global in their scope and vary enormously in the degree to which they are organized. Craig Smith has argued that their effectiveness depends on their visibility and that business seeks to get round this, as when Argentinian corned beef was (reputedly) repackaged and labelled as Brazilian to sell it in the UK during the Falklands-Malvinas 1982 War (Smith, 1990: 227). Smith also argued that consumer boycotts against food products tend to be more effective because food is a perishable good and consumed daily. Yet, the longest food boycott – against Nestlé for its sales of breastfeeding substitutes – has been well organized, has won consciousness and, on occasions, has dented sales, but has not achieved its goals (Allain, 1991).

One major study of the effectiveness of consumer boycotts found that about a quarter were successful in the USA between 1970 and 1980 (Friedman, 1985). Another study, however, found that when stock prices of the target firms are taken into the reckoning, boycotts are considerably more effective (White and Kare, 1990). The Ethical Consumer Research Association notes that a long-lasting boycott by UK students against Barclays Bank for its support of the apartheid regime was effective in dropping student use of Barclays from 27 percent of all students to 15 percent. Barclays not only lost market share of an important slice of future middle-class earnings, but also had its reputation tarnished. It bit the bullet and withdrew from South Africa.

Consumers are often keen to claim that they have boycotted products. Equally, non-government organizations (NGOs) are keen to launch a boycott to give negotiating clout. Boycotting something is rarely a majority action in mainstream culture; boycotts almost always come from, and appeal to, a minority. The issue is how big is that minority and how well-organized can it be made? In 1992, according to Hermann (Hermann, 1993), as many as 16 percent of grocery shoppers in the USA had joined a boycott as compared to 8 percent in 1984. Two larger UK studies by the Co-op found even higher percentages: 33 percent said they had boycotted a good on ethical grounds in 1994 and 29 percent in 2003 (Co-operative Group (UK), 2004: 7). Preparedness to boycott had remained firm at 60 percent. The Ethical Consumer Research Association's website gives a long list of boycotts at any time in the UK (*Ethical Consumer*, 2005).

Debating the direction of consumer activism is not new; nor is the attempt to organize disparate individual acts of consumption by appealing to higher moral or political ends. Consumerism has always been enlightened by active attempts to redirect consumer behaviour. The committed attempt to inject ethical and fair trade notions into the otherwise free trade dominated discourse about world economic development is not new. Most anti-colonial struggles have at some time appealed to external as well as internal populations not to consume products being made, owned or controlled by the oppressor. The US nonimportation movement of 1764–76 was America's first consumer revolt. Aimed against the import of goods, it was more than a rejection of colonial tax laws, an expression of cultural independence and an assertion of the local over the global. This was echoed in anti-colonial struggles elsewhere, notably by Gandhi's independence movement in India. By signing a declaration in public that they would stop purchasing British goods, his supporters also pledged, de facto, to live more frugally from local resources as an assertion of community values (Witkowski, 1989).

With the ending of the grand era of colonialism in the mid 20th-century, boycotts gradually shifted use, becoming more of a refinement tool within marketplaces. The world's largest consumer organization, the US Consumers Union (CU), was itself born out of a long and bitter struggle in the 1930s in Consumer Research Inc., another organization that the CU eventually superseded. The fight was over both formal philosophy – particularly attitudes to organized labour – and over internal management styles (Hermann, 1993). Classically, consumer organizations call on members to boycott a product or range until a perceived wrong is put right. The anti-free trade movement of the 1990s began once more to call for boycott action (Lang and Hines, 1993; Nader, 1991b).

The social historian E.P. Thompson showed how the emergence of the new corn markets in 18th-century England were 'disinfested of intrusive moral imperatives' (Thompson, 1993[1971]: 202). An a-moralized version of Adam Smith's new political economy had to be imposed on British society. This conveniently ignored Smith's prior theory of moral sentiments (1759). People's expectations and life assumptions had to be re-moulded in a process that was messy and at times bloody. In his celebrated essay on 'The moral economy of the English crowd in the eighteenth century' (1993[1970]), Thompson showed how the food riots of that century were the expression of people taking direct action against the imposition of the new free market in grain because they were hungry. More importantly, however, they were reacting to higher food prices, as the paternalism of Tudor economics gave way to the a-morality of Smith's market forces. For Forbes, contemporary consumerism is but a version of the same principle, that is, the 'organised reaction of individuals to inadequacies, perceived or real, of marketers, the marketplace, market mechanisms, government, government services, and consumer policy' (Forbes, 1987: 4).

Is consumer activism therefore inevitably oppositional? We think not. Through all the different manifestations of consumer activism explored here, there are some common characteristics:

- **Organization**: the intervention is planned and organized to deliver a coherent set of activities; the consumer bodies are to deliver that process.
- **A desire for change**: there is a moral edge to activism. Consumption is viewed as a vehicle of its own transformation; it can therefore be imbued with some mission.
- **A notion of rights informs activism**: consumers are deemed to have rights that have to be fought for or else they will (probably) be lost or subverted to others' ends.
- **Collectivity**: individual actions can be strengthened by acting in concert with others. Like workers in the workplace, individual consumers can be used and manipulated. Together they will be stronger and more effective at achieving change or negotiation towards change.
- **Values**: consumption is not merely a set of market transactions but has moral messages too, and consuming can be good or bad.
- **Implications**: consuming has effects on other people, on society or on the environment that go beyond the act, good or service itself.

First Wave: Co-operative Consumers

The first widespread, organized consumer movement began as a working-class reaction to excessive prices and poor quality goods, food in particular. The Co-operative movement took off in its modern form in Rochdale in north-west England in 1844, at the height of the industrialization process. The first co-operatives in fact date from even earlier and were co-operative corn mills established by skilled artisans. These were set up in opposition to local monopolies who in the words of one co-op historian 'had conspired to supply that most basic of commodities, bread, at very high prices' (Birchall, 1994: 4). In the 1760s, at Woolwich and Chatham just to the south-east of London, not only were there co-operative mills but bakeries too. The Woolwich co-op mill was burned down and the other local bakers were accused of the arson.

Drawing on such experiences and the example of utopians such as Robert Owen, whose thoughts and practices had developed at New Lanark Mills in Scotland, the movement developed its creed. As Dr William King, one of the key early thinkers said: 'These evils may be cured: and the remedy is in our own hands. The remedy is CO-OPERATION' (Birchall, 1994: 9). By 1832, there were 500 local co-operative societies, but the movement collapsed in 1834 in the face of outright state repression of working-class movements and internal weaknesses, which were exacerbated by lack of rights and legal status. In some cases, such as Brighton's 1830s co-op, the success was such that its members were lured into selling their shares for cash (Birchall, 1994: 31). Co-operative consumerism has always managed to amass assets (there are no profits to shareholders), which have offered temptations. In 1997, an attempt to break up and sell off the UK Co-operative Wholesale Society was foiled and ended in court.

Despite its chequered start in the 1830s, co-operation offered enough practical proof that consumers could exercise power over production to attract others to try. In the 1840s, another co-operative enterprise in Rochdale, England set up a shop – now a museum – to sell goods to those who joined up. Profits, instead of being allowed to be accumulated and ploughed back into manufacture, as in Owen's model, were divided amongst the co-operators (Redfern, 1913: 1–11). Co-operation rather than Adam Smith's self-interest should, so it was felt, be able to function as the basis for meeting consumer needs. It prospered.

The principle of this new movement, which was extraordinarily successful both in business and ideological terms, was 'self-help by the people'. No distinction was made between people as consumers and as producers. Business, co-operators argued, divided producers from the output of their own hands. Co-operation was the great social alternative to the capitalists' economic armoury, which merely divided and ruled the mass of working people (Thompson, 1994). This principle was summed up by Percy Redfern in one of the classics of consumer activism:

> In our common everyday needs the great industries of the world take their rise. We – the mass of common men and women in all countries – also compose the world's market. To sell to us is the ultimate aim of the world's business. Hence it is ourselves as consumers who stand in a central relation to all the economies of the world, like the king in his kingdom. As producers we go unto a particular factory, farm or mine, but as consumers we are set by nature thus to give leadership, aim and purpose to the whole economic world. That we are not kings, but serfs in the mass, is due to our failure to think and act together as consumers and so to realise our true position and power. (Redfern, 1913: 12)

The appeal was to ordinary people to build from the bottom, and not to accept their lot. Co-operation offered a richer, more fulfilled social existence, a chance for working people to build a better world. To allow this mass to participate, a new civic society had to be created, and vice versa. Co-operatives were a subversive combination of theory and practice, means and ends, which were and still are deeply threatening to prevailing market theory. The co-operator Holyoake parodied the movement's detractors as follows:

> The working class are not considered to be very rich in the quality of self-trust, or mutual trust. The business habit is not thought to be their forte. The art of creating a large concern, and governing all its complications, is not usually supposed to belong to them. (Holyoake, 1872: 1)

The movement grew rapidly and proved the Jeremiahs wrong. The Rochdale Pioneers, as they became known, had their own corn mill within 6 years. The practice of local co-ops spread like wildfire – and its legacy continues to this day (Thompson, 1994). Co-operation from below, rather than Owen's benign paternalist vision of production led from above, for mutual benefit, put the consumer in charge, probably for the only time ever. In the mid 19th-century, the co-operative movement expanded into hundreds of local co-operative societies, each fiercely independent, but gradually merging in the next century. Despite hundreds of mergers, there are still over a hundred co-operative societies in the UK alone.

With time, and as 20th-century abundance weakened the case for defensive co-operation, markets lost their threat and the mutuality principle weakened. Co-ops became more like tenuous and tiny share holdings at the point of sale. For most British people in the late 20th-century, the co-operation meant a process by which customers at only one chain, the Co-op, received a coupon with the bill at the check-out counter – the famous 'divi' or dividend. The scheme was closed in the 1960s, overtaken by the nakedly capitalist savings stamps schemes run by the rival private or stock-holder retailers, who in turn dropped it. The practice of consumer co-operation for mutual benefit had become a trading stamp.

Nevertheless, a century and a half after its foundation, the Co-operative movement has spread throughout the world. As Kofi Annan, Secretary-General of the United Nations, wrote in 2003, the Co-operative movement

> is one of the largest organized segments of civil society, and plays a crucial role across a wide spectrum of human aspiration and need. Co-operatives provide vital health, housing and banking services; they promote education and gender equality; they protect the environment and workers' rights. [...] they help people in more than 100 countries better their lives and those of their communities. (Annan, 2003)

There are 700 million people signed up to co-ops worldwide in those 100 countries.

Banks, factories, insurance, farming and retailing companies all reside under the Co-op movement umbrella, even in the UK. In the 1990s, however, the UK movement began to sell off huge parts of its food industrial empire. Vertical integration, owning everything from land to point of sale, for so long a strength of the movement, had by the end of the 20th-century become an economic liability. This was now the era of flexible specialization and post-fordism, characterized by tough contracts and specifications policed by ruthless retail giants to cut prices (Blythman, 2004; Lawrence, 2004). This was a far cry from the 1840s co-operators' dream of an autonomous empire with everything kept within the co-op family. The active consumer could be born, eat, live and die, all serviced from within the movement. With time and scale of operations, the direct control of consumers slipped away and the co-operative societies were forced to retrench, amalgamate and restructure. The Co-op had become associated with old values. Many began to write it off.

Today however there is a return of interest. The UK Co-operative Group has started growing again in the 21st-century, after decades of decline in the face of the conventional supermarket giants. A new generation of consumers, as we note below, has emerged unhappy with the corporate giants open to what marketing specialists call the 'offer' of co-ops. The UK Co-operative Bank, for instance, made a virtue of what it said it would *not* invest in, and saw its client base increase and rise up the social scale. The Co-operative Insurance Society, one of the UK's largest household insurers, managing £20 billon of business, undertook a massive consultation with its users and decided to follow the Co-operative Bank's example, applying ethical criteria to its business model. These were to include acting against fraud and excessive top management ('fat cat') pay to arms manufacturing, labour rights, genetic modification of food and environmental sustainability (Jones, 2005).

In other countries, the social class connotations of co-ops has not been so stifling, so they have not had to fight to rebuild a modern image and business practice. In Japan, the Seikatsu Clubs, a network of 700 consumer co-ops, prospered from the 1960s (Nelson, 1991). The Seikatsu Club movement was started in

1965 by a Tokyo housewife to buy milk more cheaply in bulk. When members joined the Seikatsu Club, they made an initial investment of 1000 yen and paid a similar sum every month. The clubs made a virtue of the duty to be harmonious with nature by 'taking action from the home' (Gussow, 1991: 101–3). By the 1990s, there were 25,000 local groups turning over an annual £260 million (Ekins, 1992). Japan's economic stagnation ensured that the no-profit message still appealed.

Despite, or indeed because of, a remarkable revolution in how foods were processed and sold, food continued to be a key area of consumer disenchantment with conventional modes of market relationship in the 20th-century. From the 1990s, scandals and crises were experienced around the globe over food quality, safety, information, price, environmental damage and public health (Lang and Heasman, 2004). Urban societies with long supply chains rely upon a trust relationship, which if damaged takes time to repair. Not just in Japan, but in the heartlands of capitalism such as the USA and Europe, co-operatives have often been a lifeline for 'alternative' visions, from the wholefood co-ops of the 1970s (Hines, 1976) to community-supported agriculture of the 1990s. Small direct farmer to consumer links such as box schemes and farmers' markets have emerged as highly visible loci of activism. So-called box schemes build links between the consumer who pays a fixed sum each week and the grower who provides a box of fresh food, whatever is in season (Festing, 1993).

These initiatives are small and in formal economic terms barely register as irritants to the big supermarket chains that now dwarf food retailing and frame supply chains regionally and globally. Yet they have been very successful in capturing attention, offering a critique of conventional production, an appeal to immediacy and an authenticity that the larger chains now also try to offer. In the early 1990s, the Co-operative Group in the UK began to realize the opportunities this shifting consumer consciousness offered and began a slow process of injecting ethical, health, environmental and information advantages to its users (Co-operative Group (UK), 2004). Many within the movement saw this as a return to roots: a mix of enlightened self-interest and citizenship, but above all the Co-op becoming once more an active consumer organization after decades in retreat. The Co-op is also reconnecting with its social mission, as a voice for the disenfranchised (Birchall, 2003).

The Co-operative movement now has a big challenge: how simultaneously to address, confront, service, deliver on consumer appetites that are contradictory – damaging ecology and health yet being bought with apparent free-will and awareness! In the past, the co-operatives had an easier time; associated with decent but low income working people, value-for-money was assumed to be a driver. The hard work, zeal and commitment of the 19th-century pioneers who built the local societies, who saved and invested in new shops, factories and land to serve working people, all this brought good-quality goods and services to those who hitherto had lacked them. The co-ops made consumerism affordable. But with the arrival of the mass consumer society in the late 20th-century, that rationale for the movement waned. Others could do it cheaper, faster, with modernity, without the ideological worthiness. The co-op's affairs were inevitably conducted by professional managers, whose vision became more pragmatic, though it never collapsed into quite the ethos of other retail organizations. Despite these limitations, the active co-operator/consumer retains its potency even if today's global markets and the international division of labour make it hard to realize. Will co-operatives be able to rebuild and combine ethics with efficiency? Be associated with flair and panache rather than solid respectability – or recapture respectability as more potent than flair and excitement? It remains to be seen.

Second Wave: Value-for-money Consumers

The second wave of the consumer movement is today by far the highest profile wave of consumer activism, to such an extent that it is often wrongly regarded as being the entire consumer movement. We term this 'value-for-money' consumerism. This emerged in its modern form in the 1930s, but built upon tentative US consumer initiatives in the late 19th- and early 20th-centuries.

A Consumers League was formed in New York in 1891. In 1898, the National Consumers League was formed from local groups and by 1903 had 64 branches in 20 states. The movement took off after a celebrated exposé of wide-scale food adulteration and bad trade. Upton Sinclair, a radical journalist, was sent to write newspaper articles on the insanitary condition at the Chicago stockyards and the meat packing plants. The result was *The Jungle*, a novel published in 1906 (Sinclair, 1985[1906]). A socialist, he hoped to proselytize with the political message that market forces served neither worker nor consumer; he hoped to bring down US capitalism – instead he changed US food law. 'I aimed at the public's heart and by accident hit it in the stomach', he wrote, anticipating many a single issue consumer campaign which launches a simple message, from which it generalizes (Sinclair, 1985[1906]). As a result of the reaction to Sinclair's book, legislation was rushed through Congress, the Pure Food and Drug Act of 1906 and the Meat Inspection Act of the same year, an extraordinary impact for a book (Forbes, 1987: 4). The Federal Trade Commission and a variety of anti-monopoly laws were also set up at the turn of the century.

These early US consumer groups placed heavy emphasis on the containment of the emergent powerful corporations. Their writings were full of concerns about the power of the new combines over individuals, both as workers and as consumers. Unlike the first wave of consumerism, these groups were concerned about the threat posed to consumers by increasing concentration and monopoly capital. In the roaring 1920s with its unprecedented explosion of consumption, *Your Money's Worth*, (Chase and Schlink, 1927) a best selling book, tried to show how consumers were being exploited even as they were first tasting the fruits of mass production – the beginnings of what we term the Fordist bargain, pleasurable consumption as compensation for alienated work. A year later, one of the authors, Schlink, founded Consumers Research Inc. to carry out consumer product testing on a large scale. Its purpose was to provide research and information to consumers. This was the first time that consumer activism saw itself as enabling consumers to take best advantage of the market, rather than trying to undermine the market through co-operative action or political agitation and lobbying.

In 1936, following a bitter confrontation over Schlink's authoritarian management, a group from Consumers Research Inc. split to form the Consumers Union. Consumers Union is now a huge organization, with 450 staff in 2005. It proudly states: 'Since 1936, our mission has been to test products, inform the public, and protect consumers' (Consumers Union, 2005). At its publishing peak in the mid 1990s, it had around 5 million subscribers to its magazine *Consumer Reports*, which epitomizes the principle of second-wave consumerism, namely enabling its members to get best value for money by offering authoritative information. The principle of value-for-money took root in the consumer movement and reached its heyday in President John F. Kennedy's 1962 'Consumer Message to Congress' (Forbes, 1987: 37).

Some value-for-money organizations besides those in the USA have grown into very substantial operations. The UK Consumers' Association magazine *Which?* had a 700,000 subscriber list by the mid 1990s, but this was down from a million at the start of the decade, while The Dutch Konsumenten Bond had 660,000, the highest membership for any consumer movement in the West proportionate to national population. The Belgian *Test Achats*, whose own subscriber list is 320,000, has considerable extra weight due to its formal link with similar Spanish, Portuguese and Italian groups who have 230,000, 150,000 and 350,000 subscribers respectively. Smaller organizations with the same ethos and publishing a regular magazine can be found in many other countries, such as Germany, Belgium, Denmark, Australia, New Zealand, and the newly independent countries in transition, ex-Soviet or Eastern bloc, such as Slovenia.

But the recipe is the same. These magazines test products for safety, ease of use, price, durability, task effectiveness; in short, overall value-for-money. Readers are informed about the 'best buy' and warned about cons and bad buys. Large sums of money are spent testing the products, usually in the consumer organization's own laboratories or test benches. And with the web, surveys and requests to hear stories and problems from members has grown, a new more interactive consumerism *inside* the consumer activist organizations themselves.

Unlike the co-operative movement, this second wave of consumer organizations has no pretensions of offering a radically different vision for society. Its adherents see their role as ameliorative, to make the marketplace more efficient and to champion the interests of the consumer within it. Their aim is to inform and educate the consumer about the features that will enable them to act effectively as consumers (John, 1994). The value-for-money model places considerable stress on rights to information and labelling and the right of redress if something goes wrong. John Winward, former Director of Research at the UK Consumers' Association, conceived of these non-profit organizations as 'information co-operatives' (Winward, 1994: 76–7).

Currently, second-wave consumerism is facing a number of difficulties. On the one hand, post-Fordism and the proliferation of niche markets undermine the possibility of meaningful comparisons between broadly similar products. On the other hand, the number of subscribers of these organizations, which had risen alongside rises in disposable income, began to drop from the early 1990s. This happened for a number of reasons.

First, the pace and impact of technological change meant that consumer organizations' capacity to deliver durable consumer information became harder. As producers delivered ever more nuanced 'niche' products into the marketplace, product information was almost inevitably out-of-date almost before consumers got the data. Models of everything from cars to computers were driven by post-Fordist production. If the sheer range and proliferation of products make testing infinitely harder and render such benchmarking quickly obsolete, one compensation is that consumers have become more market savvy. Consumers compare and contrast products quickly directly, without needing the mediation or championing of the organization.

Second, the emergence of retail giants across national borders gave unprecedented buying power to large retail corporations that could then offer consumers bargains. This pitched them, rather than consumer advocates, as the consumers' champion. Retailers usurped the organizations as the consumers' friend.

And third, value-for-money second-wave consumerism began to be hoist by its individualist stance. This had been both its strength and its weakness. John Beishon, a former Chief Executive of the UK Consumers' Association, recognized this in the early 1990s. He stated that the 'main difficulty is that there is no strong commonality of interest among consumers. [...] Another serious difficulty lies in raising the revenue to support a powerful, independent consumer body' (Beishon, 1994: 5). This is a candid admission of the limitations of second-wave consumerism, coming as it does from one of the richest consumer organizations in the world and coinciding with deeply critical assessments of that organization's narrow outlook (Barker, 1994; Nicholson-Lord, 1994).

The main criticisms raised of second-wave consumerism have been that it fails to address longer-term environmental and social issues; that it has an overwhelmingly middle-class orientation based on the assumption of ever-increasing standards of living; that, as a child of middle-class affluent consumption, it tends not to focus on the plight of poorer consumers; and that it has an inappropriately conservative approach to consumption. Second-wave consumerism has:

> ... rarely questioned the fundamental premise on which American industrialism is based: the desirability of technical efficiency and of technological and economic growth. Instead, consumerism has focused most of its attention on such problems as the lack of product safety or of adequate consumer information. (Bloom and Stern, 1978: 14)

These criticisms apply to second-wave consumerism everywhere, not just in the USA. However, they should not obscure the constraining effect that second-wave groups have had on business. Their independence, their unwillingness to accept advertising revenue and their sometimes religious obsession with accuracy has given them an authority which companies and governments can only disregard at their cost. Even if magazine subscriptions are down, influence is very high, helped ironically by a rise in vociferousness and presence of two subsequent waves of activism.

Third Wave: Naderism

The third wave of consumer activism, like the second, emerged in the USA. Its figurehead, Ralph Nader, became one of the most admired US citizens in national polls for years, until his presidential campaign in 2000 was blamed by many for allowing George W. Bush to win the presidency. His 2004 campaign barely registered and he received accordingly less opprobrium. Nader is not someone to worry about unpopularity. He initially shot into global, not just US, prominence with the publication of his book *Unsafe at Any Speed* in 1965, an exposé of the car industry (Nader, 1991b). The book argued that one automobile model in particular, the Chevrolet Corvair, and automobiles in general were poorly designed and had built-in safety short-cuts. The industry had resisted giving priority to safety, he alleged, a policy that, according to Nader, resulted in an annual slaughter of

Americans: 51,000 in 1965. Highway accidents cost $8.3 billion in property damage, medical expenses, lost wages and insurance overhead expenses (Nader, 1991b: vii). Relying on independent tests, Nader showed how the Corvair easily went out of control at 22 miles per hour, contrasting with its advertising claims of 'easy handling', being 'a family sedan' and a car that 'purrs for the girls' (1991a[1965]: 27). Yet the car's road-handling on corners meant that it demanded 'more driving skill in order to avoid collision than any other American automobile'. As though that was not bad enough, he catalogued how General Motors had failed to come clean on the Corvair's design faults and how when aware of these, it calculated that it would be cheaper not to correct them. Overnight, Nader became a consumer activist hero. What marked his approach as special was that he not only generalized from the particular, documenting how the Corvair may have been an extreme case of consumer safety being a low priority, but that he spelt out at great length how the case was only the tip of an iceberg. His perspective – much expanded and expounded – posited the consumer activist against the corporate giants. In so doing, he brilliantly voiced the interests of mainstream as well as radical consumers emerging in the phenomenally affluent US society of the 1960s.

Nader, a Harvard-educated lawyer, quickly expanded his activities, setting up the Center for Study of Responsive Law and the Project for Corporate Responsibility in 1969. By the end of the 1970s he had spawned a series of organizations, staffed by young professionals, nick-named 'Nader's Raiders', many of them lawyers like himself, young, keen and prepared to be David to corporate Goliaths. By the 1990s, there were 29 organizations with combined revenues of $75–$80 million under the Nader umbrella (Brimelow and Spencer, 1990). The common themes of these organizations were a distrust of corporations, a defence of the individual against the giants, a demand that the state protect its citizens and above all, an appeal for Americans to be citizens, not just consumers. Naderism assumed that the consumer is relatively powerless in a world dominated by corporate giants, whether these be automobile or insurance companies, the health sector or the government–industry complex. The nature of commerce is stacked against the customer, unless regulations or standards of conduct are fought for. This is a hard fight, so the consumer organizations have to be tough, well briefed, well organized and able to make optimum use of the mass media.

Nader brought a new punch to consumer politics and tapped a deep well of public unease about the power of large corporations vis à vis the individual customer. He saw the role of consumer organizations as going beyond getting the consumer the best deal in the marketplace. He made the case for confronting the market itself. Writing about the US food industry in 1970, for instance, Nader made a number of charges about what it will do if left to its own devices:

> Making food appear what it is not is an integral part of the $125 billion food industry. The deception ranges from the surface packaging to the integrity of the food products' quality to the very shaping of food tastes. [...] In fact, very often the degradation of these standards proceeds from the cosmetic treatment of food or is its direct cost by-product. [...] For too long there has been an overwhelmingly dominant channel of distorted information from the food industry to the consumer. [...] Company economy very often was the consumer's cost and hazard. As a result, competition became a way of beating one's competitor by racing for the lowest permissible common denominator. (Nader, 1970: v)

The role of the state, in the absence of consumer pressure, is to collude with this downward spiral, which disadvantages good businesses. The consumer activist's role was and is to confront, to expose, to stand up for public rights, to be a citizen. A persistent theme is to bring the corporate state under the control of democratic forces, and away from the grip of big business (Krebs, 1992: 440–3).

Like the second wave of the consumer movement, Naderism is adamant on the role of information and that information should be free and fair. If the first wave saw capitalism as something to be stepped away from (co-ops are non-profit organizations that share out rather than accumulate or privatize profits), the second wave sees its own role as that of providing information for the consumer to be able to operate more effectively in the marketplace. And the third wave, Naderism, sees capitalism as something to be accepted, but which has to be worked hard on to prevent its excesses becoming its norms.

Naderism places great emphasis on information from consumer bodies as debunking the misinformation systematically disseminated by companies. Nader has described the situation thus: 'It is time for consumers to have information that will provide them with an effective understanding of the secrecy-clouded situation' (Nader, 1970: vii). Freedom of information – rather than product information or mere labelling on a packet – has been a persistent theme for Nader. Indeed, he helped inspire the UK Campaign for Freedom of Information in its uphill task to reform the British state's reflex for secrecy. (Britain only achieved an overarching Freedom of Information Act in 2000, although there had been some incremental improvement prior to that.) For Nader, secrecy is often a collusion between state and commercial interests and it is the duty of the consumer activist to break that collusion, or else she or he becomes an accomplice to it. Only vigilant consumers can break the pact, said Nader:

> Major corporations like their consumers to remain without a capacity for group purchasing action, group legal action, group participating action before regulatory agencies. …The possibility that consumers banding together can muster their organised intelligence to play a major role in shaping economic policy and the future of our political economy is an unsettling one for the mega corporations that play much of the world's economy. So too would be an organised consumer initiative to assess the hazards of technology or forestall the marketing of products which use consumers as test subjects or guinea pigs. (quoted in Beishon, 1994: 9)

Nader's views have fed on the deep apprehension of American consumers, and the public in general, towards anything big and unfettered corporate power in particular. Unlike second-wave organizations, Nader and his colleagues believe that only active involvement by citizens at the local level can counteract these forces. Whereas second-wave groups are reformist and 'top-down' in their strategies, preferring lobbies to rallies, Naderism has been equally content to lobby and rally, priding itself upon building up grassroots citizens action. In the marketplace, the message is to be frugal, to get wise in 'the vital art of self defense' to 'protect yourself in the marketplace', whether buying a car, health insurance, food or a house (Nader and Smith, 1992). These are terms that echo the early American nonimportation movement resisting the British in the late 18th-century (Witkowski, 1989).

Unlike second-wave consumerism, Naderism, though admired, has not easily been grafted onto the consumer cultures of other countries. Neither the political culture nor the legal system nor the scale of consumption in other countries has until recently favoured the growth of Nader-like organizations. But with global de-regulation in the 1990s and the emergence of regional trade blocs such as the EU and NAFTA, Naderism's persistent charge at the collusion of big business and the state has found new allies. These have included environmental groups, animal welfare groups, trades unions, as well as other consumer groups (Lang and Hines, 1993).

The globalization of consumer activism

Consumers' International, formerly the International Organisation of Consumers Unions (IOCU), is a global network founded in 1960, which has over 250 affiliated organizations from 115 countries (Consumers International, 2004). These vary in size and wealth, with the larger and wealthier tending to be in affluent Western countries, but activists are strong in developing countries too and the Western groups have funded consumer activism in new markets of the South and, for instance, in the former Eastern bloc after the USSR collapsed in the late 1980s. Developing countries produced a new generation of consumer activists such as Anwar Fazal, Martin Khor, Vandana Shiva and others, who have not only applied the lessons of Naderism in their own countries but have taken on corporations outside their national boundaries. But they have not done so for consumer rights within the marketplace per se. Their vision has tended to be more social than consumerist, reflecting development concerns. They were particularly active in the anti-globalization movement from the 1990s. Developing countries, they argue, are particularly vulnerable to the globalization of capital, equally for the well-being of their consumers, as for their workers. The stress on citizenship is more important than value for money in the strict sense. In the words of Khor:

> Traditional value for money consumerism (what brand of washing machine to buy) is not important for the Third World. What is important is pollution, world resources, what products should be promoted and what products should be banned. Should we have washing machines at all? (Interview with the authors, January 1994)

The presence of this more questioning approach to consumerism within the umbrella of consumerism has been problematic. Consumers International states that it:

> promotes the establishment of legislation, institutions and information that improve quality of life and empower people to make changes in their own lives. It seeks to ensure that basic human rights are recognised, and promotes understanding of people's rights and responsibilities as consumers. (Consumers International, 2004)

Rights and responsibilities are equally important. The rights are: for basic needs to be satisfied, for safety, to be informed, to choose, to be heard, to redress, for consumer education and for a healthy environment. Consumer responsibilities should also 'use their power in the market to drive out abuses, to encourage ethical practices and to support sustainable consumption and production.' Consumers International members believe that developing and protecting consumers' rights and their awareness of their responsibilities are integral to the eradication of poverty, good governance, social justice and respect for human rights, fair and effective market economies and the protection of the environment (Consumers International, 2004).

Fourth Wave: Alternative or Political Consumers

A new wave of consumer organizations emerged slowly in the 1970s and accelerated in the 1980s, which in 1995 we termed 'alternative consumerism'. A decade ago, we sensed that while this fourth wave had many elements – green, ethical, Third World solidarity and fair trade orientations – it as yet lacked any overall coherence. Nonetheless, we felt there was sufficient commonality for these apparently disparate groups to be one wave. We called it 'alternative consumerism'. Since the first edition of this book, that coherence has definitely emerged. A new progressive consumer activism is building an ethical, social and ecological dimension into marketplace thinking (Harrison et al., 2005). It is now being called by some 'political activism'. The claims and arguments are increasingly confident.

Today, we detect an important coming together of what were different strands of new wave thinking. These strands are different – animal welfare, health, food, ethics, fair-trade, labour rights and more – but their linkages are being recognized even by companies. The largest food retailers in Europe, for instance, now routinely monitor consumer sentiment, and one detects a Maslow-like hierarchy of priorities emerging within European consumerism. The thesis is simple: as consumers become more affluent, their room to think about 'ethical' and wider issues grows, putting new demands on retailers and the supply chain.

Ethics sit at the top of this retailer's pyramid, highest or last-to-be-aspired-to in the supposed consumer priority list. And indeed, over the last 30 years, ethically derived coffees have moved from the consumer fringe to become everyday commodities, despite costing more. By 2003, fair trade had achieved 14 percent of the UK roast and ground coffee market. Cafédirect, all of whose products carry the Fairtrade Mark, had become the UK's sixth largest coffee brand (Fairtrade Foundation, 2005). Giant companies like Starbucks and Costa Coffee now promote fair trade; Pret A Manger switched all its filter coffee (15% of sales) to fair trade in 2002. The motives for the switch are important. When people consume food or drink, they are mostly (not all) uncomfortable with connotations of harm. In brand terms, this had a triple message: a good product in its own right, has *extra special connotations* and by consuming it, one can *feel* good.

If ethical consumerism is now the 'hot' strand within alternative or political consumer activism, at the end of the 1980s, the most influential of the strands we outlined was green consumerism, an attempt to inject environmental consciousness into product choice. This was driven by a then new environmental consciousness to consume wisely in a manner that did not damage the capacity of future generations to consume at all. Green consumers should protect the environment in a number of ways, from purchasing more environmentally friendly products to resisting consumption altogether. For the first time since the early Co-operative movement, consumers were offered a message that it was politically right to set out to influence production directly: buy this rather than that product and you can help good producers to out-compete bad producers. 'Good' and 'bad' were defined in environmental but also moralistic terms. If you consume badly, the implications will be felt by more than you the consumer. Other generations, the environment, climate, might be affected. Suddenly, the environment movement shifted from being oppositional to staking a claim in the marketplace. The impact was significant, although right from its onset, some argued that it would be temporary (Cairncross, 1991: 153).

The green consumer movement began in Europe and spread west to North America. As Cairncross noted 'the sheer speed with which green consumerism erupted in some countries will also leave its mark' (Cairncross, 1991). Seemingly overnight, aerosols with CFCs and apples with pesticide residues became no-go areas in the supermarket. The green consumer movement forced companies to listen to them and spawned new ranges of products such as phosphate-free detergents and cars with recyclable components, which gave consumers the option of choosing 'green'. Often these products, however, remained at the margins of mainline consumption. Perhaps the more important role of green consumerism was to question market supremacy that had dominated the 1980s. Green consumerism represented a significant shift from the rampant individualism, short-termism and venality of the Reagan–Thatcher years, assuming the role of primary opposition to the New Right.

One effect of pressure from green consumer groups was that companies started to undertake environmental audits as a way of gaining competitive advantage over their competitors and fending off criticism. One branch of green consumer activism monitored companies and pursued an approach akin to that of second-wave consumerism by comparing products for their environmental soundness and the green credentials of the company that produced them (Elkington and Hailes, 1988). Its fundamental message was less apocalyptic than it was in the early 1970s and more accommodating to productionism. 'Consume carefully' it proclaimed, rather than 'don't consume' or 'consume less'.

By the early 21st-century, environmentalism had fragmented, with green consumerism a niche in the mainstream. A whole new category of green businesses and green product ranges had consolidated, ranging from cosmetics to electrical goods and even cars, leading to a green producer–consumer nexus, where environmentalists began to act as referees of corporate behaviour. Green consumer activism had generated another niche in the product mix on offer. It is up to the consumer to chose whether to save or destroy the planet. A MORI poll in Britain suggested that half the country's adult consumers had made at least one purchase where the product was chosen rather than another because of its environment-friendly packaging, formulation or advertising (Elkington and Hailes, 1988: 3).

But the tension between the reformists and radicals among consumer activists continued. In one camp lay the proponents of a more caring, considerate capitalism: use purchasing power to reduce energy use; the Factor Four approach, for instance, argues that technologically it is possible for advanced societies to reduce their energy use by a factor of four and to become much more efficient than at present, thus staving off ill-effects of emissions, and climate change (von Weizacher et al., 1996). In the other camp were those who argued that the thrust of green consumers should be to consume less altogether (Irvine, 1989). In some respects, the first camp was charged by the latter with coming to the rescue of consumer capitalism and giving it new opportunities for niche products, at the very moment when tradition markets were being saturated.

Like earlier generations of reformers, green activists have been victims of their own success, a process recognized by activists themselves, many of whom have harboured no illusions about the limitations of green activism when restricted to consumption. As a result, radical segments within the movement advocated the case for more structural change (Irvine, 1989).

If green consumerism became mainstream by the early 1990s, by the early 2000s, another previously fringe strand had become the high-profile new entrant: ethical consumption. Reaffirming the moral dimension of consumer choice, ethical consumerism initially seemed doomed to the margins (much as these authors willed it to succeed). Who would push its case? Who would fund the necessary organizations? Yet that funding and support emerged. In the UK, the fair trade-oriented New Consumer organization rose and fell, but the Ethical Consumer Research Association (ECRA) consolidated and thrived. In the USA, the Council on Economic Priorities introduced a guide that rated 1300 US brands thus:

> Every time you step up to a cash register, you vote. When you switch from one brand to another, companies hear you clearly. You can help make America's companies socially responsible by using this guide. (Will et al., 1989: 143)

Ethical consumer groups grade products and companies on criteria such as these, taken from *Ethical Consumer* magazine in 2004:

- **Environmental**: reporting, pollution, nuclear power, other;
- **Animals**: testing, factory farming, other;
- **People**: support for oppressive regimes, workers' rights, code of conducts, irresponsible marketing, armaments;
- **Extras**: genetic engineering, boycott calls, political activity, action alert.

These criteria have altered and deepened since the 1990s (Adams et al., 1991; *Ethical Consumer*, 1993). When the ECRA was founded in Manchester, close to Rochdale of co-operative pioneer fame, in the late 1980s, it was advised not to use the word 'consumer' in its title 'because the word is too narrow a definition of what people do' (Rob Harrison, interview with the authors, February 1994). The word 'consumer' places an emphasis on only one aspect of people's behaviour, one that tends to deny the political and moral goals the organization had come into existence to promote. By the mid 1990s, Rob Harrison of ECRA argued that the organization's goal is really to change culture and to promote a consumer awareness of the global implications of Western consumption. Issues such as fair trade, aid and exploitation of Third World workers, far from being marginal to the ethics and politics of Western consumption, lie at its very heart (Wells and Jetter, 1991). Globally aware consumers, argued Anwar Fazal of IOCU Asia Office, 'cannot ignore the conditions under which products are made – the environmental impact and working conditions. We are linked to them and we have a responsibility for them' (quoted in Wells and Jetter, 1991: 3).

The fair trade movement has sought to encourage links between producers and workers of the South and consumers of the North by delivering products from developing countries directly to rich consumer markets. It asks consumers to buy these products in part because they return more money to the original producer than does conventional trade and in part as a way of supporting non-exploitative firms operating in the South. In this way, they hope to revitalize the old co-operators' goal of bringing the consumer and producer into closer relationship (Barratt Brown, 1993: 184–6).

One particularly successful product in Europe, for instance, has been a coffee branded as Cafédirect in the UK and as Max Havelaar in the Netherlands, named after a famous Dutch novel of the same name, published in 1860, which denounced the use of slaves in the coffee trade, an early appeal to consumers (Mulatuli, 1987 [1860]). This coffee was adopted by the European Parliament as its official brand. The Cafédirect brand sold its millionth packet in 1994, just 2 years after its launch. By 2004, fair trade was an important force in 17 affluent food countries, particularly for product sectors such as tea, confectionary and coffee, linking 350 commodity producers, representing 4.5 million farmers in developing countries, to developed world markets (Fairtrade Foundation, 2005). Britain had become the biggest market in the world for fair-traded products.

The Future: Convergence or Continued Divergence?

Since we outlined our waves of consumer activism, a number of important changes have occurred all pointing to some convergence and cross-fertilization across the waves of activism.

First, the fourth wave's ethical and environmental values began to be absorbed by the dominant and powerful second-wave or value-for-money consumer groups. Corporate social responsibility (CSR) advocates became influential in auditing company behaviour. The crises and bankcruptcies of giant firms such as Enron in the USA and Parmalat in Italy encouraged financiers to see the economic value of viewing companies through an ethical and longer-term filter (Harrison, 2003). CSR has been, in part, a response to consumer activists whose legitimacy grew with the crises.

Second, co-operatives, the first wave, took note of, helped and began to adopt the vitality and appeal of the fourth wave by making new commitments to position co-operatives as more trustworthy sources of the necessities of life. The Co-operative Bank's pioneering return to ethics-led banking had been proven to be good business as well as ethics. As we noted above, the Co-operative Insurance Society decided in 2005 to do likewise. Co-op food retailing had tentatively begun earlier, launching its 'responsible retailing' campaign in 1995 and consolidating this in 2004 (Co-operative Group, 2004). Whatever final shape this takes, the overt reconnection with ethics, health and social justice is interesting. Whereas other retailers, for instance, may offer an 'ethical range', this is not done out of conviction but to respond to consumers, to keep people coming who might otherwise go elsewhere. The Co-op says it does it because it believes in it.

Third, in December 1999, the disparate strands of consumer activism came together in Seattle in opposition to the proposed revision of the WTO's GATT. Suddenly, what had been 'single issues' in a wider activist agenda was brought together by a realization that the same trade rules that threatened, say, animal welfare also affect public health, the environment, labour rights, fair trade access. In the 1990s, some within the single issue groups had learned that they shared a more common agenda, but after Seattle it became legitimate to build alliances. Thus, globalization reinvigorated consumer activism (Klein, 2000; Vidal, 1997).

Fourth, as we argued in our notion of the 'twilight of consumerism', a certain ennui set in within consumer society. As Alan Durning asked: how much is enough? (Durning, 1992). How much can one consume? There are no signs of an end to consumption – far from it – but the activists began to feel the law of diminishing returns. Ethical consumption began to experience what green consumerism had undergone a decade earlier. Might the activists burn themselves out or, worse, win the publicity war but not alter mass consumer behaviour? Cheap airfares and cheap food still win more consumer 'votes' than the social issues, however much the polls suggest consumers want to act honourably.

One of the most effective globally organized consumer activist campaigns, the International Baby Foods Action Network (IBFAN) has been struggling for over two decades to achieve its ends. This heroic campaign has much to teach consumer activists. It began as an alliance of health and religious workers, but quickly took on the biggest food company in the world Nestlé (Lang et al., 2004). At moments IBFAN dented Nestlé and the sales of other companies seeking to promote breast-feeding substitutes, but the fact is that the company and products are still there. But cynicism is not in order. We use the term 'heroic' not lightly. A small number of dedicated workers worldwide have built the only really genuine *global* consumer activist organization.

In Conclusion

How can we judge consumer activists? Is the consumer as activist doomed to struggle endlessly against the odds, only achieving 'success' if it is narrowly defined? A few cents or pence on or off a share price here; a dent in a company's market share there? If the ultimate goal is to redirect consumer culture, to give it a particular moral bent, this is an enormous task and surely way beyond any consumer organization, however rich, however well staffed.

All waves of consumer activism undoubtedly rely on people of considerable skill and vision. As morally and politically driven individuals, they work hard, long hours, often for low pay. Their rewards are a strange pleasure most easily observable in single issue campaigns. Victories in such campaigns come by forcing governments to recognize their errors (for example, over the risks of BSE-infected meat), companies to make policy u-turns (for example, Shell dumping the Brent Spa at sea) or sought-after pieces of legislation reaching the statute books. To the outsider, the reaction to such successes might be 'so what?'; to the activist, these are occasions for some cheer, a reassertion of consumer rights, a sense of winning against superior forces. This moral certainty maintains the effort.

The consumer as activist struggles daily to redefine the notion of progress and quality of life, to pursue happiness by consumption and to promote or create debate. Crucially, it is the consumer as activist who confronts consumption, explicitly seeking to alter its meaning and to redefine the cultural dynamic of goods by reintroducing the validity of the idea of needs and wants. Few movements apart from the feminist and gay movements have had such a discernible effect in truly remoulding culture. And yet the consumer as activist seems to be the great absentee from many celebrations of contemporary consumer culture. This absence has left discussions on the subject seriously impoverished.

From this short review, very different strands of consumer activism emerge. We have outlined our four waves, but across these waves are visible some other characteristics, summarized in Table 9.1. Consumer-activists may be diverse, but their efforts and successes constitute a stubborn rejection of the anarchism of the market, by persistently stressing that right and wrong, damaging and beneficial, useless and useful, needs and wants are concepts that cannot be written out of consumption. The vast majority of consumers recognize these terms even as they

Table 9.1   Some dimensions of consumer activism

Dimension of activism	Ranges from ...	To ...
Organizational form	Individual consumerist 'heroes'	collectivist
Size of organization	Small	Large
Range of action	Single issue	Entire consumer culture
Focus of action	The state	Corporations
Nature of activism	Direct action	Sentiment
Values	Reform markets	Constrain or reduce markets

continue to be driven heavily, but not exclusively by price, to be tempted by advertising and to be seduced by images. Ironically, consumer activists today perhaps achieve influence less in the marketplace and more via public relations departments of companies which are now so finely tuned to neutralize or reduce any potential shocks such as activists can deliver.

Many activists acknowledge that consumer capitalism can redefine itself in ways that accommodate many of their demands. This may take the form of creating niche markets (for ethical or green products) or by accepting a degree of regulation as a necessity for its continuing legitimation. Some consumer-activists recognize this as an inevitable limitation of much reformist activity. This in no way annihilates the value of their efforts or undermines the objectives, but does mean that there is a ceaseless process of incorporation and accommodation, as ideas are 'cherry-picked' and modifications made to products and processes, ranging from slight to significant. Cynics might argue that this relegates ethical consumption and other progressive movements to a process of being unpaid revisionists of advanced capitalism. In some respects, this might be, and is, inevitable, but in important ways, their contribution lies in acting as the moral conscience of the existing system, a set of principles that is above price or minor product amelioration and diversification. Others go further and view palliative reform as inadequate in stopping the ruinous path of consumer capitalism. For them, the concept of the consumer must now be itself overcome, having become fatally flawed and compromised. Only by redefining how they think and act as consumers can individuals today individually and collectively recover some of the control that they have lost to the organizations and objects that now dominate their lives and through which they express themselves.

In this important sense, the new wave of political consumerism incorporating animal welfare, fair trade, ethical consumption and more, maps one clear if complex path for consumers, a route for translating consumerism into citizenship. The contrast between consumers and citizens is one conventional ideological contrast. Much as we would like consumers to take the 'high' road, evidence suggests that there are powerful forces pushing and pulling consumers in different and 'low' roads, too; consumer less versus consumer ever more. Political consumer activism, by internalizing otherwise externalized social, environmental and human costs, almost inevitably adds to the price of goods and services. Ultimately, we feel, consumer activism has to face this fact. If humanity wants a decent society, it has to be paid for. If it doesn't, or enough don't, society and the biosphere will pay anyway. The stakes are high. Consumers as activists are unlikely to fade away!

CHAPTER **10**

The Consumer as Citizen

We are witnessing the swift debasement of the concept of
'citizen' – the person who actively participates in shaping society's
destiny – to that of 'consumer', whose franchise has become his or
her purchasing decisions.

Stuart Ewen, 1992: 23

C
O
ARGUMENTS
E

The increasing universality of consumerism has eroded an older tradition that approached people as citizens with rights and responsibilities. This tradition looked at political action as the key to ensuring a
better and fairer quality of life. In the 20th-century, this democratic tradition delivered a welfare system in many countries, where the state
acted as the guarantor that core human needs, such as education and
health, be met independently of ability to pay. Consumerism, on the
other hand, in the later part of the 20th-century proposed a model of
freedom and happiness through individual choice exercised in a
market environment. Currently, political culture is poised between giving primacy to voting or shopping. Consumerism has encroached core
citizenship terrain, including housing, healthcare and education. There
are, however, signs that a number of key obstacles may halt or even
reverse further erosion of citizenship. We single out three: casualization and job uncertainty, which undermine the Fordist Deal, problems
of information (including overload and access) and environmental
constraints.

The idea of the citizen to some Anglo-Saxon ears has a rather quaint, old-fashioned ring to it; citizenship was what liberal political theorists referred to, civics was what children were taught in class. For other cultures, following the legacy of the French Revolution, the concept of citizen is foundational to their national and political identity. The contrast between consumer and citizen has been the subject of considerable debate. Does the triumph of consumerism and the omnipotence of markets consign the notion of citizenship to the history text-books? Can consumerism replace citizenship as the guarantee of social rights? Does the notion of citizenship add any value in societies where markets dominate social relations? Can the consumer replace the citizen as the agent of social change and become the basis of platform of opposition?

Many consumer activists, as we saw in Chapter 9, have also sought to proclaim the ideal of citizenship in contradistinction to the notion of the consumer, which they saw as too individualistic, restrictive, in short irrecoverably hi-jacked by the political Right (Goldsmith and Mander, 2001; Khor, 2001; Korten, 2001; Martin, 2002; Nader, 1991a [1965]; Shiva, 2002). In this way, they have resurrected an older idea propounded by the founder of the UK's *Which?* (formerly the Consumers' Association) and National Consumer Council, Michael Young, who had envisaged organized consumers as a new third force for the citizenry, alongside organized labour and organized capital and management. Even earlier in 1920, the co-operative theorist, Percy Redfern, had called on consumers to unite to:

> build a new social order – an order which may restore the primitive social unity, but now upon a world scale instead of within the narrow circle of the township and village. (Redfern, 1920: 42)

> In the past the consumer has paid. In the future he and she together must live and act as citizens in the commonwealth of man. (Redfern, 1920: 57)

Yet almost as soon as the idea of citizenship re-emerged as the focus for progressive opposition in the late 1980s, attracting to it demands for freedom of information, written constitutional rights, electoral reform, and so on, the idea was seized by New Right (Pirie, 1991) as a lifeline to keep the neo-liberal project on course, even as it was beginning to be questioned. More recently, the idea of choice that has prospered on the back of a consumerist ethos has been re-introduced into discussions of citizenship to the point where consumerism may have colonized citizenship.

In this chapter, we examine the chronic tension that has existed between the idea of the consumer and that of the citizen, and assess whether the two represent conflicting tendencies. We also examine whether one of them can usurp the other or whether there remains a place for both of them in contemporary culture. Finally, we provide a provisional assessment on whether the concept of the citizen can form the basis of a co-ordinated opposition to consumer capitalism. We will see that the idea of citizenship is itself often commodified and corrupted by consumer capitalism and the political and ideological powers that underpin it. Yet we shall also note that whenever a vocabulary of opposition and defiance is required it is as likely as not to proceed from the ideal of the citizen.

Citizens and Consumers

We have no serious difficulty thinking of ourselves as consumers. Thinking of ourselves as citizens is more problematic, even for those of us who spent our childhood saluting the flag daily. 'In this society, citizenship is an archaic term. It is not part of the language of everyday life. Its value for understanding this life is not evident either' (Wexler, 1990: 166). Demands for citizenship and the right to vote might be high on the popular agenda in a country engaged in mass struggle for enfranchisement, such as South Africa during the five apartheid decades, but in the so-called mature democracies like the USA and countries of the EU, the right to vote and broader notions of citizenship have become more problematic. Voting rates have declined, though citizenship re-asserts itself whenever voters question a political agenda, such as the European Constitution.

The idea of citizen implies mutuality and control as well as a balance of rights and duties that is neither evident nor especially attractive to us. Citizens are active members of communities, at once listened to, but also prepared to defer to the will of the majority. Citizens have to argue their views and engage with the views of others. In as much as they can make choices, citizens have a sense of superior responsibility. Choosing as a citizen leads to a very different evaluation of alternatives from choosing as a consumer. As a citizen, one must confront the implications of one's choices, their meaning and their moral value. The notion of citizenship has at its core a 'bond', as T.H. Marshall noted, 'a direct sense of community membership based on loyalty to a civilization which is a common possession' (Wexler, 1990: 169).

Consumers, on the other hand, need not be members of a community, nor do they have to act on its behalf. Consumers operate in impersonal markets, where they can make choices unburdened by guilt or social obligations. Both Marx and Simmel remarked on how the cash nexus dissolves social bonds, the former to criticize it as the root of alienation under capitalism, the latter to praise it as the liberation from the fetters of the gift economy (Marx, 1972[1844]: 780: 1967[1867]: 770; Simmel, 1978: 660).

The two ideas have very different pedigrees. The citizen, the foundation of Athenian democracy and reinvented and expanded by the American and French revolutions, implies an equality among citizens, even if it denies it to others – slaves, immigrants or refugees. It is essentially a political concept, defining individuals standing within a state and a community, according them rights and responsibilities (Rawls, 1971: 699). The citizen is an impersonation of what Philip Rieff called 'political man', the cultural ideal based on the notion that the good life, justice and happiness can be attained through political action, rather than through religious faith; the latter had been the recipe for salvation of political man's predecessor, the 'religious man' (Rieff, 1959, 1966). Common to both religious and political ideals was the presupposition that each individual is an organic part of a whole, unable to achieve full individuality and happiness except as a member of that whole. Where the ideal of the citizen dramatically deviated from that of the religious believer was in the inalienable rights of citizens to hold their own opinions and views. One can be a citizen while disagreeing and criticizing the government; this was a new form of freedom.

The consumer, on the other hand, originates in a very different ideal, referred to by Rieff as economic man, who seeks the good life in markets. Few variants of this ideal are as clear-cut as the Protestant work ethic, or, in the 20th-century, the backbone of modern consumerism, the Fordist Deal (see Chapter 1, 'The Emergence of Contemporary Consumerism'). Here individuals act as atoms, unencumbered by social responsibilities and duties, free from the obligation to account for their preferences and choices. They are never required to endure sacrifices for a superior goal, nor do their actions represent anybody other than themselves. They need not defer to any collective majority.

The idea of the citizen can become easily idealized, becoming the focus of nostalgia for a time when individuals were meant to be active members of political communities and when economies where conceived as having national boundaries, when a vote created a political assembly which could control a national economy. However, if such a notion of citizenship implies control, commitment and bonding, it also carries since its earliest origins disturbing resonances of exclusion and discrimination. Non-citizens, stateless persons, immigrants, refugees, exiles, people without official papers and fixed addresses, vagrants, these are people who may be legitimately harassed, exploited and discriminated against in most societies, especially those which place a high premium on citizenship. The outsider can be used as a mechanism of social division. Consumers, on the other hand, generally face no such discrimination, so long as they can afford to pay. Through money they may acquire a wide variety of things, including in many cases 'citizenship', the right to participate in a way of life, a dream.

How then is it possible that two ideas so different as citizen and consumer can become part of the same discourse? Two main avenues have led to this convergence. The Left, having lost faith in the consumer as the hero of right-wing economics has sought to enlarge the consumer into a responsible consumer, a socially aware consumer, a consumer who thinks ahead and tempers his or her desires by social awareness, a consumer whose actions must be morally defensible and who must occasionally be prepared to sacrifice personal pleasure to communal well-being. In other words, the Left has stretched the idea of consumer in the direction of citizen. The US organization Public Citizen and all the other organizations started by Nader (See Chapter 9, 'The Consumer as Activist') have been prolific in campaigning and promoting the idea of the citizen and of consumers as citizens. So concerned was his team about the decline of meaningful US citizenship by the early 1990s that it produced a civics package for use in schools (Isaac and Nader, 1992). This profiled a number of key citizens' movements representing the rights of women, minorities, consumers, unions and environment. More importantly, the civics package took students through the options a citizen has for participating in civil society: whistle-blowing, pamphleteering, getting organized, arranging meetings, conducting research, legal action, direct action, becoming a shareholder activist, and so on. The book, to some extent, was a 'how to' and 'what' summary of much of third- and fourth-wave consumer activism and was a classic statement, as Nader wrote in the 'Foreword', of 'practicing civics, becoming a skilled citizen, using one's skills to overcome apathy, ignorance, greed or abuses of power in society at all levels ...' Nadar, 1991a[1965: iv]). Similar moves followed the election of New Labour (a centrist rather than left government) in 1997 in the UK. The message was that the only route to rebuilding citizenship from a consumer starting point was involvement with others.

The Right (which has repeatedly reinvented itself and even incorporated some of the old centre), on the other hand, has sought to incorporate the citizen into its image of the consumer by using the spurious concept of 'votes' and ballots. According to this argument, consumers vote in the marketplace in exactly the same way as citizens voted in the Athenian agora of old. The marketplace becomes a surrogate for political discourse or, in their view, incorporates political discourse, rendering it redundant. The citizen is being redefined as a purchaser whose 'ballots ... help create and maintain the trading areas, shopping centres, products, stores, and the like' (Dickinson and Hollander, 1991: 12). Buying becomes tantamount to voting, market surveys the nearest we have to a collective will (Ewen, 1992: 23). In this way, the more wealth or purchasing power the consumer has, the more 'votes' she or he gets, thus transmogrifying the old political principle of one-person-one-vote.

So, when the idea of the citizen emerges in discussions of consumption, it assumes different meanings. Nowhere is this more clear than in discussions of TV (McRobbie, 1994, 1999). Market enthusiasts want unregulated TV, where individuals choose to watch what they want. In an age of multi-channel, satellite and cable TV, if they do not like a programme, they vote by switching to a different channel or by switching off and turning to their game consoles, their computer or other personal entertainment systems. Public service advocates, on the other hand, believe that if individuals act merely as consumers, they end up with a profusion of virtually indistinct channels appealing to the lowest common denominator. Their choice is narrowed to minutiae (Brown, 1991). If, however, they act as citizens, they seek to control and regulate what is shown on their screens, voting for a particular range of options and stopping others. Ultimately, the citizens do not take markets as given but will seek to regulate them, control them and tame them. They seek to do so either through direct action and active participation, or indirectly, through the state. And this is where the state comes into discussions of citizens and contemporary consumption.

The Dilution of the Citizen? Or Resurrection?

The nature of the state, however, is furiously contested. On the traditional Left, critics have long seen the state as the club of the ruling class, a mechanism for facilitating the interests of capital and oiling the wheels of commerce (Miliband, 1969; O'Connor, 1973; Poulantzas, 1975). Social democrats and liberals have taken a more accommodating position, arguing that the state can be used to ameliorate the conditions of the poor, notably through welfare, educational and health provisions (Beveridge, 1942; Bobbitt, 2002; Rawls, 1971). Conservatives of the older paternalist school did not deviate much from the idea of the state as safety-net, though they would draw a line between those deserving assistance and those not.

> [Conservatism] regards it as the duty of the modern State to ensure to the subject pure air and water, to see that his food is unadulterated, and to assist him to maintain himself and his family in sickness and old age. It lays it down as a cardinal principle that every citizen shall have a right, so far as is humanly possible, to a good education, open spaces, and healthy conditions of life. The modern State is the assurance company which assures these benefits to its citizens. (Bryant, 1929: 17)

Under the New Right of the 1980s, the state disowned such responsibilities. Throughout the 1980s and 1990s (the Thatcher–Reagan years and their legacy), it set out, first, to dismantle the welfare philosophy through privatization and contracting services to independent firms, and then explicitly they sought to redefine it (Osborne and Gaebler, 1992; Pirie, 1991), turning citizens into consumers (HM Government, 1991). According to this view, it is up to the citizens as consumers to decide whether they want a service from the state and what quality they are prepared to pay for. In simple terms, why bother voting for politicians to provide public parks and clean air, if the Chicago futures market will trade pollution permits and if parks can be supplied by Disneyland and others? Public space, from parks to pavements, is seen as an opportunity to sell, not to commune; it becomes a marketplace, not a social place (Worpole, 2000). This marketization has been most rigorously applied into the education, healthcare and pension sectors, with even the social democratic welfarist countries under pressure to reform their public sectors. The principles of consumer choice and individual responsibility are subverting the idea of universal rights to health, education and pensions.

Critics of marketization draw upon three stands of analysis, broadly, sociological, economic and political. One strand argues that government has been taken over by totally unaccountable forces that corrupt the possibility of anyone having control, whether termed consumer or citizen (Greider, 1992; Korten, 2001). For both citizens and consumers, rights have become dependent upon wealth. For Bauman, the poor have been made to look like failed citizens who mishandled their exercise of choice and are now forced to accept the state's choices on their behalf (Bauman, 1998). As Golding has said, 'to be poor is to endure conditional citizenship' (Lister, 1990: vii). The poor, of course, are marginalized by consumerism but further fractionalized by gender and position in the workforce (Lister, 2004; Lister and Campling, 2003; Toynbee, 2003).

The second strand of criticism asserts that the very idea that consumers or market forces can govern affairs of state is absurd and that a public sector, distinct from the private sector, has to be retained.

> The analogy between government and firms doesn't hold water. Since the public sector is not driven by the same profit motive – citizens' priorities are different from stockholders' – it has not inherent reason to price its services more expensively. (Lynch and Makusen, 1993: 128)

According to this view, fundamental resources such as water, air, open space and wildernesses should not be treated as commodities but as common goods to be husbanded and cared for by agencies that are not penetrated by market forces (Barlow and Clarke, 2002; Morgan, 2003).

The third strand set out to reclaim the notion of citizenship from the clutches of the New Right (Crick, 2001, 2004; Lynch and Makusen, 1993). This strand argues that the modern Anglo-American 'hands off' state with its individualistic and pro-business orientation marks the nadir of true citizenship (Pollock and Leys, 2004). David Rieff views the US citizen as no more than a supermarket cultural browser: 'For better or worse (probably both), ours is a culture of consumerism and spectacle, of things and *not* ideas' (Rieff, 1993: 63).

Where does the consumer movement stand in all this? In the UK, the consumer movement was initially divided by the Right's attempt to redefine the citizen as consumer. The second-wave value-for-money organizations generally supported initiatives such as John Major's Citizen's Charter and privatization, with minor reservations (HM Government, 1991). They believed that such moves offered a better deal for consumers, raising the quality of service and widening the range of options available to them. Few can argue that before the wave of privatization, nationalized industries were perfect models of responsiveness, efficiency or consideration for the needs of their customers. In doing so, second-wave organizations acknowledged the argument of the New Right that the state is unable to conduct economic activity effectively, whether this amounts to running a transport network, a health service or an automobile manufacture.

The third and fourth waves of consumer organizations, on the other hand, were dismissive of both privatization and performance targets for the state sector (Harrison et al., 2005; Lang, 1991). Privatization is seen as accelerating the dilution of citizenship, accentuating social inequality and making public services contingent on the ability to pay (Pollock and Leys, 2004). If the ideological principle of progressive taxation is on the defensive, the idea that all citizens are entitled to certain services on an equal basis is also under attack from dominant political culture. Many third- and fourth-wave thinkers were disparaging of the New Right's efforts to resurrect an ideal of citizen, even as it fostered inequalities and divisions within their societies. These efforts were even more risible when seen against the tone of political and cultural discourse set by the mass media. The days of the agora, of reasoned debate and personal involvement have long been overtaken by the politics of the sound-bite, the image, the simulation and the passive evaluation of policies and politicians after the manner of soap-powders. Even governments genuinely committed to the ideal of citizenship would find it hard to take independent political or economic action in an age of free trade, capital globalization and transnational institutions (Lang and Hines, 1993: 49; Nader, 1991a[1965]).

The rest of this chapter explores further the arguments above through three important arenas, which are currently at the centre of political debate: privatization and sub-contracting of public services, advice and information, and the environmental impact of consumption.

Privatization and sub-contracting

The privatization of state industries is one of the central arenas in which these arguments are currently being fought over. State industries were targeted by Thatcherism as inefficient, failing to give value for money to the customer and ripe for market discipline. Prior to that, certain consumer bodies had already argued the case for increased competition in public services (National Consumer Council, 1978, 1979). They found themselves overtaken by the Thatcher government, which went well beyond their recommendations and, in a wave of spectacular privatizations, sold off water, telephone, electricity, gas, the state airline and even public transport all to the private sector. Thatcher was a pioneer whose example has been emulated worldwide, from Italy and the Netherlands to India and Russia. The main opposition to these moves, outside party politics, came from unions and, occasionally, environmental groups which took a broader citizen's approach, expressing a series of concerns regarding standards, public health and safety implications, increased costs for low-income groups and lack of democratic accountability. Reaction to privatization has been strongest in Latin American countries, such as Venezuela and Brazil, where there has been fierce debate over retention of public assets such as oil (Gott, 2000).

The consumer might in the short-term benefit from competition, smarter packaging, greater choice, but even the consumer bodies expressed reservations about monitoring by independent regulators, financial redress, and so on. The citizen, on the other hand, stood to lose massively from these moves. Not only were a number of national assets taken away from them, but, subject to the market mechanism, unprofitable operations were run down. More importantly, these moves symbolized the ideological triumph of the neo-liberal and neo-conservative creed that only free enterprise could run business efficiently and that all state-run enterprise was doomed to dip endlessly into the tax-payers pocket. A service or a commodity that did not attract purchasers in the market, according to the Thatcherite logic, could be dispensed with. A wedge had been driven between citizen and consumer. Under the rhetoric of a share-owning democracy, the concept of the citizen was itself being privatized.

Another prong of the strategy to reduce citizens into consumers consisted of the introduction of compulsory competitive tendering for local authority services. In the UK, services such as street cleaning, school meals and direct labour organizations in building maintenance were all contracted out in the early 1980s (Whitfield, 1983). Subsequently in the 1990s, middle-class professional services such as architects, legal services and residential care homes were all contracted out too. What had previously been a nexus of national and local services regarded as integral parts of the British state's support structure for the citizen, became markets. The privatization ethos spread in many other countries worldwide (for example, Walker and Wang, 2005). Integrated services were now internally split into purchasers and providers; as was seen in Chapter 2, 'The Consumer as Chooser', this did not on the whole lead to an automatic shift of power in favour of the consumer, but the citizen was certainly lessened.

The introduction of a new language of 'empowerment', 'internal markets' and 'mixed economy of care', 'public–private partnerships' and 'private finance initiatives' into public service organizations is significant. A service becomes a commodity, even as a hollow vocabulary of empowerment, choice and quality was rehearsed to justify it (Mather, 1991; Pirie, 1991; Walker and Wang, 2005). What the rhetoric of the consumer achieved beyond doubt was to put business in the driving seat, while constantly undermining the idea of citizens with rights and obligations. The buzz-word of empowerment, hi-jacked from minority right movements, was to provide both the *coup de grâce* to the old notion of citizen and its banalization in the Citizen's Charter, a UK government initiative launched in 1991 promising certain 'rights' for customers of state services (HM Government, 1991). This was a misnomer and might have been more accurately described as a customers' charter for public services about to be privatized. Academic critics viewed it as 'an exercise in improving supplier responsiveness to customers but unaccompanied by any real shift in power to consumers' (Hambleton and Hoggett, 1993). Utilities were made to promise targets such as the length of delay before answering a phone, the percentage of trains arriving within a few minutes of the promised arrival time, the number of crime enquiries completed, and so on. Over the next decade, this discourse took root and became accepted as the normal framework for policy-making. Tony Blair's government enlarged the discourse, tempering the rhetoric of consumer empowerment by injecting the Rawlsian notion of balancing rights and responsibilities.

Advice and information

The second issue that has highlighted the distance between older traditions of citizenship and its reinvention by the neo-liberals has been the information required to operate effectively as a consumer in a marketplace. Consumer advocates are in agreement on this one. Since the earliest days of the consumer movement, they have argued for the value of information, notably product information and labelling, on the one hand, and general consumer education on areas like nutrition and health which then enables them to discriminate between products and to make good use of labelling information, on the other. As seen in the previous chapter (Chapter 9, 'The Consumer as Activist'), one of their earliest arguments was that markets cannot operate as effective mechanisms against unscrupulous or inefficient suppliers unless consumers have the requisite information and right of redress. All strands of consumer activism have also been in agreement that it is essential for consumers to know their rights in front of the law (Cranston, 1984). Consumers International, the umbrella group of consumer organizations, argues that without information, markets cannot work; new institutions have to be created to deliver this if they do not exist. In the UK, a national system of law centres, offering legal advice to consumers on a collective basis, started in the 1970s, borrowing heavily from the US experience, and proposed by the Society of Labour Lawyers (UK) (1968). The aim was to offer everybody access to the law, irrespective of their means to pay.

A separate scheme aimed at giving consumers information and advice emerged in the 1970s, the Consumers Advice Centres. These had been pioneered by the Consumers Association (now *Which?*), based on experience elsewhere in Europe. The aims of the centres were to offer pre-shopping advice to help people decide which product to purchase, as well as to assist them with complaints when purchases had gone wrong. In practice, people did not use the pre-shopping advice that much, but they did make extensive use of the complaint support schemes (National Consumer Council (UK), 1977). Some of the centres handled as many as 40,000 enquiries a year, no mean index of interest at a local level. By 1975, there were 75 in the UK and they processed half a million complaints in a year. By 1977, there were 120 centres, 79 of which had been set up without central government help (Fulop, 1977: 22–3). Better evidence of the consumers' thirst for support and information cannot be supplied than the success of this scheme. Yet one of the very first things that the new Thatcher government did was to cut central government funds to the Consumer Advice Centres. Part of this function now resides with the older established Citizens' Advice Bureaux, which cover all aspects of legal redress.

And what of information? Capitalist societies are not all the same. They have starkly contrasting cultures and notions of rights, community and individualism – in short, of citizenship (Hampden-Turner and Trompenaars, 1993). Yet consumer activists have insisted that unless there is information about goods and services, inadequate goods will be left on the market, when with due information they would not survive. The market alone cannot be left to discriminate between safe and unsafe products, such as medical drugs or food additives. Information, in the form of independent findings, are an essential prerequisite for consumer and citizen safety. And what was the solution of Thatcherism to this? To commodify information and advice, just as it encouraged the commodification of public services and of the idea of the citizen itself. If consumers wants advice, was the argument, let them pay for it individually; there is no need for government to supply such information. Companies, watch-dogs and, not least, consumer organizations themselves can do this very effectively. Consumer activists, on the other hand, argued that in the light of the massive resources devoted to advertising by capitalist organizations, state involvement and some funding is vitally needed to counter the vast inequality in resources companies put behind sales information for products (through advertising, marketing, and so on), compared to the resources available for consumer information and education (Loudon and Della Bitta, 1993).

Since the first edition of this book, the arrival of the Internet has opened vast new opportunities for consumers to obtain information. The media, including the older ones like TV, radio and papers, have embraced the consumer as an opportunity to provide a variety of services and information. The role of the media in relation to consumerism is complex. On the one hand, the media are a conduit of facts about consumers and consumer news reports; conduct product tests on behalf of consumers, report results, make judgments of best and worst buys; champion causes on behalf of consumers, conducting investigations and delivering exposés; inform consumers of products and processes, rights and wrongs, responsibilities and opportunities. On the other hand, the media also sell goods and services to consumers, directly or indirectly, promote celebrities as archetypes of consumption and are the major carriers of the consumerist ideology that the good life is to be found in material goods (see Chapters 1 and 3).

Citizens, consumers and the environment

The environment is another key location from which to explore the differing outlooks between consumer and citizen. It also is a litmus test for distinguishing between the citizen as a mechanism for self-discipline and control and the citizen as a vehicle for seeking to re-establish a deeper spirit of community and general welfare. The consumer's role in either damaging or protecting the environment is an issue that has generated considerable rancour within the organized consumer movement, sections of which initially did not see the environment as a consumer issue at all. Some of them went as far as seeing environmental regulations as anti-consumer, a back door into protectionism and, therefore, higher prices in the shops. 'The environment is not a consumer issue' is a position that now only rarely, if at all, appears in consumer circles. The older waves of the consumer movement were slow to integrate even weak environmental criteria into their value-for-money assessments of consumer goods. But today it is de rigeur for responsible consumerism to include environmental strategies ranging from pale green to dark green. The former focuses on environmental labelling, energy audits and niche products with marginal green gain; the latter ranges from stringent recycling and product footprints (see below) to a more generalized advocacy to consume local products and even to consume less, if possible.

Environmentalists, for their part, have since the late 1960s urged retailers to cut down on packaging and shoppers to recycle or reuse where possible. As a result, appeals to consumers to clean up their own back-yard and use their purchasing power to force industry to tidy up its act have become part of the cultural landscape. Jay Hair, then President of the National Wildlife Federation, urged Americans to take 10 practical steps if they wish to act as citizens rather than consumers (Hair, 1989). These included actions such as cutting down on trash, using cloth diapers (nappies), not leaving water running needlessly, reusing grocery bags, planting a tree and using public transport or car pools. Such encouragements to act responsibly, to consume wisely and to think of the eco-sphere as one consumes seek to reintroduce a citizen's ethic of social responsibility, which goes beyond the consumer's narrow self-interest, countering the ethos of a throw-away society (*Ecologist*, 2001). What this vision of planet-Earth citizenship was accused of lacking was any wider notion of social solidarity, civic debate, co-ordinated action or sacrifice. It individualized the idea of citizenship, as if becoming a citizen was a matter of individual choice alone. In this way, citizenship became a lifestyle, however praiseworthy and necessary, which could easily degenerate into tokenism and was hardly likely to alter the politics of consumption.

A more collective appeal to consumers as citizens resorts to communal citizens' action to restrain the free market and introduce 'green' measures through legislation or taxation, at international, national or local levels. European environmental groups have turned to the EU as the state forum on which campaigns for the protection of the environment and individual consumers could be debated and acted upon. It was at this forum that measures such as the setting of standards for controlling pesticide residues, genetic engineering and the pollution of European beaches, as well as access to environmental information, recycling electrical goods and cars and eco-labelling (such as labelling washing-machines or refrigerators for their energy efficiency) were debated. Some of these debates went in the environmentalists' favour and some went against. However, the important matter is that European institutions emerged as an important new terrain for citizenship and as political bodies delivering environmental protection.

Citizenship, at a local level, can go beyond choosing as an individual whether to recycle the aluminium can of your soft drink or beer into acting in concert with other citizens. The UN Conference on Environment and Development in 1992 enshrined this community basis for citizenship and consumption in the Local Agenda 21 strategy (UN, 1992). This proposed that localities should define their own goals, in consultation with local populations, and should then be supported by central government to deliver those objectives. This strategy built upon the experience of pioneering green citizen local economies. For instance, in the German town of Kassel, citizens forced the authorities to institute a local tax charged on fast-food packaging, against bitter legal opposition from well-known fast-food companies and canned-drink dispenser machine companies. The tax dramatically altered consumer behaviour and also led to a reduction in packaging. Its success encouraged 500 other towns to follow suit (Tomforde, 1994). Such measures re-affirm the power of citizens to regulate consumption, even when this implies a reduction of choice for the individual consumer or costlier products. One is denied the option of choosing to pollute, just as one may on public health grounds be denied the right to spit on pavements. Despite the success of the Local Agenda 21-type initiatives, the fundamentals of consumerism have not been altered.

The diverging outlooks of consumer and citizen over the environment is encapsulated in the notion of 'environmental space' or 'ecological footprints' (van Brakel and Buitenkamp, 1992; van Brakel and Zagema, 1994; Wackernagel et al., 1996). This notion proposes that every consumer action leaves a 'footprint' on the ecological system and that every consumer takes up a certain amount of ecological space. By using a battery, by driving a car, by purchasing a computer, or by eating meat every day, contemporary Western consumers are leaving disproportionately large and deep imprints on the environment, in comparison to earlier generations and to the vast majority of the world's consumers. It is possible to calculate the overall footprint of a city, such as London, helping thereby set policy goals (Lyndhurst and Greater London Authority, 2003). To achieve any goal of sustainable development, rich Northern consumers will have to reduce their consumption of the earth's resources. In the Netherlands, for instance, it has been calculated that consumers will have to reduce their fresh water usage by 30 percent by the year 2010 and reduce their consumption of meat and milk (the production of which are notoriously heavy users of agricultural space and energy) if the drop in available Netherlands land per citizen is to be met without using other countries as 'hidden' supporters of supposed Netherlands' farming efficiency (van Brakel and Zagema, 1994: 18). In the decade following this study and its recommendations, little has been done to meet these targets.

In spite of initiatives like these, some environmentalists have argued that Western consumption (including its consumer organizations) have become part of a new class system (Harrison et al., 2005). A new ruling class, the 'consuming class', oppresses everybody else both materially and ideologically, consuming unequally while selling an impossible dream of happiness through consumption. Political economy in the 21st-century will be dominated by this new class dynamic and rich consumers, unless they have a change of heart politically and re-orient what they define as a good quality of life, will argue for a retention of their 'rights' to consume unequal shares of resources. Consumerism and citizenship, according to this view, are incompatible (Durning, 1992; UNEP, 2001). Consumer capitalism, say these environmental thinkers, cannot continue at the current pace without meeting its nemesis – resources will run out, the eco-sphere will be irreparably damaged, and the choices of future generations severely curtailed to the point, say the more apocalyptic proponents of this view, at which life itself is threatened (see also Chapter 1, 'The Emergence of Contemporary Consumerism'). It has long been recognized that elite consumers have to do more than adopt a token 'green' product if a more just citizenship is to be available for all.

> On the basis of massive borrowing and massive sales of national assets, Americans have been squandering their heritage and impoverishing their children. They have done so for the sake of present consumption, the enjoyment of shopping that accompanies it, and most of all as a way to postpone questioning the efficacy of free trade and continuous growth. (Daly et al., 1990: 367)

From this perspective, the Western citizen's paramount duty is to alter and reduce consumption and to help change the rules, such as taxes and laws, to this end. Failure to do so would lead to what Meadows and Colleagues, authors of the pioneering *Limits to Growth* report in the 1970s, in a review 20 years later called 'overshoot', a style of living running beyond its limits (Meadows and club of Rome, 1972; Meadows et al., 1992).

There can be little doubt that the efforts of environmentalists and the more radical elements of the consumer movement have played a part in the rediscovery of the citizen in recent years. However, is it possible for this idea to have any practical value in the modern world when politics itself threatens to collapse into an offshoot of consumption? 'The culture and entertainment industry has helped make politics a spectator sport. The pursuit of happiness now means amusement and diversion ...' (Barnet and Cavanagh, 1994: 41). When politicians compete for votes via sound-bites and television commercials, and when political debate is conducted at the level of slogans, does not the idea of citizenship itself collapse too? When so many political decisions are taken outside the public's view or in another country (what is referred to as the problem of multi-level governance), could it even be that the idea of citizenship has become a smoke-screen behind which green fundamentalists are pushing their own political agendas, as the ideologues of the free market sometimes claim? And could the idea of the EU as a forum for the new citizenry not be laughed out of court by those who have sought to portray all European institutions as parapets on Bluebeard's bureaucratic castle? Can it not be argued that behind the ideal of the global or European citizen, unelected civil servants and unaccountable politicians keep themselves in jobs by dreaming up unwarranted regulations and standards that tie up the hands of business and restrict the choice of consumers? It is unclear yet whether the mainstream second-wave consumer organizations see it as their primary responsibility to protect the planet by reducing consumption or to help reduce the price of cars.

The question of whether the battle over the citizen is worth fighting against the narrow self-interest of the consumer is not one that environmental groups and other progressive forces have resolved yet. Some are arguing that instead of setting up the citizen to fight the beast of consumerism, as a latter-day St George against the dragon, a preferable strategy might be to tame the beast and redirect its powers. Why not combine an effective consumer education campaign about the environmental impact of consumption, for example, and tap its market potential at the same time? An early illustration of this strategy was the initiative of Greenpeace Germany in the 1990s, which saved an East German refrigerator plant from closure by the Treuhand by using it to produce a radically new environmentally friendly product, called the Greenfreeze, which it successfully marketed to its membership. With one stroke, this assured, first, the factory's future; second, it proved that refrigerators need not use ozone-depleting CFCs, now a standard feature of all European refrigerators; third, this forced other mainstream manufacturers to produce similar models, which they had previously denied was commercially possible; and fourth, it pioneered a more benign technology for use in developing countries (Lang and Hines, 1993: 90–1). In this way, an environmental group turned green entrepreneur, Paul Hawken, argued that this kind of action prefigures what he called the 'restorative economy', arguing that if business thinks more about its waste and takes longer-term responsibility for products, not only will this be good for it, but it will allow buyers to become customers rather than consumers of the earth's resources (Hawken, 1993: 155–7). But the leap from present economics to future economics envisaged by Hawken or Daly, Cobb and Cobb, or the Factor Four technology thinkers is daunting (von Weizacher et al., 1996). The question of strategy for progressive social movements as to whether to champion the green consumer or the citizen is still being fought over. This dichotomy lies at the heart of attempts to tackle immense issues such as climate change, the state of the seas and the capacity of the world to feed itself (Lang and Heasman, 2004).

In Conclusion

In this chapter, we have examined the battle that is being fought over the concept of the citizen. We have considered the efforts to present the consumer as citizen as a force that may potentially oppose contemporary Western consumerism, as well as those forces that seek to reduce the citizen to but another face of the consumer, like those investigated in other chapters of this book.

At the moment, the prospects for the citizen do not look good. For the last 30 years, voters in Western countries have listened to appeals to act in more socially responsible ways. However, by and large, in the privacy of the ballot booth they have often voted for governments that are wary of tax increases and favour increased opportunities for individuals to spend their pay packets as they wish.

Government in the global age and global marketplace is increasingly driven by large corporations and groupings of the powerful such as the G-8 and OECD groups of rich countries. Power is exercised in transnational fora, such as the WTO or regional institutions such as the EU and the NAFTA. Global economic institutions such as the World Bank and International Monetary Fund, founded in the mid 20th-century, are now hugely more powerful than national governments that citizens vote for (Bello, 2002; Jawara and Kwa, 2003; Monbiot, 2000).

Even if people wish to be citizens, the flow of economic history appears to offer them little choice but to be more or less socially aware consumers. This pessimistic assessment suggests that a majority of people may give strong backing to broader notions of civic responsibility in opinion polls, while voting against those who point out the consequences in the polling booth. As one UK commentator noted:

> Our collective hypocrisy about the state needs no encouragement. We already treat government spending as if it were gold from a magic sack hidden under the Bank of England, while treating attempts to tax us as confiscation, to be avoided by all means possible. (Marr, 1994: 4)

At the moment the consumer-citizen appears as a timid figure at the borders of contemporary consumption. Embarrassed by the Right's attempts to embrace them or set them up as a bulwark against unwanted aliens, citizens feel uneasy amidst the din of modern advertising and the clamour of the mass media. Yet citizens are figures who, from time to time, raise their voices, to the surprise of many. It is too early to assess their ultimate impact, but by the beginning of the 21st-century, all over the world citizen-like protests and demands for new rights, as well as the assertion of old ones, were heard in response to the economic restructuring and globalization of decision-making (Klein, 2000; Korten, 2001; Monbiot, 2003; Soros, 2000, 2004). Some targeted governments and others business, seeking, for instance, to inject more 'transparency' into the process of granting companies charters of incorporation (Grossman and Adams, 1993; Held and Koenig-Archibugi, 2005; Keasey et al., 2005). Whether to protect a piece of countryside from a proposed commercial development, or to stop the export of live animal stock (from becoming foreign consumers' cheap beefsteak or veal *escalope*) or to protest against the introduction of identity cards, citizens can make their presence felt.

It can be argued that today people make their voices heard as citizens only in single issues, marginal activities or local communities, which can themselves be corralled, trivialized or commodified by the mass media. The sacrifices of local campaigners against hypermarketization, environmental protesters or human rights activists can be decoded as media stunts and attempts at sensation, devoid of commitment and moral force. No sooner do individuals discover in citizenship one of the last remaining defences against the rule of markets, than they also discover what a precarious defence it turns out to be. All the same, it is telling that whenever a vocabulary of organized and conscious opposition to consumer capitalism and its powerful accoutrements is required, citizenship, especially global citizenship, citizenship without frontiers, citizenship defending the interests of future generations, even if it is an assertion and celebration of the community, invariably appears on the agenda. It remains to be seen whether, under the force of things to come, the idea of citizen, redefined and reformulated, can form the basis of an alliance that mounts a serious challenge to consumer capitalism. The tension between consumer and citizen looks set to endure.

CHAPTER **11**

The Unmanageable Consumer

The world is too much with us; late and soon,
Getting and spending, we lay waste our prowess:
Little we see in nature that is ours;
We have given our hearts away, a sordid boon!

William Wordsworth, 'The World'

C O ARGUMENTS E

We see no end to continuing consumer unmanageability and unpredictability. The Fordist Deal is under immense strain. Changes in production, rapid technological innovation, population and environmental pressures, political uncertainties and trends toward globalization of the media, all conspire to undermine the comfortable assumption of ever-increasing consumption. Moreover, while large segments of the world embrace consumption as the way to happiness and the good life, questions and evidence continue to mount as to whether consumerism is sustainable and the extent to which it enhances human quality of life. We suggest that a number of scenarios are discernible: business as usual, dramatic constraint on consumption and increasing popular pressure for sustainable consumption. These scenarios are fighting for political dominance.

Few concepts have been claimed by so many interest groups, ideologies and academic traditions as that of the consumer. It is rare for an idea to have such diverse meanings as 'to consume'. As we have seen, economists, sociologists, social psychologists, cultural critics, postmodernists, Marxists, Conservatives, advertisers, journalists, pop-semioticians, marketers and marketeers, historians of ideas, environmentalists and activists all come up with their own visions and images. The consumer has become a cultural fetish, something that people get obsessed about to the point at which it can dominate their lives.

This book has, from the beginning, brought together traditions that do not normally address each other enough. Each chapter of this book has critically assessed a core idea of who consumers are, how they behave, what drives them, what concerns them and how they see the world. Each one can be thought of as a landscape of consumption, highlighting different features and disguising others. We have disagreed with some, supported others, offered our own. We are not suggesting that contemporary consumption is the totality of these, nor do we recommend that readers should pick and choose which image they most or least identify with and discard the others. What we are suggesting is that each image represents a position within a contested terrain. It is what the French refer to as a *prise de position*, in other words an initial gambit on which one is prepared to place a stake.

Why has the consumer become such a hotly contested terrain, the point where so many contradictions of contemporary society converge? Why do so many claim it as their own and, if it is not, struggle to appropriate it? Why do so many political parties now claim to speak on consumers' behalf? Why do so many different academic traditions seek to define the consumer, criticize the consumer or praise the consumer? At the outset of the book, we stated that numerous historical factors have contributed to raising the consumer to the first line of recent academic and political debates. These include the decline of the Protestant work ethic in the West, the ideological role of Western consumerism throughout the Cold War, the adoption of the consumer by the political Right, which sought to redefine itself as the party of the consumer rather than just the party of business, as well as the emergence of new forms of mass communication and information.

Through the pages of this book we have established that much hinges on the consumer, whether for example, he or she is seen as sovereign (requiring no self-appointed spokespeople to defend his or her interests) or victim (easily manipulated and outwitted by the apparatuses of capital), explorer (thirsting after new experiences and meanings) or activist (campaigning on behalf of collective rights), communicator (using objects as bridges to relate to fellow humans) or rebel (using objects to express rejection and rage), identity-seeker (trying to find a real self in the objects he or she consumes) or hedonist (concerned above all with personal pleasure). These are all attempts to frame the consumer, and, more often than not, to sell particular self-views to the consumers themselves, either by flattery, by cajoling, by moralizing, by seduction or by straight manipulation.

But while all these battles are raging above and around the heads and wallets of the consumer, people get on with their everyday lives, trying to make the best of them, whatever their lot, and also to make sense of them. It would be plausible and attractive to envisage consumers in this way, that is, as oblivious to the consternation they are causing to the chattering classes and theoreticians. At a stroke, this analysis would halt any systematic attempt to understand people's behaviour as reflexive, self-conscious consumers, leaving the terrain to those who have an interest in defining them in particular ways. Market researchers and opinion pollsters, for instance, would claim the consumer as theirs, but so too would consumer activists and political parties. We are profoundly opposed to ending our pursuit of the consumer in this book in this fashion, by abandoning him or her to those who claim to speak on his or her behalf.

For better or for worse, many of us think of ourselves, at least part of the time, as consumers. Whether reading the consumer pages of newspapers, listening to exhortations from politicians or consumer organizations, visiting theme parks and supermarkets, or trying to stretch the family budget at the end of a week, we unavoidably have to confront ourselves as consumers, and make decisions as consumers. Why else do individuals become so preoccupied with what they buy, give and eat? Why do they seek advice, turning to the consumer agony aunts that fill the media? For the most part, one cannot opt out of being a consumer, living in a non-consumer fashion, in a non-consumer landscape. Even those who find themselves excluded from the bonanzas of consumerism – including an estimated 1.3 billion of our fellow humans who live on less than $1 per day – cannot escape defining themselves in terms of lack and dreaming of a better life. Consumerism, in the diverse forms examined in this book, has become part of almost all of humanity's daily reality.

The Fordist Deal and its Aftermath

We began this book by suggesting that modern consumers have to be understood in their relationship to production, as the outcome of what we called the Fordist Deal (see Chapter 1, 'Introduction: The Faces of the Consumer'). By this we meant the unwritten understanding that ever-increasing living standards and steady employment would be the reward for accepting potentially alienating work without excessive dissent. From birth, the modern consumer has been connected to the methods and politics of mass production, just as earlier generations of consumers, too, had been dependent on the vagaries of production, harvests and warfare for their subsistence.

The Fordist Deal is currently unravelling under pressure from multiple directions that affect production as deeply as consumption. New technologies enable the easy migration of jobs and transfer of information, resulting in a dramatic restructuring of the international division of labour – who makes what, where and how. The ideas of 'steady job' or 'job for life' in much of the industrialized West, to say nothing of the formerly centrally planned economies of the Communist bloc have virtually lost meaning. Instead, many jobs have become casualized and careers have become fragmented – rapid job moves, being constantly on the lookout for better opportunities and work prospects; frenetic periods of work on specific projects followed by almost certain periods of self-employment or under-employment (Bunting, 2004; Sennett, 1998). Casualization does not necessarily mean unemployment; on the contrary, it implies impermanence in work as the new benchmark. Indeed, vast new opportunities of employment have been created in the service sectors, involving either the manipulation of symbols on screens and the clicking of computer mice, or alternatively front line work with customers in hospitality, entertainment, retail, sport and tourist sectors.

The Fordist Deal is also unravelling as a result of deep-rooted changes in consumption patterns. In most countries, consumers are becoming younger; and, due to demographic pressures and healthcare, they are becoming older. New areas of consumption, such as education, health (including fertility and voluntary euthanasia), the voluntary and not-for-profit sector and transport, are rapidly being colonized by a consumer ethos of choice and identity politics. New parts of the world are seized by the excitement of consumerism. New forms of resistance are making themselves felt, ranging from music piracy, to anti-globalization and environmental protests, from fundamentalist and militant religious resurgence to economic downshifting and career moratoriums. New vulnerabilities such as Internet crime and identity theft are added to enduring old ones, such as terrorism and fraud. Consumerism may absorb or co-opt some of these challenges, although in the longer run, the challenges posed by ecological and demographic factors leave no doubt about troubled times ahead or even coming crises.

If the comfortable co-habitation of mass consumption and mass production that characterized the Fordist Deal is coming to an end, production and consumption continue to be tied together, neither one determining the other but in constant and mutual definition. Understanding consumption requires that we understand production, and understanding production requires that we understand consumption. This is not a new insight. A century and a half ago, Marx was keenly aware that production and consumption cannot be separated: 'Without production, no consumption; but also, without consumption, no production' (Marx, 1993[1859]). Every form of production involves the consumption of resources and every type of consumption results in some production, even if only waste. But, as we have seen through the pages of this book, consumption is also *work* – it requires patient or breathless searches through high-streets, shopping malls or Internet sites; it involves minuscule comparisons and painstaking choices; it demands continuous updating and vigilance. Some consumption, such as working out in a gym or reading this book is almost *just work*. By the same token, a great deal of consumption, including what are referred to as corporate hospitality and corporate travel, takes place while we are notionally *at work*.

Part of what ties consumption and production together is the new politics of meaning and identity (Du Gay, 1996a). Meaning and identity are not fashioned solely in the realm of consumption as some theorists of postmodernity have argued, but emerge through what is referred to as lifestyle choices – loosely connected sets of tastes, behaviours, ideas and values (Chaney, 1996; Gershuny, 1988). These lifestyles may entail coherence in work, leisure and home, or may entail dissonances and discontinuities. The holiday, that lifestyle emblem, may complement work, home and income or, equally, may be extravagantly out of tune with them. Under the regime of the Fordist Deal, identity and meaning were tied to one's work and one's living standards as enabled by their working situation, themselves the product of class position (Sennett, 1998). Today, by contrast, identity and meaning are more fluid, tentative and inconsistent – choice has made such inconsistencies possible.

Globalization

If Henry Ford's assembly lines represented the kernel of the Fordist Deal, today's interdependence of consumption and production may best be observed in the call centre (Frenkel et al., 1999; Korczynski, 2001, 2003; Sturdy et al., 2001), late modernity's answer to those satanic mills of early industrialization. In the Indian call centre servicing customers in Toronto and Manchester at all times of day and night, we find many of the contemporary global interconnections between production and consumption. The consumer, that reputed sovereign, stuck to his or her telephone in New York, cursing the umpteenth return of Vivaldi's *Four Seasons* while being put on hold, waiting to buy his or her railway ticket to the suburbs through a busy call centre located somewhere in Bangalore. And the worker at the call centre, a member of the local consumer aristocracy in his or her own right, servicing a global clientele, caught between a relentless pressure for 'orders taken' and a much drummed requirement to offer a quality, personalized service with the telephone equivalent of a smile.

A closer look at the inter-relations of production and consumption, however, suggests that the call centre falls short of embodying all the complexities of this relationship. Much of what is traded today is still goods and services, but an increasing proportion is information itself. This is what Castells calls the new 'informational capitalism' (Castells, 1996, 1997, 1998); the productivity and competitiveness of different economic units, such as firms, countries or trading networks, lies in their ability to handle, process and manage information and knowledge. Crucial for this capitalism is the free flow of information across networks of economic agents, a flexible workforce, capable of working around the clock when and as required. The very concept of a job, argues Castells and others, is replaced by what he terms *self-programmable labour*, in which the stock of knowledge and information in the minds of workers is constantly expanded and modified throughout their working lives. Work, then, becomes tantamount to learning or more specifically learning how to learn or being prepared to learn. In an economy changing at Internet speed, specific information and knowledge becomes obsolete in a few years. What becomes essential is the ability to transform generic information into specific knowledge to be applied in concrete situations (Castells, 2001: 90) and always ready to engage with and understand the new.

When thinking of information, most commentators envisage reams of spreadsheets, astronomical sequences of digitized figures on computer memories, in short, data on every conceivable detail of social, personal and economic life. Undoubtedly, we live in a society drowning in such information, a society in which the ability to navigate in shortcuts, around the endless detours of mostly useless information, accords individuals, organizations and networks considerable power. Some authors (Brown and Duguid, 1994; Gherardi et al., 1998; Orr, 1996; Wenger, 1998, 2000) have sought to defend narrative knowledge, the knowledge stored in stories, anecdotes and narratives, as precisely such shortcutting knowledge, knowledge developed and shared creatively by what are currently referred to as 'communities of practice'. Whether a medical practitioner, an advertising executive, an airline pilot, a stockbroker, a midwife or a traveling salesperson, you realize that some of the most valuable is not contained in books, manuals and computer programmes of your trade but in the stories and narratives you exchange informally with people on your wavelength, people who share your assumptions, interests and problems (Gabriel, 2000, 2002). A telling story may shortcut through swathes of information, supplying the idea behind a quick, relevant and appropriate solution.

Narrative knowledge can also supply much of value to consumers of all kinds of products and services. The experience of those who had plastic surgery in a particular clinic, the stories they tell about the staff, the pain endured and the eventual success of their treatment may be decisive in whether a potential customer decides to avail of the clinic's service, or indeed to have the treatment at all. The stories of owners or users of particular objects, ranging from books, music, mobile telephony, and so forth can now be easily found in the Internet. Amazon, apart from everything else, offers a prospective customer a wonderful opportunity to sample what he or she is about to purchase and also to read the stories of those who have purchased it before. In this sense, at least, the Internet has created a type of knowledge that is quite distinct from the ones and zeroes on those spreadsheets.

Society of Image?

For all its importance, narrative knowledge is not the main currency of informational capitalism. Ours is not a narrative society, although narratives subsist and even prosper in some of its domains. Ours is more a society of visual representations, images, spectacles and shows. Our daily universe has become saturated with images, jumping at us from our TV sets, our magazines and newspapers, our computer screens and our digital cameras, advertising billboards and shop windows. We are bombarded by PowerPoint® presentations, a template of presenting ideas that marginalizes finely turned arguments and analysis. As image replaces words, pithiness replaces subtlety. Shops and malls, the cathedrals of consumption, are minutely engineered mega-shows, to stimulate and delight the eye, to whet appetites and to excite emotions. Saturated by images, most of us have given up trying to fit them into stories and have learnt to accept them as spectacle pure and simple, pleasing or annoying, evoking, prompting, comforting, upsetting, entertaining or irritating.

The idea that we live in an era saturated by spectacle where image reigns supreme is, of course, not new. Parodying Marx, Guy Debord opened his 1960s situationist manifesto with:

> In societies where modern conditions of production prevail, all life presents itself as an immense accumulation of *spectacles*. Everything that was directly lived has moved away into representation. (Debord, 1977: para. 1)

Allowing for the obvious hyperbole, Debord's premise seems to be even more powerful today than in the 1960s when he made it the basis of his then fashionable critique (Debord, 1977). Numerous theorists, including Bauman, Ritzer and Baudrillard, have since argued that spectacle has become the primary type of experience in late modernity, dominating every aspect of our public and private lives. Spectacle liquefies most forms of social exchange, colonizing politics, sport, religion and education. The society of spectacle probably reaches its apotheosis in the Olympic Games, a truly global brand that lands on Earth every 4 years. What has changed since the situationist critique is the more nuanced evaluation that we accord spectacle today, the less unequivocal equation of spectacle with passivity and stupefaction. Thus, inspired by Bauman, Ritzer (1999) has argued that spectacle has led to a re-enchantment of the world in late modernity's cathedrals of consumption. Shopping malls, glass buildings, tourist resorts, sports venues and theme parks, are all minutely planned and orchestrated shows, with spectators themselves becoming part of the display. Immense amounts of money are spent in advertising and packaging, films and TV shows, magazines and printed images. Politics, education, sport, religion, charity, journalism, to say nothing of the entertainment and leisure sectors become dominated by spectacle. Spectacle becomes the archetypal experience of our time, they argue, offering 'the promise of new, overwhelming, mind-boggling or spine-chilling, but always exhilarating experience' (Bauman, 1997: 181).

According to this view, we are now deep in the era of spectacle. It is estimated that in 2004, 28 billion digital pictures were taken in the USA alone. The figure is likely to continue rising exponentially as life gets lived as a series of photo-opportunities and consumption becomes substantially a consumption of images or a consumption for the benefit of generating images. The media are themselves inviting the public to amplify this process by submitting their own digital images of events ranging from pop festivals to tsunamis and from everyday crime to terrorist outrages. The media themselves produce a constant sequence of images which create, as Boorstin (1962) understood before Debord or Baudrillard, illusions of reality, swamping us with images and pictures. Our consciousness is now saturated with image and our memories are to a large extent visual ones. As Susan Sontag put it succinctly following the publication of the horrendous images of prisoner abuse from the Abu Ghraib prison camp in Iraq:

> The memory museum is now mostly a visual one. Photographs have an insuperable power to determine what people recall of events. ... To live is to be photographed, to have a record of one's life, and therefore, to go on with one's life, oblivious, or claiming to be oblivious, to the camera's non-stop attentions. But it is also to pose. To act is to share in the community of actions recorded as images. ... Events are in part designed to be photographed . (Sontag, 2004: 3)

Under the regime of the Fordist Deal, automobiles symbolized the link between production and consumption. The product of hard manual labour, the automobile captured the aspirations of the affluent working-classes, promising freedom, mobility, speed, style and comfort. By contrast, in a society dominated by image, labour assumes aesthetic and emotional qualities, previously only available to the super-rich. Looking smart and sounding right are qualities every bit as important in getting a job in the new service economy, over and above physical strength or formal qualifications and cognitive competences. The notion of emotional intelligence has emerged as the way of capturing and commodifying these aptitudes (Fineman, 2000; Goleman, 1996).

If image, including the employees' looks, the buildings, clothes, logos, and atmosphere, now permeates production, it totally saturates consumption. The most mundane or innocuous object or service can be beautified to make it an object of desire. The aestheticization of every day life, as epitomized by Italy's love affair with style (*bello stile*), becomes an end in itself (Calinescu, 1987; Featherstone, 1992).

Unmanageability and the Consumer

Inequalities among consumers are already sharp, leaving substantial numbers of them window-shopping with only restricted opportunities to make a purchase and many, in the developing countries, without even windows to window-shop. This is contributing to the fragmentation of consumers' experiences. While some consumers throughout the world may spend inordinate amounts of time deliberating whether to invest in a new swimming-pool, a new car or a second home abroad, others have to choose between feeding their children or buying them a new pair of shoes. Given such social chasms, it is difficult to talk about *all* consumption and *all* consumers as coming under the same ethos or constraints, i.e. as being uniform entities or acting as a unified force. The fragmentation of images of consumption is itself a symptom of the malaise of contemporary consumerism.

In the first edition of this book, we argued that the Fordist Deal was weakening and suggested that Western consumerism may have entered a twilight phase. During the high noon of consumerism in the latter half of the 20th-century, we argued, the face of the consumer was clear, as was the significance of his or her every movement. The pursuit of happiness through consumption seemed a plausible, if morally questionable, social and personal project. Today, that analysis is inadequate. The economic conditions have become more fraught, the social inequalities have widened further, insecurity is experienced on a massive scale. Cultural fatigue threatens to overcome even the well-off, raising questions of pursuing simpler lives and spiritual and community values. The Fordist Deal can no longer promise happiness; it has become a museum piece.

When we surveyed the consumption landscape ten years ago, we were unsure about the future of consumerism and we felt that it was open. In the intervening period, the implications of several factors have become more salient. Key among them are the continuing expansion of consumerism to different parts of the globe and different areas of social life; the increasing domination of image and spectacle; the pursuit of meaning through consumption; enduring global inequalities; emerging new forms of activism and resistance; and continuing casualization of work and consumption.

It is now clear that casualization of work is accompanied by casualization of consumption. People lead precarious and uneven existences, one day enjoying unexpected boons and the next feeling overwhelmed by insecurity and debt. Precariousness, unevenness and fragmentation will continue to characterize Western life prospects. Marginality has paradoxically become central. The notion of an average consumer has become a fiction. In a world where everyone claims the consumer for her- or himself, the consumer must now be deemed *unmanageable*, claimed by many, but controlled by nobody, least of all by consumers themselves. The notion of unmanageability seems to us to be entirely appropriate for an era where the capacity to plan must give way to opportunism, living for the present. Deeming the consumers to be unmanageable does not mean that vast resources are not expended in seeking to control them, cajole them, predict and mould their behaviour and consciousness. Vast amounts of information is collected at the point of sale, the point of thinking about a purchase, in order to make consumers appear predictable and amenable to typologies of marketing efforts. And yet, the best attempts at managing consumers easily comes undone, as when a fad or a fashion seizes their imagination and, just as quickly, goes. Even as they are constantly typecast and pigeon-holed, consumers are becoming more unmanageable, eccentric and paradoxical.

The argument then is that, like today's producers, today's consumers (after all, even in a globalized division of labour they are often the same people) must rely on opportunism, and seeking to be in the right place at the right times. As Bauman has argued,

> In the life-game of the postmodern consumers the rules of the game keep changing in the course of playing. The sensible strategy is therefore to keep each game short – so that a sensibly played game of life calls for the splitting of one big all-embracing game with huge stakes into a series of brief and narrow games with small ones. ... To keep the game short means to beware long-term commitments. To refuse to be 'fixed' one way or the other. Not to get tied to the place. Not to wed one's life to one vocation only. Not to swear consistency and loyalty to anything and anybody. Not to *control* the future, but to *refuse to mortgage* it: to take care that the consequences of the game do not outlive the past to bear on the present. (Bauman, 1996: 24)

To retailers and producers of goods and services, this unmanageability may not be a terminal difficulty and, for some, it may represent an opportunity. So long as a certain proportion of the population at any one time is in a position to spend, there will be markets, and entrepreneurs will discover opportunities to capitalize on people's desire to celebrate and enjoy themselves. After all, the opportunism of consumers is matched by the opportunism of business. To other consumers, however, a future based on mortgages, careful husbanding of resources and long-term financial commitments could become routine. Within someone's life, periods of both of these experiences are likely to feature, periods of both feast and famine.

Market researchers and the agents of production endlessly pursue the Holy Grail of control, seeking to anticipate consumer trends on behalf of capital, which stands to gain massively from accurate predictions, coupled with investment, in attempts to shape or tempt consumption to its benefit. The task of those who seek to anticipate trends is inevitably partisan, their goal to mould the future to their ends.

But planning a future for the consumer is one thing; delivering it is another. Even at the mundane level of anticipating what objects will be popular in the future, prognostication is fraught with danger. The history of consumption is full of dead-ends. Products that pundits were once sure would become objects of mass consumption and desire in the future now stand as quaint reminders of the pitfalls of futurology. In the 1960s, for instance, the merchants of tomorrow's world were offering us throw-away paper clothes, holidays on the moon, living in geodesic domes, eating food in tablet form, undertaking less work. In practice today, precious few houses are in dome form; there has been a meteoric rise in nutritional supplements but only in addition to more 'ordinary' food; no-one has been to the moon almost since the first landings; mountains of paper are thrown away – despite that the age of the electronic office once promised paperlessness – but not having been worn on human bodies; and people who are in work often work harder and longer. The future of the 1960s failed to materialize, in more senses than one. Equally, we suspect, the future as envisaged by today's brave prognosticators has more to do with their own fantasies and wishes than future facts.

There is a disparity, however, between the fantasies of industrialists and retailers and those of consumers themselves. The former ever dream of managing consumers, while the latter's dreams make them ever unmanageable. The former seek to put their vision into practice; the latter subvert, refuse, accept, interpret, surrender or embrace, in the manner this book has explored. Consumers have proven that in spite of the best efforts to constrain, control and manipulate them, they can act in ways that are unpredictable, inconsistent and contrary.

The Future(s)

If, as we have just argued, on the one hand, unpredictability, inconsistency and contrariness all characterize today's consumption, on the other hand, governments persist in their policy of 'business as usual', by which well-being is equated to ever-higher national income and higher spending power. Public discourses are dominated by the discipline of economic forecasts and narrow conceptions of value and utility. Faith in the market as the mechanism that will deliver this higher standard of living is undiminished in the world's power elite, even if it is being more openly contested by some critics and some oppositional movements. An increasing number of voices is heard arguing that environmental, demographic and social factors will combine in the longer term to undermine this conception of well-being as increased wealth.

The environmental challenge to consumerism is now clear to almost all thinking people. The evidence is very strong for coming shortages of key resources that have underpinned the consumerist expansion of the 20th-century. These include oil, water, land, soil, clean air and minerals (Lang and Heasman, 2004; Millennium Ecosystem Assessment (Program), 2005). Without these, even an information-based economy cannot be delivered and some forward-thinking companies are preparing exit strategies or technical fixes to leave the present mode of production and to experiment with alternative modes. The success of such strategies should not be relied upon; nor should they be dismissed out of hand. Even tougher environmental challenges are already apparent. The most significant of these is undoubtedly climate change, which heralds dramatic discontinuities and ruptures in current form of consumption. Pollution, waste and desertification are also looming.

The demographic challenge is likely to prove as severe and politically unsettling. The world population passed 6 billion at the beginning of the 21st-century, and is predicted by the UN Population Fund to rise to 9–10 billion by 2050. Feeding, housing and providing water for such escalating demands would be awesome enough across centuries. But these problems will be exacerbated by the environmental problems noted above and by the demographic disequilibria created by aging populations of most industrialized countries, alongside the youthfulness of other countries. The combination of environmental and demographic factors have led some pessimistic theorists to speculate that social unrest, disease and warfare will reach unprecedented scale in the longer term. Optimists, on the other hand, argue that, as ever, the problem is not absolute numbers of people and production, but relative inequalities and distribution of public goods within and across those populations.

In the last resort, however, even environmental and demographic factors are mediated by social and cultural forces. It is people, after all, who consume, people who aspire and people who can make a difference. There is increasing evidence that decades of consumerism have not delivered unequivocal happiness and have created discontents of their own. Mental illness, family dislocation and the enduring social inequalities, are in themselves measures of the failure of consumerism to fulfil its promise of pleasure for all. Happiness, some people come to believe, is not a destination to travel towards, but a way of travelling. Speaking at the peak of the Fordist Deal in the USA, Robert F. Kennedy, then running for President and shortly before his assassination, captured the limitations of equating consumption as measured by GNP with social well-being.

> For too long we seem to have surrendered personal excellence and community value in the mere accumulation of material things. Our gross national product now is over 800 billion dollars a year, but that gross national product, if we judge the United States of America by that, that gross national product counts air pollution, and cigarette advertising, and ambulances to clear our highways of carnage. It counts special locks for our doors and the jails for people who break them. It counts the destruction of the redwoods and the loss of our natural wonder in chaotic squall. It counts Napalm, and it counts nuclear warheads, and armored cars for the police to fight the riots in our city. It counts Whitman's rifles and Speck's Knives and the television programs which glorify violence in order to sell toys to our children. Yet, the gross national product does not allow for the health of our children, the quality of their education, or the joy of their play. It does not include the beauty of our poetry or the strength of our marriages; the intelligence of our public debate or the integrity of our public officials. It measures neither our wit nor our courage; neither our wisdom nor our learning; neither our compassion nor our devotion to our country; it measures everything, in short, except that which makes life worthwhile. [...]' (University of Kansas, Lawrence, Kansas, 18 March, 1968)

Forty years ago, a leading politician such as Kennedy could see clearly the limits of consumerism for the richest consumer society in the world. Today, as the Fordist Deal unravels even as more nations are sucked into its legacy, leaving us with a far more fragile promise of happiness and a far greater burden for future generations, there are more people, across nations, who have started to share his concerns and foreboding. It remains to be seen whether these concerns will find organized expression in new popular movements or in a political will to bring about genuine social change.

References

Aaker, D.A. and Biel, A.L. (1993) *Brand Equity and Advertising: Advertising's Role in Building Strong Brands*. Hillsdale, NJ: Lawrence Erlbaum Associates.

Aaker, D.A. and Day, G.S. (1982) *Consumerism: Search for the Consumer Interest* (4th edition). New York: Free Press.

Abercrombie, N. (1994) 'Authority and consumer society', R. Keat, N. Whiteley and N. Abercrombie (eds), *The Authority of the Consumer*. London: Routledge. pp. 43–57.

Abolafia, M. and Biggart, N. (1992) 'Competitive systems: A sociological view', in P. Ekins and M. Max-Neef (eds), *Real-life Economics: Understanding Wealth Creation*. London: Routledge. pp. 315–22.

Accum, F.C. (1820) *A Treatise on Adulterations of Food and Culinary Poisons: Exhibiting the Fraudulent Sophistications of Bread, Beer, Wine, Spirituous Liquors, Tea, Coffee, Cream, Confectionery, Vinegar, Mustard, Pepper, Cheese, Olive Oils, Pickles and Other Articles Employed in Domestic Economy; and Methods of Detecting Them*. London: Longman Hurst Rees Orme and Brown.

Adams, R., Carruthers, J. and Fisher, C. (1991) *Shopping for a Better World: A Quick and Easy Guide to Socially Responsible Supermarket Shopping*. London: Kogan Page.

Allain, A. (1991) 'Breastfeeding is politics: A personal view of the international baby milk campaign', *The Ecologist*, 21 (5): 206–13.

Anderson, B. (1983) *Imagined Communities*. London: Verso.

Anderson, S. and Cavanagh, J. (2000) *The Rise of Corporate Power*. Washington, DC: Institute of Policy Studies.

Anderton, A.G. (1991) *Economics*. Ormskirk: Causay Press.

Andreasen, A.R. (1982) 'The differing nature of consumerism in the ghetto', in D.A. Aaker and G.S. Day (eds), *Consumerism: Search for the Consumer Interest* (4th edition). New York: Free Press. pp. 96–107.

Annan, K. (2003) 'Message for International Cooperation Day, June 25', UN Press Release SG/SM/8762 OBV/359. New York: United Nations.

Anthias, F. (1982) 'Connecting 'race' and ethnic phenomena', *Sociology*, 26 (3): 421–38.

Appadurai, A. (1990) 'Disjuncture and difference in the global cultural economy', *Theory, Culture and Society*, 7: 295–310.

Armistead, N. (1974) *Reconstructing Social Psychology*. Harmondsworth: Penguin.

Aron, R. (1967) *18 Lectures on Industrial Society*. London: Weidenfeld and Nicolson.

Barker, I. (1991) 'Purchasing for people', *Health Services Management*, 87 (5 October): 212–15.

Barker, P. (1994) 'Is *Which?* still best buy?', *The Times*, 8 June: 15.

Barling, D. and Lang, T. (2005) 'Trading on health: Cross-continental production and consumption tensions and the governance of international food standards', in N. Fold and B. Pritchard (eds), *Cross-continental Food Chains*. London: Routledge. pp. 39–51.

Barlow, M. and Clarke, T. (2002) *Blue Gold: The Battle against Corporate Theft of the World's Water*. London: Earthscan.

Barnet, R.J. and Cavanagh, J. (1994) *Global Dreams: Imperial Corporations and the New World Order*. New York: Simon and Schuster.

Barratt Brown, M. (1993) *Fair Trade: Reform and Realities in the International Trading System*. London: Zed Press.

Barthes, R. (1973) *Mythologies*. London: Paladin Books.

Barthes, R. (1977[1966]) 'The rhetoric of the image', in S. Heath (ed.), *Image – Music – Text*. Glasgow: Collins. pp. 32–51.

Bateson, G. (1972) *Steps to an Econolgy of Mind*. London: Intertext Books.

Baudrillard, J. (1983) *Simulations*. New York: Semiotext(e).

Baudrillard, J. (1988a[1968]) 'The system of objects', in M. Poster (ed.), *Jean Baudrillard: Selected Writings*. Cambridge: Polity Press.

Baudrillard, J. (1988b[1970]) 'Consumer society', in M. Poster (ed.), *Jean Baudrillard: Selected Writings*. Cambridge: Polity Press.

Baudrillard, J. (1988c[1981]) 'Simulacra and simulations', in M. Poster (ed.), *Jean Baudrillard: Selected Writings*. Cambridge: Polity Press. pp. 166–84.

Baudrillard, J. and Gane, M. (1993) *Baudrillard Live: Selected Interviews*. London, New York: Routledge.

Bauman, Z. (1988) *Freedom*. Milton Keynes: Open University Press.

Bauman, Z. (1992) *Intimations of Postmodernity*. London: Routledge.

Bauman, Z. (1996) 'From pilgrim to tourist – or a short history of identity', in S. Hall and P. Du Gay (eds), *Questions of cultural identity*. London: Sage. pp. 18–36.

Bauman, Z. (1997) *Postmodernity and its Discontents*. Cambridge: Polity Press.

Bauman, Z. (1998) *Work, Consumerism and the New Poor*. Buckingham: Open University Press.

Bauman, Z. (2001) 'Consuming life', *Journal of Consumer Culture*, 1 (1): 9–30.

Baumeister, R.F. (1986) *Identity: Cultural Change and the Struggle for Self*. Oxford: Oxford University Press.

Beishon, J. (1994) 'Consumers and power', in R. John (ed.), *The Consumer Revolution: Redressing the Balance*. London: Hodder and Stoughton. pp. 1–11.

Belk, R.W. (1988) 'Possessions and the extended self', *Journal of Consumer Research*, 15 (2): 139–68.

Bell, D. (1976) *Cultural Contradictions of Capitalism*. New York: Basic Books.

Bello, W.F. (2002) *Deglobalization: Ideas for a New World Economy*. London: Zed Books.

Benson, J. (1994) *The Rise of Consumer Society in Britain, 1880–1980*. London, New York: Longman.

Berger, P. and Luckman, T. (1967) *The Social Construction of Reality*. Garden City, NY: Anchor.

Best, A. (1981) *When Consumers Complain*. New York: Columbia University Press.

Bettman, J.R. (1979) *An Information Processing Theory of Consumer Choice*. Reading, MA: Addison-Wesley.

BEUC (1994) 'Consumer guarantees and after-sales service', report and press release, Bureau Europèen des Unions des Consommateurs, Brussels.

Beveridge, S.W. (1942) 'Social insurance and allied services', Cmd 6404, HMSO, London.

Bingham, L. (1992) 'The inquiry into the supervision of the bank of Credit and Commerce International' (The Bingham Report), HC 198, HMSO, London.

Birchall, J. (1994) *Co-op: The People's Business*. Manchester: Manchester University Press.

Birchall, J. (2003) *Rediscovering the Co-operative Advantage: Poverty Reduction through Self-help*. Geneva: International Labour Office.

Bloom, P.N. and Greyser, S.A. (1981) 'Exploring the future of consumerism', research program, July 1981, Marketing Science Institute (USA), Cambridge, MA.

Bloom, P.N. and Stern, L.W. (1978) 'Consumerism in the year 2000: The emergence of anti-industrialism', in N. Kangun and L. Richardson (eds), *Consumerism: New Challenges for Marketing*. Chicago: American Marketing Association.

Blythman, J. (2004) *Shopped: The Shocking Power of British Supermarkets*. London: Fourth Estate.

Board of Trade (UK) (1962) 'Final report of the Committee on Consumer Protection' (The Molony Committee), Cmnd. 1781, HMSO, London.

Bobbitt, P. (2002) *The Shield of Achilles: War, Peace and the Course of History*. London: Allen Lane.

Bocock, R. (1993) *Consumption*. London: Routledge.

Boje, D.M. (2001) *Narrative Methods for Organizational and Communication Research*. London: Sage.

Boorstin, D.J. (1962) *The Image or What Happened to the American Dream*. New York: Atheneum.

Bourdieu, P. (1979) *Outline of a Theory of Practice*. Cambridge: Cambridge University Press.

Bourdieu, P. (1984) *Distinction: A Social Critique of the Judgement of Taste*. London: Routledge.

Brandt, W. (1980) *North–South: A Programme for Survival*. London: Pan Books.

Brimelow, P. and Spencer, L. (1990) 'Ralph Nader Inc.', *Forbes*, 146 (6): 117–29.

British Retail Consortium (2004) '11th Retail Crime Survey', British Retail Consortium, London.

Britt, S.H. (1966) *Consumer Behavior and the Behavioral Sciences: Theories and Applications*. New York: Wiley.

Britt, S.H. (1970) *Psychological Experiments in Consumer Behavior*. New York: Wiley.

Broad, R. and Cavanagh, J. (1993) *Plundering Paradise: The Struggle for the Environment in the Philippines*. Berkeley, CA: University of California Press.

Brown, D.H. (1991) 'Citizens or consumer: US reactions to the European Community's directive on television', *Critical Studies in Mass Communication*, 8: 1–12.

Brown, D.M., Cameron, B.A. and Meyer, S.S. (1993) 'A survey of commercial laundry detergents: How effective are they? Part 1: Powders', *Journal of Consumer Studies and Home Economics*, 17: 145–52.

Brown, J.S. and Duguid, P. (1994) 'Organizational learning and communities of practice: Toward a unified view of working, learning and innovation', in H. Tsoukas (ed.), *New Thinking in Organizational Behaviour*. London: Sage. pp. 165–87.

Brown, R.L. (1958) 'Wrapper influence on the perception of freshness in bread', *Journal of Applied Psychology*, 42: 257–60.

Brown, S.A. (1997) *Revolution at the Checkout Counter*. Ca nbridge, MA: Harvard University Press.

Brownell, K.D. and Horgen, K.B. (2004) *Food Fight: The Inside Story of the Food Industry, America's Obesity Crisis, and What We Can Do About It*. Chicago: Contemporary Books.

Bryant, A. (1929) *The Spirit of Conservatism*. London: Methuen.

Bull, D. (1982) *A Growing Problem: Pesticides and the Third World Poor*. Oxford: OXFAM.

Bunting, M. (2004) *Willing Slaves: How the Overwork Culture is Ruling our Lives*. London: HarperCollins.

Burnett, J. (1969) *A History of the Cost of Living*. Harmondsworth: Penguin.

Burton, S. and Babin, L.A. (1989) 'Decision-making helps make the sale', *Journal of Consumer Marketing*, 6 (2): 15–25.

Cairncross, F. (1991) *Costing the Earth: The Challenge for Governments, the Opportunities for Business*. Boston, MA: Harvard Business School Press.

Calinescu, M. (1987) *Five Faces of Modernity: Modernism, Avant-garde, Decadence, Kitsch, Postmodernism*. Durham, NC: Duke University Press.

Cameron, B.A., Brown, D.M. and Cameron, B.A. (1993) 'A survey of commercial laundry detergents: How effective are they? Part 2: Liquids', *Journal of Consumer Studies and Home Economics*, 17: 267–73.

Campbell, C. (1989) *The Romantic Ethic and the Spirit of Modern Consumerism*. Oxford: Macmillan.

Camus, A. (1971) *The Rebel*. Harmondsworth: Penguin.

Carruthers, I. and Holland, P. (1991) 'Quality assurance for the individual', *Journal of Health Care Quality Assurance*, 4 (2): 9–17.

Castells, M. (1996) *The Information Age: Economy, Society and Culture. Vol. 1: The Rise of the Network Society*. Oxford: Blackwell.

Castells, M. (1997) *The Information Age: Economy, Society and Culture. Vol. 2: The Power of Identity*. Oxford: Blackwell.

Castells, M. (1998) *The Information Age: Economy, Society and Culture. Vol. 3: The End of the Millennium*. Oxford: Blackwell.

Castells, M. (2001) *The Internet Galaxy: Reflections on the Internet, Business, and Society*. Oxford, New York: Oxford University Press.

CEC (2005) 'Healthier, safer, more confident citizens: A health and consumer protection strategy', Commission of the European Communities, Brussels. Released 6 April 2005.

Chaney, D. (1996) *Lifestyles*. London: Routledge.

Chase, S. and Schlink, F.J. (1927) *Your Money's worth: A Study in the Waste of the Consumer's Dollar*. New York: Macmillan.

Chesterfield Evans, A. (1987) *Confessions of a Simple Surgeon* (video-tape). Sydney: Technical and Further Education Association (TAFE).

Clammer, J. (1992) 'Aesthetics of the self: Shopping and social being in contemporary Japan', in R. Shields (ed.), *Lifestyle Shopping: The Subject of Consumption*. London: Routledge.

Coley, N.G. (2005) 'The fight against food adulteration', *Education in Chemistry*, March. Accessed 1 November 2005 from www.rsc.org/Education/EiC/issues/2005Mar/Thefightagainst foodadulteration.asp.

Commission on the Nutrition Challenges of the 21st Century (2000) 'Ending malnutrition by 2020: An agenda for change in the millennium. Final Report to the ACC/SCN', *Food and Nutrition Bulletin*, 21 (3 Supplement): whole issue.

Competition Commission (UK) and Department of Trade and Industry (UK) (2000) *Supermarkets: A Report on the Supply of Groceries from Multiple Stores in the United Kingdom*. London: The Stationery Office.

Confederation of British Industry (2002) 'CBI's response to the European Commission's Green Paper on Consumer Protection', CBI, London.

Consumers International (2004) *About CI: Rights and Responsibilities*. London: Consumers International.

Consumers International (2005) 'Competition – more for everybody information kit', Consumers International, London. Accessed 3 July 2005, from www.consumerinterna tional.org.

Consumers Union (2005) 'About CU', Yankers, NY, Consumers Union. Accessed 27 June 2005 from www.consumersunion.org/aboutcu/about.html.

Co-operative Group (UK) (2004) *Shopping With Attitude*. Manchester: Co-operative Group.

Coupey, E. (1994) 'Restructuring – constructive processing of information displays in consumer choice', *Journal of Consumer Research*, 21 (1): 83–99.

Coupey, E. and Narayanan, S. (1996) 'Effects of knowledge types on choice quality and perceptions of choice performance', *Psychology & Marketing*, 13 (7): 715–38.

Cox, A.D., Cox, D. and Anderson, R.D. (2005) 'Reassessing the pleasures of store shopping', *Journal of Business Research*, 58 (3): 250–9.

Cranston, R. (1979) *Regulating Business*. London: Macmillan.

Cranston, R. (1984) *Consumers and the Law* (2nd edition). London: Weidenfeld and Nicolson.

Crawford, R. (1977) 'You are dangerous to your health: The ideology and politics of victim blaming', *International Journal of Health Services*, 7 (4): 663–80.

Crick, B.R. (2001) *Citizens: Towards a Citizenship Culture*. Oxford: Blackwell.

Crick, B.R. (2004) *Essays on Citizenship*. London: Continuum.

Csikszentminhalyi, M. and Rochberg-Halton, E. (1981) *The Meaning of Things: Domestic Symbols and the Self*. Cambridge: Cambridge University Press.

Culler, J. (1981) *The Pursuit of Signs: Semiotics, Literature, Deconstruction*. London: Routledge.

Cunliffe, V., Gee, R. and Ainsworth, P. (1988) An investigation into some aspects of the efficiency of low-temperature laundering', *Journal of Consumer Studies and Home Economics*, 12: 95–106.

Daly, H.E., Cobb, J.B. and Cobb, C.W. (1990) *For the Common Good: Redirecting the Economy toward Community, the Environment, and a Sustainable Future*. London: Green Print.

Davidson, M.P. (1992) *The Consumerist Manifesto: Advertising in Postmodern Times*. London: Routledge.

de Certeau, M. (1984) *The Practice of Everyday Life*. Berkeley, CA: University of California Press.

Deaton, A. and Muellbauer, J. (1980) *Economics and Consumer Behavior*. Cambridge, New York: Cambridge University Press.

Debord, G. (1977) *Society of the Spectacle*. Detroit: Black and Red.

Deighton, J., Henderson, C.M. and Neslin, S.A. (1994) 'The ethics of advertising on brand switching and repeat purchasing', *Journal of Marketing Research*, 31 (1): 28–44.

Department of Trade Industry (UK) (2005) *Guide to the 1987 Consumer Protection Act*. London: DTI Consumer Affairs Directorate.

DG SANCO (2005) 'Health and consumer protection programme 2007–2013', Commission of the European Communities, Luxembourg. Accessed 3 July 2005 from europa.eu.int/comm/consumers/overview/programme_2007–2013_en.htm.

Dibb, S.E. (1993) *Children: Advertisers' Dream, Nutrition Nightmare*. London: National Food Alliance.

Dickenson, N. (1993) 'Catering for the ethical shopper: A look into a growing consumer trend', *Financial Times*: 15 April.

Dickinson, R. and Hollander, S.C. (1991) 'Consumer votes', *Journal of Business Research*, 22: 335–42.

Dinham, B. (1993) *The Pesticide Hazard: A Global Health and Environmental Audit*. London, Atlantic Highlands, NJ: Zed Books.

Dittmar, H. (1991) 'Meanings of material possessions as reflections of identity: Gender and social-material position in society', *Journal of Social Behavior and Personality*, 6 (6): 165–86.

Doll, R., Peto, R., Boreham, J. and Sutherland, I. (2004) 'Mortality in relation to smoking: 50 years' observations on male British doctors', *British Medical Journal*, 328: 1519.

Douglas, M. (1975) 'Deciphering a meal', in M. Douglas (ed.), *Implicit Meanings: Essays in Anthropology*. London: Routledge. pp. 179–92.

Douglas, M. and Isherwood, B. (1978) *The World of Goods: Towards an Anthropology of Consumption*. London: Allen Lane.

Dowler, E., Turner, S.A., Dobson, B. and Child Poverty Action Group (UK) (2001) *Poverty Bites: Food, Health and Poor Families*. London: Child Poverty Action Group.

Du Gay, P. (1996a) *Consumption and Identity at Work*. London: Sage.

Du Gay, P. (1996b) 'Organizing identity: Entrepreneurial governance and public management', in S. Hall and P. Du Gay (eds), *Questions of Cultural Identity*. London: Sage. pp. 151–69.

Durning, A.T. (1992) *How Much is Enough? The Consumer Society and the Future of the Earth* (1st edition). New York: Norton.

Ecologist (2001) *Go M-A-D: Go Make a Difference – 365 Daily Ways to Save the Planet*. London: Think Publishing Limited.

Economist (2003) 'Filling the world's belly', December 13. Accessed 1 November 2005 from www.economist.com/surveys/displayStory.cfm?story_id = 2261775.

ECRA (1994) 'Culture-jamming', *The Ethical Consumer*, 29: 20–1.

Edge, A. (1999) *Faith of our Fathers: Football as a Religion*. Edinburgh: Mainstream.

Ehrenreich, B. (1994) 'Smoke signals of defiance', *The Guardian*, 19 March: B9.

Ekins, P. (1992) 'Towards a progressive market', in P. Ekins and M. Max-Neef (eds), *Real-life Economics: Understanding Wealth Creation*. London: Routledge.

Ekins, P., Hillman, M. and Hutchison, R. (1992) *Wealth Beyond Measure: An Atlas of New Economics*. London: Gaia Books.

Elkington, J. and Hailes, J. (1988) *The Green Consumer Guide: From Shampoo to Champagne: High-street Shopping for a Better Environment*. London: Victor Gollancz.

Engel, J.F., Blackwell, R.D. and Miniard, P.W. (1990) *Consumer Behavior* (6th edition). Chicago: Dryden Press.

Erikson, E.H. (1959) *Identity and the Life Cycle*. New York: Norton.

Erikson, E.H. (1968) *Identity: Youth and Crisis*. London: Faber and Faber.

Ethical Consumer (1993) 'The Ethical Consumer guide to everyday shopping', *The Ethical Consumer* 26: whole issue.

Ethical Consumer (1994) 'The *Ethical Consumer*: Special anti-consumer issue', *The Ethical Consumer* 27: whole issue.

Ethical Consumer (2005) 'About boycotts Manchester', *The Ethical Consumer*. Accessed 27 June 2005 from www.ethicalconsumer.org/boycotts/aboutboycotts.htm.

Evans, P. (1990) *Unpacking the GATT: A Step by Step Guide to the Uruguay Round*. London: International Organization of Consumer Unions.

Evans-Pritchard, E.E. (1940) *The Nuer, A Description of the Modes of Livelihood and Political Institutions of a Nilotic People*. Oxford: Clarendon Press.

Ewen, S. (1990) 'Marketing dreams: The political elements of style', in A. Tomlinson (ed.), *Consumption, Identity and Style: Marketing, Meanings and the Packaging of Pleasure*. London: Routledge.

Ewen, S. (1992) 'From consumer to citizen', *Intermedia*, 20 (3): 22–3.

Eyre, A. (1997) *Football and Religious Experience: Sociological Reflections*. Oxford: Religious Experience Research Centre.

Fairtrade Foundation (2005) 'Annual Report 2004', Fairtrade Foundation, London.

FAO (2004) 'Farmworkers need to be better protected against pesticides', Food and Agriculture Organization of the United Nations, Rome. Accessed 3 July 2005 from www.fao.org/newsroom/en/news/2004/50709/print_friendly_version.html.

Featherstone, M. (1991) *Consumer Culture and Postmodernism*. London: Sage.

Featherstone, M. (1992) 'Postmodernism and the aestheticization of everyday life', in S. Lash and J. Friedman (eds), *Modernity and Identity*. Oxford: Blackwell.

Ferlie, E., Ashburner, L., Fitzgerald, L. and Pettigrew, A. (1996) *The New Public Management*. Oxford: Oxford University Press.

Fernstrom, M.M. (1984) *Consumerism: Implications and Opportunities for Financial Services*. USA: American Express Company.

Festing, H. (1993) 'Is there life after supermarkets?', *New Economics*, 28 (Winter): 8–9.

Fineman, S. (2000) 'Commodifying the emotionally intelligent', in S. Fineman (ed.), *Emotion in Organizations* (2nd edition). London: Sage. pp. 101–15.

Firat, A.F. (1992) 'Fragmentations in the postmodern', *Advances in Consumer Research*, pp. 101–15. 19: 203–6.

Fiske, J. (1987) *Television Culture*. London: Methuen.

Fiske, J. (1989) *Understanding Popular Culture*. London: Unwin Hyman.

Fleishman, E.A. (1951) 'An experimental consumer panel technique', *Journal of Applied Psychology*, 35: 133–5.

Fleishman, E.A. (1967) *Studies in Personnel and Industrial Psychology* (revised edition). Homewood, IL: Dorsey Press.

Forbes, J.D. (1987) *The Consumer Interest*. Beckenham: Croom Helm.

Forman, A.M. and Sriram, V. (1991) 'The depersonalization of retailing – its impact on the lonely consumer', *Journal of Retailing*, 67 (2): 226–43.

Foxall, G.R. (1977) *Consumer Behaviour: A Practical Guide*. Corbridge: Retail and Planning Associates.

Frank, T. (1997) *The Conquest of Cool*. London: University of Chicago Press.

Frenkel, S.J., Korczynski, M., Shire, K.A. and Tam, M. (1999) *On the Front Line: Organization of Work in the Information Economy*. Ithaca, NY: Cornell University Press.

Freud, S. (1920) *Beyond the Pleasure Principle* (standard edition). London: Hogarth Press.

Freud, S. (1984a[1914]) 'On narcissism: An introduction', in S. Freud, *On Metapsychology: The Theory of Psychoanalysis*, Vol. 11. Harmondsworth: Pelican Freud Library. pp. 59–97.

Freud, S. (1984b[1923]) 'The ego and the id', in S. Freud, *On Metapsychology: The Theory of Psychoanalysis*, Vol. 11. Harmondsworth: Pelican Freud Library. pp. 341–406.

Freud, S. (1985a[1921]) 'Group psychology and the analysis of the ego', in S. Freud, *Civilization, Society and Religion*, Vol. 12. Harmondsworth: Pelican Freud Library. pp. 91–178.

Freud, S. (1985b[1930]) 'Civilization and its discontents', in S. Freud, *Civilization, Society and Religion*, Vol. 12. Harmondsworth: Pelican Freud Library. pp. 91–178.

Friedman, M. (1985) 'Consumer boycotts in the United States, 1970–1980: Contemporary events in historial perspective', *Journal of Consumer Affairs*, 19 (1): 96–117.

Friedman, M. and Friedman, R.D. (1980) *Free to Choose: A Personal Statement* (1st edition). New York: Harcourt Brace Jovanovich.

Fritsch, A.J. (1974) *The Contrasumers: A Citizen's Guide to Resource Conservation*. New York: Praeger.

Fromm, E. (1966[1941]) *Escape from Freedom*. New York: Avon Library.

Fukuyama, F. (1992) *The End of History and the Last Man*. New York: Free Press.

Fulop, C. (1977) *The Consumer Movement and the Consumer*. London: Advertising Association.

Furnham, A., and Okamura, R. (1999) 'Your money or your life: Behavioral and emotional predictors of money pathology', *Human Relations*, 52 (9): 1157–77.

Gabriel, Y. (1993) 'Organizational nostalgia: Reflections on the golden age', in S. Fineman (ed.), *Emotion in Organizations*. London: Sage. pp. 118–41.

Gabriel, Y. (1995) 'The unmanaged organization', *Organization Studies*, 16 (3): 481–506.

Gabriel, Y. (1999) *Organizations in Depth: The Psychoanalysis of Organizations*. London: Sage.

Gabriel, Y. (2000) *Storytelling in Organizations: Facts, Fictions, Fantasies*. Oxford: Oxford University Press.

Gabriel, Y. (2002) '*Essai*: On paragrammatic uses of organizational theory: A provocation', *Organization Studies*, 23 (1): 133–51.

Galbraith, J.K. (1967) *The New Industrial State*. New York: Signet.

Galbraith, J.K. (1974) *Economics and the Public Purpose*. London: Deutsch.

Gelb, B.D. (1992) 'Why rich brands get richer', *Business Horizons*, 35 (2): 43–47.

George, S. (1988) *A Fate Worse than Debt* (1st edition). New York: Grove Press.

George, S. (1992) *The Debt Boomerang: How Third World Debt Harms Us All*. Boulder, CO: Westview Press.

Gershuny, J. (1988) 'Lifestyle, innovation and the future of work', *International Journal of Development Banking*, 6 (1): 65–72.

Gershuny, J. (1992) 'Are we running out of time?' *Futures* (January/February): 3–22.

Gherardi, S., Nicolini, D. and Odella, F. (1998) 'Toward a social understanding of how people learn in organizations: The notion of the situated curriculum', *Management Learning*, 29 (3): 273–97.

Giddens, A. (1991) *Modernity and Self-identity: Self and Society in the Late Modern Age*. Stanford, CA: Stanford University Press.

Gilmore, F. (1999) *Brand Warriors: Corporate Leaders Share their Winning Strategies*. London: HarperCollinsBusiness.

Gilmore, F. (2003) *Warriors on the High Wire: The Balancing Act of Brand Leadership in the Twenty-first Century*. London: Profile.

Ginzburg, C. (1980) 'Morelli, Freud and Sherlock Holmes: Clues and scientific method', *History Workshop*, 9: 5–36.

Global Environment Facility, UNEP: GEO Section and UNEP: Division of GEF Coordination (2002) *Change and Challenge: A State of the Environment Briefing for the Global Environment Facility: A Report from the Global Environment Outlook*. Nairobi: United Nations Environment Programme.

Goldsmith, E. and Mander, J. (2001) *The Case against the Global Economy and for a Turn Towards Localization* (new edition). London: Earthscan.

Goldsmith, E., Allen, R., Allaby, M., Davoll, J. and Lawrence, S. (1972) 'A blueprint for survival', *The Ecologist*, 2 (1): 1–43.

Goleman, D. (1996) *Emotional Intelligence*. London: Bloomsbury.

Gorey, H. (1975) *Nader and the Power of Everyman*. New York: Grosset and Dunlap.

Gott, R. (1993) *Land without Evil*. London: Verso.

Gott, R. (2000) *In the Shadow of the Liberator: Hugo Chavez and the Transformation of Venezuela*. London: Verso.

Goulart, R. (1970) *The Assault on Childhood*. London: Gollancz.

Gray, J. (1993) *Beyond the New Right: Markets, Government and the Common Environment*. London, New York: Routledge.

Gray, J. (1994) *The Undoing of Conservatism*. London: Social Market Foundation.

Gray, J. (2002) *Straw Dogs: Thoughts on Humans and Other Animals*. London: Granta.

Gray, J. (2003) *Al Qaeda and What it Means to be Modern*. London: Faber.

Greider, W. (1992) *Who Will Tell the People? The Betrayal of American Democracy*. New York: Simon and Schuster.

Greyser, S.A. and Diamond, S.L. (1983) 'US Consumers' views of the marketplace', *Journal of Consumer Policy*, 6: 3–18.

Grossman, R.L. and Adams, F.T. (1993) *Taking Care of Business: Who Will Produce Tomorrow's Food*. Cambridge, MA: Charter Ink.

Gussow, J.D. (1991) *Chicken Little, Tomato Sauce, and Agriculture: Who Will Produce Tomorrow's Food?* New York: Bootstrap Press.

Guzzardi, W.J. (1982) 'The mindless pursuit of safety', in D.A. Aaker and G.S. Day (eds), *Consumerism: Search for the Consumer Interest* (4th edition). New York: Free Press. pp. 363–75.

Hair, J.D. (1989) 'Changing from "consumers" to citizens', *EPA Journal*, 15 (4): 37–9.

Hall, S. (1996) 'Who needs "identity"?', in S. Hall and P. Du Gay (eds), *Questions of Cultural Identity*. London: Sage. pp. 1–17.

Hall, S. and Du Gay, P. (eds) (1996) *Questions of Cultural Identity*. London: Sage.

Hall, S. and Jacques, M. (eds) (1989) *New Times*. London: Lawrence and Wishart.

Hambleton, R. and Hoggett, P. (1993) 'Rethinking consumerism in public services', *Consumer Policy Review*, 3 (2): 103–11.

Hampden-Turner, C. and Trompenaars, A. (1993) *The Seven Cultures of Capitalism: Value Systems for Creating Wealth in the United States, Japan, Germany, France, Britain, Sweden, and the Netherlands* (1st edition). New York: Currency/Doubleday.

Harrison, R. (2003) 'Corporate social responsibility and the consumer movement', *Consumer Policy Review*, 13 (4): 127–31.

Harrison, R., Newholm, T. and Shaw, D. (2005) *The Ethical Consumer*. London: Sage.

Harvey, D. (1990) *The Condition of Postmodernity: An Enquiry into the Origins of Cultural Change*. Oxford: Blackwell.

Hastings, G., Stead, M., McDermott, L., Forsyth, A., MacKintosh, A.M., Rayner, M., Godfrey, C., Caraher, M. and Angus, K. (2003) *Review of Research on the Effects of Promotion to Children*. London: Food Standards Agency.

Hawken, P. (1993) *The Ecology of Commerce: A Declaration of Sustainability* (1st edition). New York: HarperBusiness.

Heath, J. and Potter, A. (2005) *The Rebel Sell: How The Counter Culture Became Consumer Culture*. Chichester: Wiley.

Held, D. (1999) *Global Transformations: Politics, Economics and Culture*. Cambridge: Polity Press.

Held, D. and Koenig-Archibugi, M. (2005) *Global Governance and Public Accountability*. Oxford: Blackwell.

Held, D. and McGrew, A.G. (2000) *The Global Transformations Reader: An Introduction to the Globalization Debate*. Cambridge: Polity.

Hennessy, P. (1992) *Never Again: Britain 1945–51*. London: Jonathan Cape.

Hermann, R.O. (1982) 'The consumer movement in historical perspective', in D.A. Aaker and G.S. Day (eds), *Consumerism: Search for the Consumer Interest* (4th edition). New York: Free Press. pp. 23–32.

Hermann, R.O. (1993) 'The tactics of consumer resistance: Group action and marketplace exit', *Advances in Consumer Research*, 20: 130–4.

Hetherington, K. (1992) 'Stonehenge and its festival: Spaces of consumption', in R. Shields (ed.), *Lifestyle Shopping: The Subject of Consumption*. London: Routledge. pp. 83–98.

Hines, C. (1976) *Food Co-ops: How to Save Money by Getting Together and Buying in Bulk*. London: Friends of the Earth.

Hirsch, J. (1991) 'Fordism and post-Fordism: The present crisis and its consequences', in W. Bonefeld and J. Holloway (eds), *Post-Fordism and Social Form: A Marxist Debate on the post-Fordist state*. Houndmills: Macmillan Academic and Professional.

HM Government (1991) 'The citizen's charter', white paper, Cmnd 1599, HMSO, London.

Hobsbawn, E. (1983) 'Inventing traditions', in E. Hobsbawn (ed.), *The Invention of Tradition*. Cambridge: Cambridge University Press.

Hobsbawm, E.J. (1994) *Age of Extremes: The Short Twentieth Century, 1914–1991*. London: Michael Joseph.

Holyoake, G. (1872) *The History of Co-operation in Rochdale*. London: Trubner.

Home Office (UK) (2004) *Recorded Crime Statistics 1898–2004/05*. London: Home Office.

Homer (1974) *Iliad* (trans, E.V. Rieu). Harmondsworth: Penguin.

Homer (1988) *The Odyssey* (trans. Richmond Lattimore). Bristol: Bristol Classical Press.

Horkheimer, M. and Adorno, T. (1997[1947]) *Dialectic of Enlightenment* (trans. J. Cummings). New York: Herder and Herder.

Hull, C.L. (1974) *A Behavior System: An Introduction to Behavior Theory Concerning the Individual Organism*. Westport, CT: Greenwood Press.

Hutton, W. (1995) *The State We're In*. London: Jonathan Cape.

Icon Group International (2002) *The 2003–2008 World Outlook for Men's Outerwear Jeans*. San Diego, CA: Icon Group.

International Organization of Consumers' Unions (1993) *Time to Put Consumers First: Statement on the Uruguay Round*. The Hague: International Organization of Consumers Unions.

Irvine, S. (1989) 'Beyond green consumerism', Friends of the Earth Discussion Paper no. 1, September, Friends of the Earth, London.

Isaac, K. and Nader, R. (1992) *Ralph Nader Presents Civics for Democracy: A Journey for Teachers and Students*. Washington, DC: Essential Books.

Jackson, T. and Michaelis, L. (2003) *Policies for Sustainable Consumption*. London: Sustainable Development Commission.

Jacobs, M. and Dinham, B. (2003) *Silent Invaders: Pesticides, Livelihoods, and Women's Health*. London: Zed Books.

James, J. (1983) *Consumer Choice in the Third World: A Study of the Welfare Effects of Advertising and New Products in a Developing Country*. New York: St Martin's Press.

James, W. (1891) *Principles of Psychology*. London: Macmillan.

James, W. (1961[1892]) *Psychology: The Briefer Course*. New York: Harper and Row.

Jameson, F. (1983) 'Postmodernism and consumer society', in H. Foster (ed.), *The Anti-Aesthetic: Essays on Postmodern Culture*. Port Townsend, WA: Bay Press.

Jawara, F. and Kwa, A. (2003) *Behind the Scenes at the WTO: The Real World of International Trade Negotiations*. London Bangkok: Zed Books; Focus on the Global South.

Jencks, C. (ed.) (1992) *The Post-Modern Reader*. London: Academy Editions.

Jenkins, R. (1992) *Pierre Bourdieu*. London, New York: Routledge.

Jessop, B. (2001) *Regulation Theory and the Crisis of Capitalism*. Cheltenham, Northampton, MA: Edward Elgar.

Jeyarraratnam, J. (1990) 'Acute pesticide poisoning: A major problem', *World Health Statistics Quarterly*, 43: 139–44.

Johansson, J.K. (1982) 'The theory and practice of Swedish consumer policy', in D.A. Aaker and G.S. Day (eds), *Consumerism: Search for the Consumer Interest* (4th edition). New York: Free Press. pp. 62–75.

John, R. (ed.) (1994) *The Consumer Revolution: Redressing the Balance*. London: Hodder and Stoughton.

Johnson, V. (1992) 'Lifestyle overload? Population and environment in balance', A report of the ActionAid seminar, Commonwealth House, London.

Jones, R. (2005) 'Bribery and corruption top Co-op's "sin-list"', *The Guardian*, 27 June: 23.

Jung, A.F. (1988) 'Car prices and the degree of buyer satisfaction', *Journal of Consumer Studies and Home Economics*, 12 (3): 237–46.

Juvenal (1999[AD 110–30]) *Satires*. Oxford: Oxford University Press.

Kallet, A. and Schlink, F.J. (1932) *100,000,000 Guinea Pigs: Dangers in Everyday Foods, Drugs, and Cosmetics*. New York: Vanguard Press.

Kant, I. (1952) The *Critique of Judgement* (trans. James Creed Meredith). Oxford: Clarendon Press.

Kapuscinski, R. (1983) *The Emperor*. New York: Harcourt.

Kardon, B.E. (1992) 'Consumer schizophrenia extremism in the marketplace', *Planning Review*, 20: 18–22.

Keasey, K., Thompson, S. and Wright, M. (2005) *Corporate Governance: Accountability, Enterprise and International Comparisons*. Chichester: Wiley.

Kellaway, L. (1993) 'Twelve acorns for a haircut', *Financial Times*: 13.

Kellner, D. (1989) *Jean Baudrillard: From Marxism to Postmodernism and Beyond*. Cambridge: Polity Press.

Khor, M. (2001) *Rethinking Globalization: Critical Issues and Policy Choices*. London: Zed Books.

Klein, N. (2000) *No Logo: Taking Aim at the Brand Bullies*. London: Flamingo.

Korczynski, M. (2001) 'The contradictions of service work: Call centre as customer-oriented bureaucracy', in A. Sturdy, I. Grugulis and H. Willmott (eds), *Customer Service: Empowerment and Entrapment*. Basingstoke: Palgrave. pp. 79–101.

Korczynski, M. (2003) 'Communities of coping: Collective emotional labour in service work', *Organization*, 10 (1): 55–79.

Korczynski, M., Shire, K., Frenkel, S. and Tam, M. (2000) 'Service work and consumer capitalism', *Work, Employment and Society*, 14 (4): 669–87.

Korten, D.C. (2001) *When Corporations rule the World* (2nd edition). Bloomfield, CT: Kumarian Press.

Krebs, A.V. (1992) *The Corporate Reapers: The Book of Agribusiness*. Washington DC: Essential Books.

Kyrtatas, D.J. (2004) 'Paradise in heaven and on earth: Western ideas of perfect (non)-organization', in Y. Gabriel (ed.), *Myths, Stories and Organizations: Premodern narratives for our times*. Oxford: Oxford University Press. pp. 66–80.

Lacan, J. (1953) 'Some reflections on the ego', *International Journal of Psychoanalysis*, 34: 11–17.

Lang, T. (1991) 'Consumers or citizens?' *The Ecologist*, 21 (4): 154–5.

Lang, T. (2005) 'Food control or food democracy: Re-engaging nutrition to civil society, the state and the food supply chain', *Public Health Nutrition*, 8 (6): 730–7.

Lang, T. and Clutterbuck, C. (1991) *P is for Pesticides*. London: Ebury.

Lang, T. and Heasman, M. (2004) *Food Wars: The Global Battle for Mouths, Minds and Markets*. London: Earthscan.

Lang, T. and Hines, C. (1993) *The New Protectionism: Protecting the Future against Free Trade*. London: Earthscan.

Lang, T. and Raven, H. (1994) 'From market to hypermarket: Food retailing in Britain', *The Ecologist*, 24 (4): 124–9.

Lang, T. and Rayner, G. (2005) Obesity: A growing issue for European policy?', *Journal of European Social Policy*, 15 (4): 301–27.

Langman, L. (1992) 'Neon cages: Shopping for subjectivity', in R. Shields (ed.), *Lifestyle Shopping: The Subject of Consumption*. London: Routledge.

Lansley, S. (1994) *After the Goldrush: The Trouble with Affluence*. London: Century Business Books.

Lasch, C. (1980) *The Culture of Narcissism*. London: Abacus.

Lasch, C. (1984) *The Minimal Self: Psychic Survival in Troubled Times*. London: Pan Books.

Lasch, C. (1991) *The True and Only Heaven: Progress and Its Critics*. New York: Norton.

Lawlor, E. (1988) 'Individual choice and higher growth: The task of European Consumer policy', Luxembourg: Commission of the European Communities.

Lawrence, F. (2004) *Hard Labour*. Harmondsworth: Penguin.

Layard, P.R.G. (2005) *Happiness: Lessons from a New Science*. New York: Penguin Press.

Le Bon, G. (1985[1960]) *The Crowd: A Study of the Popular Mind*. New York: Viking Press.

Lebergott, S. (1993) *Pursuing Happiness: American Consumers in the Twentieth Century*. Princeton, NJ: Princeton University Press.

Lee, M.J. (1993) *Consumer Culture Reborn: The Cultural Politics of Consumption*. London: Routledge.

Lee, M.J. (ed.) (2000) *The Consumer Society Reader*. Oxford: Blackwell.

LETSLINK-UK (1994) *LETS Information Pack*. Warminster: LETSLINK-UK.

LETSLINK-UK (2005) *So What Are LETS?* Warminster: LETSLINK-UK.

Levett, R., Christie, I., Jacobs, M., Therivel, R. and Fabian Society (UK) (2003) *A Better Choice of Choice: Quality of Life, Consumption and Economic Growth*. London: Fabian Society.

Lévi-Strauss, C. (1978) *Myth and Meaning: The 1977 Massey Lectures*. London: Routledge.

Levy, S. (1982) 'Symbols, selves and others', *Advances in Consumer Research*, 9: 542–3.

Levy-Bruhl, L. (1966) *The 'Soul' of the Primitive*. New York: Praeger.

Light, R., Nee, C. and Ingham, H. (1993) *Car Theft: The Offender's Perspective*. London: HMSO.

Lister, R. (1990) *The Exclusive Society: Citizenship and the Poor*. London: Child Poverty Action Group.

Lister, R. (2004) *Poverty*. Cambridge; Malden, MA: Polity.

Lister, R. and Campling, J. (2003) *Citizenship: Feminist Perspectives* (2nd edition). Basingstoke, New York: Palgrave Macmillan.

Locke, S. (1994) 'A new approach to competition policy', *Consumer Policy Review*, 4 (3): 159–68.

Loudon, D.L. and Della Bitta, A.J. (1993) *Consumer Behavior: Concepts and Applications* (4th edition). New York: McGraw-Hill.

Lury, A. (1994) 'Advertising: Moving beyond the stereotypes', in R. Keat, N. Whiteley and N. Abercrombie (eds), *The Authority of the Consumer*. London: Routledge.

Lury, C. (1996) *Consumer Culture*. Cambridge: Polity.

Lury, C. (2004) *Brands: The Logos of Global Economy*. London: Routledge.

Lynch, R. and Makusen, A. (1993) 'Can markets govern?', *The American Prospect*, 16 (Winter): 125–4.

Lyndhurst, B. and Greater London Authority (2003) *London's Ecological Footprint: A Review*. London: Greater London Authority.

Mack, J. and Lansley, S. (1985) *Poor Britain*. London, Boston: Allen and Unwin.

Mack, J. and Lansley, S. (1992) *Breadline Britain in the 1990s*. London: HarperCollins.

Madge, J. (1963) *The Origins of Scientific Sociology*. London: Tavistock.

Maffesoli, M. (1995) *The Time of Tribes: The Decline of Individualism in Mass Society*. London: Sage.

Mander, J. (1991) *In the Absence of the Sacred: The Failure of Technology and the Survival of the Indian Nations*. San Francisco: Sierra Club Books.

Marcuse, H. (1964) *One-Dimensional Man: Studies in the Ideology of Advanced Industrial Society*. Boston, MA: Beacon Press.

Marcuse, H. (1969) *An Essay on Liberation*. London: Allen Lane.

Margolius, S. (1982) 'The consumer's real needs', in D.A. Aaker and G.S. Day (eds), *Consumerism: Search for the Consumer Interest* (4th edition). New York: Free Press. pp. 48–56.

Marr, A. (1994) 'Any tax of mine must be yours too', *The Independent*, 18 August.

Martin, C.L. (1992) 'Perspectives of service consumers: Their multiple roles and challenges', *Journal of Consumer Studies and Home Economics*, 16: 139–49.

Martin, J. (2002) *Nader: Crusader, Spoiler, Icon*. New York: Basic Books.

Marx, K. (1972[1844]) 'Economic and philosophic manuscripts of 1844', in R.C. Tucker (ed.), *Marx–Engels Reader*. New York: Norton, pp. 53–103.

Marx, K. (1967[1867]) *Capital*. New York: International Publishers.

Marx, K. (1993[1859]) *Grundrisse – Outline of the Critique of Political Economy* (trans. M. Nicolaus). Harmondsworth: Penguin.

Maslow, A. (1970[1954]) *Motivation and Personality*. New York: Harper and Row.

Mather, G. (1991) 'The race to improve public services', in M. Pirie (ed.), *Empowerment: The Theme for the 1990s*. London: Adam Smith Institute.

Matsu, K. (1994) 'Demarketing', *The Ethical Consumer*, 27 (January): 24.

Matthews, D. (1973) *Sue the Bastards: The Victim's Handbook*. New York: Arbor House.

Matza, D. (1964) *Delinquency and Drift*. New York: Wiley.

Mauss, M. (1974[1925]) *The Gift: Forms and Functions of Exchange in Archaic Societies*. London: Routledge.

McCarney, W.G. (1981) 'Joy-riding: A quest for identity', *Youth in Society* 53: 16–17.

McCracken, G. (1988) *Culture and Consumpton: New Approaches to the Symbolic Character of Consumer Goods and Activities*. Bloomington, IN: Indiana University Press.

McKendrick, N., Brewer, J. and Plumb, J.H. (1982) *The Birth of a Consumer Society: The Commercialization of Eighteenth-century England*. Bloomington, IN: Indiana University Press.

McLean, B. and Elkind, P. (2004) *Enron: The Smartest Guys in the Room*. New York: Penguin Portfolio.

McRobbie, A. (1994) *Postmodernism and Popular Culture*. London, New York: Routledge.

McRobbie, A. (1999) *In the Culture Society: Art, Fashion, and Popular Music*. London, New York: Routledge.

Meadows, D.H. and Club of Rome (1972) *The Limits to Growth: A Report for the Club of Rome's Project on the Predicament of Mankind*. New York: Universe Books.

Meadows, D.H., Meadows, D.L. and Randers, J.R. (1992) *Beyond the Limits: Global Collapse or A Sustainable Future*. London: Earthscan Publications.

MEC (2005) Consolidated financial statement, Mountain Equipment Co-operative, Vancouver. Accessed 3 July 2005 from www.mec.ca/main/home.jsp

Mendelson, R.A.C., Committee on Communications (1992) 'The commercialization of children's television', *Pediatrics*, 89 (2): 343–4.

Mick, D.G. (1986) 'Consumer research and semiotics: Exploring the morphology of signs, symbols and significance', *Journal of Consumer Research*, 13: 196–213.

Miliband, R. (1969) *The State in Capitalist Society*. New York: Basic Books.

Millennium Ecosystem Assessment (Program) (2005) *Ecosystems and Human Well-being: Synthesis*. Washington, DC: Island Press.

Miller D. (1987) *Material Culture and Mass Consumption*. Oxford: Blackwell.

Miller, D. (2001) *The Dialectics of Shopping*. Chicago: Chicago University Press.

Millis, H.A. and Brown, E.C. (1950) *From the Wagner Act to Taft-Hartley: A study of National Labor Policy and Labor Relations*. Chicago: University of Chicago Press.

Mintel (2005) Jeans – UK. London: Mintel International.

Mishan, E.J. (1967) *The Costs of Economic Growth*. London: Staples.

Mitchell, V.W. and Boustani, P. (1992) 'Consumer risk perceptions in the breakfast cereal market', *British Food Journal*, 94 (4): 17–27.

Monbiot, G. (2000) *Captive State: The Corporate Takeover of Britain*. Basingstoke: Macmillan.

Monbiot, G. (2003) *The Age of Consent: A Manifesto for a New World Order*. London: Flamingo.

Morgan, B. (2003) *Social Citizenship in the Shadow of Competition: The Bureaucratic Politics of Regulatory Justification*. Aldershot: Ashgate.

Moyle, F. (1990) 'Morals of a modern major marketer', *Marketing Week*, 13 (4): 36–40.

Mukerji, C. (1983) *From Graven Images: Patterns of Modern Materialism*. New York: Columbia University Press.

Mulatuli (1987[1860]) *Max Havelaar or the Coffee Auctions of the Dutch Trading Company*. Harmondsworth: Penguin.

Nadel, M.V. (1971) *The Politics of Consumer Protection*. Indianapolis: Bobbs-Merrill.

Nader, R. (1968) 'The great American gyp', *New York Review of Books*, 11 (21 November): 28.

Nader, R. (1970) 'Foreword', in J.S. Turner (ed.), *The Chemical Feast: The Ralph Nader Study Group Report on Food Protection and the Food and Drug Administration*. New York: Grossman. pp. 24–8.

Nader, R. (1991a[1965]) *Unsafe at Any Speed: The Designed-in Dangers of the American Automobile*. New York: Knightsbridge Publishing.

Nader, R. (1991b) 'Keynote speech to the World Consumer Congress', International Organisation of Consumers Unions, Hong Kong, August.

Nader, R. and Smith, W.J. (1992) *The Frugal Shopper*. Washington, DC: Center for Study of Responsive Law.

National Consumer Council (UK) (1977) *The Fourth Right of Citizenship: A Review of Local Advice Services*. London: National Consumer Council.

National Consumer Council (UK) (1978) *Real Money, Real Choice*. London: National Consumer Council.

National Consumer Council (UK) (1979) *The Consumer and the State: Getting Value for Public Money*. London: National Consumer Council.

National Consumer Council (UK) (1981) *Shopping*. London: National Consumer Council.

National Consumer Council (UK) (1993) *International Trade: The Consumer Agenda*. London: National Consumer Council.

National Consumer Council (1994) 'Annual report', National Consumer Council, London.

National Statistics (Great Britain) and Great Britain Dept. for Environment Food and Rural Affairs (UK) (2004) 'Family food 2003–2004' TSO, London.

Nelson, D. (1991) 'The seikatsu club consumers' co-operative: Activism for alternatives', *World Consumer*, December: 4–5.

Nestle, M. (2002) *The Politics of Food*. Berkeley, CA: University of California Press.

Nicholson-Lord, D. (1994) 'Consumerism with a shrunken vision', *The Independent*, 25 May.

Nixon, S. (1992) 'Have you got the look? Masculinities and shopping spectacle', in R. Shields (ed.), *Lifestyle Shopping: The Subject of Consumption*. London: Routledge.

Norberg-Hodge, H. (1991) *Ancient Futures: Learning from Ladakh*. San Francisco: Sierra Club Books.

Nove, A. (1983) *The Economics of Feasible Socialism*. London, Boston: Allen and Unwin.

O'Connor, J. (1973) *The Fiscal Crisis of the State*. New York: St Martin's Press.

O'Connor, M.C. (2005) 'Surveys reveal dubious consumers', *RFID Journal*, 17 February 2005: Accessed 3 July from www.rfidjournal.com/article/articleview/1409/1/132.

Office of Fair Trading (UK) (1994) *A Buyer's Guide*. London: HMSO.

Omi, M. and Winant, H. (1987) *Racial Formation in the United States*. London: Routledge.

Orbach, S. (1978) *Fat is a Feminist Issue*. London: Hamlyn.

Orbach, S. (1986) *Hunger Strike: The Anorectic's Struggle as a Metaphor for our Age*. London: Faber and Faber.

Orr, J.E. (1996) *Talking about Machines: An Ethnography of a Modern Job*. Ithaca, NY: ILR Press/Cornell.

Orwell, G. (1962) *The Road to Wigan Pier*. Harmondsworth: Penguin.

Osborne, D. and Gaebler, T. (1992) *Reinventing Government: How the Entrepreneurial Spirit is Transforming the Public Sector*. New York, NY: Plume.

O'Shaughnessy, J. (1987) *Why People Buy*. New York: Oxford University Press.

Otker, T. (1990) 'The highly involved consumer: A marketing myth?', *Advances in Consumer Research*, 19: 147–54.

Packard, V. (1981[1957]) *The Hidden Persuaders* (2nd edition). Harmondsworth: Penguin.

Pandya, A. and Venkatesh, A. (1992) 'Symbolic communication among consumers in self-consumption and gift-giving: A semiotic approach', *Advances in Consumer Research*, 19: 147–54.

Pantzar, M. (1992) 'The growth of product variety – a myth?', *Journal of Consumer Studies and Home Economics*, 16: 345–62.

Parker, H.J. (1974) 'The joys of joy-riding', *New Society*, 3 January: 7.

Parsons, P.R. Rotfeld, H.J. (1990) 'Informercials and television station clearance practices', *Journal of Public Policy and Marketing*, 9: 67–72.

Paxton, A. (1994) *Food Miles*. London: Sustainable Agriculture, Food and Environment Alliance (SAFE).

Pearce, F. (1991) *Green Warriors: The People and the Politics behind the Environmental Revolution*. London: Bodley Head.

Penz, P.G. (1986) *Consumer Sovereignty and Human Interests*. Cambridge: Cambridge University Press.

Perry, M. (1994) 'The brand: Vehicle for value in a changing marketplace', Advertising Association, President's Lecture, 7 July, London.

Peters, T.S. and Waterman, R.H. (1982) *In Search of Excellence*. New York: Harper and Row.

Pines, A. and Aronson, E. (1989) *Career Burnout*. New York: Free Press.

Pirie, M. (ed.) (1991) *Empowerment: The Theme for the 1990s*. London: Adam Smith Institute.

Pollock, A. and Leys, C. (2004) *NHS plc: The Privatisation of our Health Care*. London: Verso.

Pook, S. (1993) 'Ram-raids spark talks on security', *Bath Evening Chronicle*, 2 August: 5.

Postman, N. (1986) *Amusing Ourselves to Death*. London: Heinemann.

Potter, J. (1988) 'Consumerism and the public sector', *Public Administration*, 66 (2): 145–66.

Poulantzas, N.A. (1975) *Political Power and Social Classes* (2nd edition). London, Atlantic Highlands NJ: NLB; Humanities Press.

Pountain, D. and Robins, D. (2000) *Cool Rules: Anatomy of an Attitude*. London: Reaktion Books.

Powderley, J. and MacNulty, C. (1990) 'A turbulent time ahead', *Marketing* (11 October): 33–4.

Pretty, J.N., Ball, A.S., Lang, T. and Morison, J.I.L. (2005) 'Farm costs and food miles: An assessment of the full cost of the UK weekly food basket', *Food Policy*, 30 (1): 1–20.

Ramsay, I. (1989) *Consumer Protection*. London: Weidenfeld and Nicolson.

Randall, G. (1994) *Trade Marketing Strategies: The Partnership between Manufacturers, Brands, and Retailers* (2nd edition). Oxford: Butterworth Heinemann.

Randall, G. and Chartered Institute of Marketing (1990) *Marketing to the Retail Trade*. Oxford: Heinemann Professional on behalf of the Chartered Institute of Marketing.

Raven, H., Lang, T., Dumonteil, C. and Institute for Public Policy Research (UK) (1995) *Off our Trolleys? Food Retailing and the Hypermarket Economy*. London: Institute for Public Policy Research.

Rawls, J. (1971) *A Theory of Justice*. Cambridge, MA: Harvard University Press.

Redfern, P. (1913) *The Story of the C.W.S. The Jubillee History of the Co-operative Wholesale Society, limited. 1863–1913*. Manchester, New York, etc.: The Co-operative Wholesale Society.

Redfern, P. (1920) *The Consumers' Place in Society*. Manchester: Co-operative Union Limited.

Reekie, G. (1992) 'Changes in the Adamless Eden: The spatial and sexual transformation of a Brisbane department store 1930–90', in R. Shields (ed.), *Lifestyle Shopping: The Subject of Consumption*. London: Routledge.

Reich, R. (1981) 'Business is asking for it again', *New York Times*, 22 November.

Reich, W. (1970) *The Mass Psychology of Fascism*. New York: Farrar, Straus and Giroux.

Rieff, D. (1993) 'Multiculturalism's silent partner: It's the newly globalized consumer economy, stupid', *Harper's Magazine* (August).

Rieff, P. (1959) *Freud: The Mind of a Moralist*. New York: Doubleday.

Rieff, P. (1966) *The Triumph of the Therapeutic*. New York: Harper and Row.

Ritzer, G. (1999) *Enchanting a Disenchanted World: Revolutionizing the Means of Consumption*. Thousand Oaks, CA: Pine Forge Press.

Robins, D. and Cohen, P. (1978) *Knuckle Sandwich: Growing up in the Working-Class City*. Harmondsworth: Penguin.

Rock, S. (1989) 'Are greens good for you?', *Director* (January): 40–3.

Rogers, C. (1951) *Client-centered Therapy*. Boston, MA: Houghton Mifflin.

Rose, G. (1978) *The Melancholy Science: An Introduction to the Thought of Theodor W. Adorno*. London: Macmillan.

Rudé, G.F.E. (1959) *The Crowd in the French Revolution*. Oxford: Clarendon Press.

Rutherford, J. (1990) 'A place called home: Identity and the cultural politics of difference', in J. Rutherford (ed.), *Identity: Community, Culture, Difference* London: Lawrence and Wishart. pp. 1–20.

Ryle, S. (1993) 'Crowds cheer as gang hits Jolly's', *Bath Evening Chronicle*.

Sahlins, M.D. (1972) *Stone Age Economics*. Chicago: Aldine-Atherton.

Samuelson, P.A. (1970) *Economics* (8th edition). New York: McGraw-Hill.

Schwartz, H.S. (1990) *Narcissistic Process and Corporate Decay*. New York: New York University Press.

Scitovsky, T. (1976) *The Joyless Economy: An Inquiry into Human Satisfaction and Consumer Dissatisfaction*. New York: Oxford University Press.

Seabrook, J. (1978) *What Went Wrong? Why Hasn't Having More Made People Happier?* (1st American edition). New York: Pantheon Books.

Seabrook, J. (1985) *Landscapes of Poverty*. Oxford: Blackwell.

Seabrook, J. (2004) *Consuming Cultures: Globalization and Local Lives*. Oxford: New Internationalist.

Secord, P.F. and Backman, C.W. (1964) *Social Psychology*. New York: McGraw-Hill.

Seikatsu Club (2005) 'Consumers' Cooperative Union of Japan', Seikatsu Club Consumers' Cooperative Union, Tokyo. Accessed 3 July 2005 from www.iisd.org/50comm/commdb/desc/d08.htm

Sennett, R. (1998) *The Corrosion of Character: The Personal Consequences of Work in the New Capitalism*. New York: Norton.

Seth, A. and Randall, G. (2001) *The Grocers: The Rise and Rise of the Supermarket Chains* (2nd edition). London: Kogan Page.

Sheth, J.N., Newman, B.I. and Gross, B.L. (1991) 'Why we buy what we buy – a theory of consumption values', *Journal of Business Research*, 22 (2): 159–70.

Shiva, V. (2002) *Water Wars: Privatization, Pollution and Profit*. London: Pluto Press.

SIB (1993) 'Pension transfers', report to the Securities and Investments Board by KPMG Peat Marwick, London.

Sievers, B. (1986) 'Beyond the surrogate of motivation', *Organization Studies*, 7 (4): 335–51.

Simmel, G. (1971a[1903]) 'The metropolis in mental life', in D. Levine and G. Simmel (eds), *On Individuality and Social Form*. Chicago: Chicago University Press.

Simmel, G. (1971b[1904]) 'Fashion', in D. Levin and G. Simmel (eds), *On Individuality and Social Form*. Chicago: Chicago University Press.

Simon, H.A. (1947) *Administrative Behavior*. New York: Macmillan.

Sinclair, U. (1985[1906]) *The Jungle*. Harmondsworth: Penguin.

Singh, J. (1990) 'A typology of consumer dissatisfaction response styles', *Journal of Retailing*, 66 (Spring): 57–99.

Sklair, L. (1991) *Sociology of the Global System*. London: Harvester Wheatsheaf.

Sklair, L. (1995) *Sociology of the Global System* (2nd edition). London: Prentice Hall/Harvester Wheatsheaf.

Sklair, L. (2002) *Globalization: Capitalism and its Alternatives*. (3rd edition). Oxford: Oxford University Press.

Slater, D.R. (1997) *Consumer Culture and Modernity*. Cambridge: Polity.

Smith, A. (1970[1776]) *The Wealth of the Nations*. Harmondsworth: Penguin.

Smith, N.C. (1990) *Morality and the Market: Consumer Pressure for Corporate Accountability*. London: Routledge.

Social Science Research Council (US) and United States Army Service Forces: Information and Education Division (1949) *Studies in Social Psychology in World War II*. Princeton, NJ: Princeton University Press.

Society of Labour Lawyers (UK) (1968) *Justice for All*. London: Fabian Society.

Sontag, S. (2004) 'What have we done?', *The Guardian*, 24 May: 2–3.

Soros, G. (2000) *Open Society: The Crisis of Global Capitalism Reconsidered*. New York: Public Affairs.

Soros, G. (2004) *The Bubble of American Supremacy: Correcting the Misuse of American power*. London: Weidenfeld and Nicholson.

Stiglitz, J.E. (2002) *Globalization and its Discontents* (1st edition). New York: W.W. Norton.

Sturdy, A., Grugulis, I. and Willmott, H. (eds) (2001) *Customer Service: Empowerment and Entrapment*. Basingstoke: Palgrave.

Surgeon-General of the United States (2004) *The Health Consequences of Smoking*. Washington, DC: US Department of Health and Human Services.

Tatzel, M. (2002) 'Money worlds' and well-being: An integration of money dispositions, materialism and price-related behavior', *Journal of Economic Psychology*, 23 (1): 103–26.

Taylor, I., Walton, P. and Young, J. (1973) *The New Criminology*. London: Routledge.

Taylor, J. and Taylor, D. (eds) (1990) *The Safe Book Handbook*. London: Ebury.

Thompson, D.J. (1994) *Weavers of Dreams: The Origins of the Modern Co-operative Movement* (150th anniversary edition). Davis, CA: Center for Cooperatives, University of California.

Thompson, E.P. (1993[1971]) 'The moral economy of the English crowd in the eighteenth century', in E.P. Thompson (ed.), *Customs in Common*. Harmondsworth: Penguin.

Thurow, L.C. (1993) *Head to Head: The Coming Economic Battle among Japan, Europe, and America* (Warner Books edition). New York, NY: Warner Books.

Tiemstra, J.P. (1992) Theories of Regulation and the History of Consumerism. *International Journal of Social Economics*, 19 (6): 3–27.

Tomforde, A. (1994) 'Fast food losses to 'food tax', *The Guardian*, 22 August.

Tomlinson, A. (1990) 'Introduction: Consumer culture and the aura of commodity', in A. Tomlinson (ed.), *Consumpton, Identiy and Style: Marketing, Meanings and the Packaging of Pleasure*. London: Routledge.

Townsend, P. (1979) *Poverty in the United Kingdom: A Survey of Household Resources and Standards of Living*. Harmondsworth: Penguin.

Townsend, P. (1993) *Poverty in the United Kingdom: A Survey of Household Resources and Standards of Living* (second edition) Hemel Hemstead: Harvester Wheatsheaf.

Townsend, P. and Gordon, D. (2002) *World Poverty: New Policies to Defeat an Old Enemy*. Bristol: Policy Press.

Toynbee, P. (2003) *Hard Work: Life in Low-pay Britain*. London: Bloomsbury.

Trentmann, F. (2005) *The Making of the Consumer: Knowledge, Power and Identity in the Modern World*. New York, NY: Berg.

Twitchell, J.B. (1999) *Lead Us into Temptation: The Triumph of American Materialism*. New York: Columbia University Press.

UN (1992) 'Report of the United Nations Conference on Environment and Development, Rio de Janeiro, 3–14 June 1992', Annex 1, A/CONF.151/26 (Vol. I) Annex I, United Nations Conference on Environment and Development, New York.

UN and UNEP (1990) *The Public Health Impact of Pesticides used in Agriculture*. Geneva: World Health Organization.

UNDP (2001) *Human Development Report*. New York: UNDP.

UNEP (2001) *First Africa roundtable on cleaner production and sustainable consumption: Nairobi, Kenya, 9–11 August 2000*. Paris: United Nations Division of Technology Industry and Economics and United Nations Environment Programme Regional Office for Africa, Paris.

UNFPA (2004) *State of World Population 2004*. New York: United Nations Population Fund.

UNICEF (1992) *Food, Health and Care: The UNICEF Vision and Strategy for a World Free from Hunger and Malnutrition*. New York: United Nations Childrens Fund.

van Brakel, M. and Buitenkamp, M. (1992) *Sustainable Netherlands: A Perspective for Changing Northern Lifestyles*. Amsterdam: Friends of the Earth.

van Brakel, M. and Zagema, B. (1994) *Sustainable Netherlands*. Amsterdam: Friends of the Earth.

Veblen, T. (1925[1899]) *The Theory of the Leisure Class*. London: Allen and Unwin.

Vidal, J. (1997) *McLibel: Burger Culture on Trial*. London: Pan.

von Weizacker, E.U., Lovins, A.B. and Lovins, L.H. (1996) *Factor Four: Doubling wealth – Halving Resource Use: The New Report to the Club of Rome*. London: Earthscan.

Wackernagel, M., Rees, W.E. and Testemale, P. (1996) *Our Ecological Footprint: Reducing Human Impact on the Earth*. Gabriola Island, BC: New Society Publishers.

Walker, A. and Wang, Z. (2005) *East Asian Welfare Regimes in Transition: From Confucianism to Globalisation*. Bristol: Policy Press.

Warde, A. (1994) 'Consumers, identity and belonging: Reflections on some theses of Zygmunt Bauman', in R. Keat, N. Whiteley and N. Abercrombie (eds), *The Authority of the Consumer*. London: Routledge.

Wells, P. and Jetter, M. (1991) *The Global Consumer: Best Buys to Help the Third World*. London: Victor Gollancz.

Wenger, E. (1998) *Communities of Practice: Learning, Meaning and Identity*. Cambridge: Cambridge University Press.

Wenger, E. (2000) 'Communities of practice and social learning systems', *Organization*, 7 (2): 225–46.

Wernick, A. (1991) *Promotional Culture: Advertising, Ideology and Symbolic Expression*. London: Sage.

Wexler, P. (1990) 'Citizenship in the semiotic society', in B.A. Turner (ed.), *Theories of Modernity and Postmodernity*: 164–75. London: Sage.

White, R.E. and Kare, D.D. (1990) 'The impact of consumer boycotts on the stock prices of target firms', *The Journal of Applied Business Research*, 6 (2).

Whitfield, D. (1983) *Making it Public: Evidence and Action against Privatisation*. London: Pluto Press.

Whitworth, D. (1994) 'Promoting and representing the consumer interest', in R. John (ed.), *The Consumer Revolution: Redressing the Balance*. London: Hodder and Stoughton.

Will, R., Marlin, A.T., Corson, B. and Schorsch, J. (1989) *Shopping for a Better World*. New York: Council on Economic Priorities.

Williams, R. (1976) *Keywords: A Vocabulary of Culture and Society*. London: Fontana.

Williams, R.H. (1982) *Dream Worlds: Mass Consumption in Late Nineteenth-century France*. Berkeley, CA: University of California Press.

Williamson, J. (1986) *Consuming Passions: The Dynamics of Popular Culture*. London: Marion Boyars.

Willis, P. (1990) *Common Culture: Symbolic Work at Play in the Everyday Cultures of the Young*. Milton Keynes: Open University Press.

Winnicott, D.W. (1962) *The Maturational Processes and Facilitating Environment*. London: Hogarth Press.

Winnicott, D.W. (1964) *The Child, the Family and the Outside World*. Harmondsworth: Penguin.

Winward, J. (1994) 'The organized consumer and consumer information co-operatives', in R. Keath, N. Whiteley and N. Abercrombie (eds), *The Authority of the Consumer*. London: Routledge.

Witkowski, T.H. (1989) 'Colonial consumers in revolt: Buyer values and behavior during the nonimportantion movement, 1764–1776', *Journal of Consumer Research*, 16 (2): 216–26.

Worpole, K. (2000) *Here Comes the Sun: Architecture and Public Space in Twentieth-century European Culture*. London: Reaktion.

Yalch, R.F. and Spangenberg, E. (1993) 'Using store music for retail zoning – a field experiment', *Advances in Consumer Research*, 20: 632–36.

Yalch, R.F. and Spangenberg, E.R. (2000) 'The effects of music in a retail setting on real and perceived shopping times', *Journal of Business Research*, 49 (2): 139–47.

Index

Added to a page number, 'f' denotes the entry follows on to the next page; 'ff' denotes the entry follows on to the next two or more pages.